10/07

R. Smith

The Words and Music of John Lennon

THE PRAEGER SINGER-SONGWRITER
COLLECTION

The Words and Music of John Lennon

Ben Urish and Ken Bielen

James E. Perone, Series Editor

PRAEGER

Westport, Connecticut
London

Library of Congress Cataloging-in-Publication Data

Urish, Ben.
 The words and music of John Lennon / Ben Urish and Ken Bielen.
  p. cm. — (The Praeger singer-songwriter collection, ISSN 1553–3484)
 Includes bibliographical references (p.   ), discography (p.   ), and index.
 ISBN-13: 978–0–275–99180–7 (alk. paper)
 ISBN-10: 0–275–99180–6 (alk. paper)
 1. Lennon, John, 1940–1980—Criticism and interpretation.   I. Bielen,
Kenneth G. II. Title.
 ML420.L38U75   2007
 782.42166092—dc22   2007007815

British Library Cataloguing in Publication Data is available.

Library of Congress Catalog Card Number: 2007007815
ISBN-13: 978–0–275–99180–7
ISBN-10: 0–275–99180–6
ISSN: 1553–3484

First published in 2007

Praeger Publishers, 88 Post Road West, Westport, CT 06881
An imprint of Greenwood Publishing Group, Inc.
www.praeger.com

Printed in the United States of America

The paper used in this book complies with the
Permanent Paper Standard issued by the National
Information Standards Organization (Z39.48–1984).

10 9 8 7 6 5 4 3 2 1

In 1967 we were living in Springfield, Missouri, and I had just turned nine. I was riding in the car with my mother and "Strawberry Fields Forever" came on the radio. I was terrified. It didn't sound like anything I'd ever heard before with its odd pulsing tones and droning, nearly monotonous vocals. It seemed nightmarish. To reassure me, my mother started to explain what the lyrics meant and how the sounds were supposed to approximate what was going on with the singer's emotions and in his mind.

It was one of the pivotal moments of my life.

I dedicate my work on this book to my mother, Sue. Mom: thanks for helping to keep me from living with my eyes closed.

—Ben Urish

Contents

Series Foreword

Although the term *singer-songwriters* might most frequently be associated with a cadre of musicians of the early 1970s such as Paul Simon, James Taylor, Carly Simon, Joni Mitchell, Cat Stevens, and Carole King, the Praeger Singer-Songwriter Collection defines singer-songwriters more broadly, both in terms of style and in terms of time period. The series includes volumes on musicians who have been active from approximately the 1960s through the present. Musicians who write and record in folk, rock, soul, hip-hop, country, and various hybrids of these styles will be represented. Therefore, some of the early 1970s introspective singer-songwriters named above will be included, but not exclusively.

What do the individuals included in this series have in common? Although some have collaborated as writers and some have not, all have written and recorded commercially successful and/or historically important music *and* lyrics at some point in their careers.

The authors who contribute to the series also exhibit diversity. Some are scholars who are trained primarily as musicians, while others have such areas of specialization as American studies, history, sociology, popular culture studies, literature, and rhetoric. The authors share a high level of scholarship, accessibility in their writing, and a true insight into the work of the artists they study. The authors are also focused on the output of their subjects and how it relates to their subject's biography and the society around them; however, biography in and of itself is not a major focus of the books in this series.

Given the diversity of the musicians who are the subject of books in this series, and given the diverse viewpoints of the authors, volumes in the series will differ from book to book. All, however, will be organized chronologically according to the compositions and recorded performances of their subjects. All of the books in the series should also serve as listeners' guides to the music of their subjects, making them companions to the artists' recorded output.

James E. Perone
Series Editor

Acknowledgments

Jointly we would like to thank series editor James Perone for his support for our project in particular and for the series overall. And we are grateful to Acquisitions Editor Daniel Harmon for his insights, patience, and understanding.

Our special thanks go to Jim Cummer, formerly of Madhatter Music (madhattermusic.com), for his help in getting information regarding rare Lennon recordings clarifying Beatle rumors. And we are indebted to William L. Schurk and the Music Library and Sound Recording Archives of Bowling Green State University, Bowling Green, Ohio, for access to materials as well.

Ken thanks Ben Urish for dragging me into this project; Judy Bielen Smith for sharing Beatlemania with me; Neocles and Vassiliki Leontis for friendship and encouragement; Stan and Fran Bielen for support; Joyce Bielen McNally for concern and the vinyl; and Mary, Kelly, Alex, and Dylan Bielen for helping me to be who I am.

Ben would like to thank Shari Barbour for providing safe haven literally and spiritually, and to my sister Georgia and niece Savannah (get it?) for understanding why it matters. Of course, immense gratitude and respect go to my coauthor Ken Bielen. Quite simply this book would not exist without him.

Introduction

John Lennon showed artistic talent and leaning at an early age. The double punch of British skiffle music and American rock and roll in the mid-1950s turned his creative impulses to performing music. The Quarry Men, a group named after Lennon's school and formed and led by him at age 16, developed over the next three years into The Beatles, the most significant of all rock music combos. Key among this development was Lennon's meeting and forming a musical partnership with Paul McCartney. At McCartney's suggestion and with his example, the two young men began composing songs jointly and separately.

Lennon enrolled in Liverpool Art College as The Beatles honed their skills by performing in the Liverpool area and then in Hamburg, Germany. By late 1962, Lennon and The Beatles were on the British music charts, and within several months "Beatlemania" was born and spreading, reaching the United States in full force early in 1964.

By the end of the following year, Lennon's songwriting had matured. As a craftsman, he could do what was required quite well, often to levels of brilliance. But for him, that was increasingly no longer satisfying artistically. Lennon's songs became more overtly personal in terms of topic, more freely expressive in terms of lyrics, and sonically more evocative. They had to say something meaningful, both in the form and the content, or to him they were of lesser value. For Lennon, a song of his was "good" if it expressed and communicated real emotions, ideas, or events, regardless of whether it was successful in terms of professional polish or chart success. The reverse held true as well. A song of his may have been excellent at the level of craft, structure, story, and harmony, but if it did not express and communicate something vital, he considered it empty hack work and was often the most dismissive critic of his own efforts.

The Beatles' unprecedented popularity continued as musical styles and interests changed during the socially turbulent 1960s. By early 1970, the individual Beatles went their separate artistic ways, having jointly amassed 51 singles in the top 40, 34 in the top 10, and 20 number-1 hits.[1] In the decades since, the group's recordings continued to find both relevance and sales with new, large audiences.

Lennon's pop music innovations while in The Beatles spanned music, lyrics, and recording techniques. These innovations continued as his creative partnership with Paul McCartney dissolved and another creative partnership, with avant-garde conceptual and performance artist Yoko Ono, evolved.

Lennon continued to have erratic chart successes for post-Beatles singles and albums, having 13 charting singles and 8 charting musical albums during his lifetime, with another 6 singles charting in the eight years after his murder. Yet only one of those singles topped the charts at number one during his life. It was both his at-times discomforting emotional honesty and his espousing of and devotion to controversial social and radical political causes in his music and otherwise that arguably hampered the mass appeal legacy he inherited as a former Beatle. Efforts such as "Mother" were not dance-floor friendly, and, excellent though it is, Lennon could not have expected the provocative "Woman Is the Nigger of the World" to have had much appeal in the pop market of 1972. A similar statement could be made regarding his more innovative work done in support of Ono; though readily available, such work did not find much favor with former Beatlemaniacs.

Yet he did release those recordings, and his status as a former Beatle at least garnered them some notice. Lennon naturally sought the largest possible audience for his music. His relishing of the experimental aside, he was, after all, a pop musician. When he could combine mainstream success with his need to say something of value, as with "Instant Karma!" or "Imagine," that was ideal.

After his greatest solo chart success and a flurry of collaborations with other performers, Lennon did not formally record for almost five years. Then, scarcely a month after the release of his "comeback" album, he was shot to death as he entered his apartment building in New York City. The resulting worldwide display of grief and memorials demonstrated not just nostalgia for The Beatles or their era in general or Lennon in particular, but recognition that Lennon had achieved iconic status. He had become a living legend. Lennon might have alternately been bemused by this and railed against it, but it had happened—and in the decades since, this process has only intensified.

But Lennon was an all-too-real flesh-and-blood human, both as frail and as strong as any. Many examples of his work, musical and otherwise, have become available posthumously, and they illuminate the man as well as the artist. What we are left with is the intensity of his thoughts, the clarity of his questions, the concern within his humor, and the pain within his triumphs.

SCOPE AND ORGANIZATION

As is the case with all of the books in this series, the focus of this volume is on the music, lyrics, and recordings of our subject. For this volume, that is John Lennon, but John Lennon apart from The Beatles. Some might contend that this is an artificial break, and to a certain degree it is. Yet having been made numerous times elsewhere, the case does not need to be made here for the exceptional nature of The Beatles' work and Lennon's contributions to that body of work. Compared to the academic coverage of The Beatles' material, Lennon's post-Beatle compositions and recordings, even in light of his killing, remain unfairly neglected with only a handful of attempts to do them justice.

Although this work focuses on John Lennon's "solo"—or, more accurately, post-Beatle—years, clearly, it is impossible to totally ignore his work as a singer-songwriter while a member of The Beatles. Just as clearly, his later career would not have been the same had he never been a Beatle. Much of the sociohistorical and artistic weight Lennon's post-Beatle output carries results from his having been a Beatle.

Much that is, but not all. Lennon himself saw his life's creative output as one large mosaic.[2] His solo artistry and influence not only illuminate what he gave to The Beatles (and what the experience gave to him), but comprise a significant contribution on their own.

More so than all but a few other pop music artists, Lennon was able to fuse experiments in technology, instrumentation, lyrics, and song form into artistically and commercially successful recordings. Whether expressing emotions, explaining philosophies, protesting social situations, or ruminating on the joys and pains of romantic or familial entanglements, few have been Lennon's equal and none his better.

The book is arranged chronologically with minor exceptions where some posthumously released recordings may be discussed then as opposed to when they were recorded for reasons explained in the text at those points. This is by no means a full-scale biography of John Lennon. Yet, as with many artists, and with Lennon more than most, the biography does not just underlay the art; it is directly and explicitly woven into it. Many of Lennon's musical creations are overt editorials on what was happening to him, or about what issues were of immediate concern to him at the time of their creation. In many instances, Lennon's biography and artistic enterprises mesh, and as a result our discussions do as well.

Obviously Lennon's post-Beatles body of work was first curtailed by his voluntary self-removal from the music industry, and then by his slaying. Yet he was incredibly productive from the start of The Beatles' recording career until his withdrawal from recording early in 1975. Since his shooting, several composition tapes, home demos, studio recordings, and even completed songs have been released and may continue to be. But it is not the mere number of Lennon's compositions and recordings that intrigues; it is their content and quality. An analysis of Lennon's work that aims to straddle academic and mainstream audiences is, we hope, a welcome addition to the Beatles and Lennon literature available.

In keeping with the scope of the Praeger Singer-Songwriter Collection, we have focused on Lennon's musical compositions that he recorded, and have further focused on particularly notable songs from each of his albums. That said, we have not left out any studio recording that Lennon composed and completed recording during his lifetime, and we have included uncompleted compositions and recordings that we deem most significant.

In addition, we have commented as thoroughly as seems appropriate, given the focus of this series, on Lennon's significant musical works in collaboration with others (again, post-Beatles), notably with Yoko Ono. The full range of Lennon's efforts in conjunction with other musicians—whether vocal, instrumental, in composition, or in production—is discussed in the context of his other musical endeavors.

Because of his status as a former Beatle, Lennon had enormous artistic control over his work. Outside of a handful of collaborations as a "guest star," he produced all of his post-Beatle recordings, often in collaboration with Ono, Phil Spector, or both. The one exception to that rule, the *Oldies but Goldies* project, fell apart and Lennon had to take over complete control to finish the project. His recordings may have at times been unsettling enough to be censored or outright banned from broadcast or sales, but during his lifetime they were as he wanted them or they did not get released. Naturally, this does not apply to the uncompleted, posthumously released recordings.

Because the aim of this series is to provide a guide to the recordings and compositions of the singer-songwriters under discussion, we have provided a discography of Lennon's key post-Beatles recordings. The index includes all of the songs mentioned in the text, including those written, co-written, and/ or recorded by Lennon; songs he recorded but did not write; and songs which Lennon neither wrote nor recorded, but which we have discussed in the text.

Lennon had a playful, adventurous, questioning, and concerned spirit. Those attributes variously imbued his artistic endeavors. Both in The Beatles and beyond, there is usually a sense of joyful wonder coupled with an intense honesty underlying Lennon's work that is frequently difficult to adequately explain. The more we attempt to put our finger on it, the more it slips away— to paraphrase something we heard somewhere. No matter what his topic—be it a straightforward love song, an angry polemic, or a surreal bit of nonsense— Lennon expressed some aspect of himself that was real, and in so doing, either clarified it for all of us or at least shed some light on it for future understanding. We hope we have done something similar with his words and music.

In My Life: The Early Years

John Winston Lennon (later John Ono Lennon) was born on October 9, 1940, in the midst of a bomb raid during the Second World War in the port city of Liverpool, England.[1] His father, Fred Lennon, was a merchant seaman who had only sporadic contact with his family during the war; he moved away within a year after the war's end, having no further contact with his son until after fame had arrived. Later in life, Fred Lennon remarried and fathered another two sons. Lennon and his father had minimal contact until Fred Lennon's death in 1976.[2]

At an early age, Lennon's mother, Julia (maiden name Stanley), by most accounts a free spirit, turned over her son's rearing to her stern sister Mimi and Mimi's husband George Smith, though she kept in sporadic contact with him. Julia soon had three daughters by two different men. As Lennon entered his teens, she began to have closer contact with him, including teaching him rudimentary banjo playing. This deepening relationship was cut short by her accidental killing by an inebriated, off-duty police officer in the summer of 1958, when Lennon was 17 years old. Lennon maintained sporadic contact with his two youngest half-sisters (the eldest had been adopted by a family in Sweden shortly after her birth) until his slaying.[3]

Bright enough to be bored and disenchanted enough to be rebellious, by all accounts Lennon slid through his schooling, only applying himself to expressive projects such as artwork or writing. Talented but disinterested and directionless, Lennon spent his early teens withdrawn into a small circle of close friends, and bonding with his affable uncle George, who died unexpectedly in 1955, when Lennon was just 14.

LYRICAL INFLUENCES

While not evident in his earliest songwriting, the short stories, sketches, and essays that made up Lennon's first two books clearly evidence the influence of the fantasy, illogic, and nonsense literary achievements of Edward Lear, Lewis Carroll, and W. S. Gilbert. What in Lennon's lyrics many have attributed to the influence of psychedelic drugs more properly has its roots in Victorian-era wordplay humor.[4]

Lennon's imagination and tart sense of humor were also in accord with the absurdist drolleries of such British comedy troupes as The Crazy Gang and The Goons, a humor tradition that led to Lennon's contemporaries such as Beyond the Fringe and Monty Python's Flying Circus. As Lennon's lyrical composing matured, he often combined his comical wordplay and imaginative flights, sometimes just for the absurdity itself, but often for more poetic or thoughtful ends. While such Beatles' classics as "Lucy in the Sky with Diamonds," "I Am the Walrus" (where the Lewis Carroll inspiration is most overt), and "Glass Onion" are well-known examples, his post-Beatles career has numerous illustrations as will be shown.

MUSICAL INFLUENCES

Lennon grew up during the tail end of the big-band swing era in postwar Europe, where the pop music scene was heavily influenced by the American presence through military bases, economic trade, and war recovery efforts. Additionally, homegrown artists, national and regional, from traditions such as the British Music Hall, were still very popular. For example, both Lennon and his Beatles band mate George Harrison were lifelong George Formby fans, and outtakes of The Beatles rehearsals show them playing a wide variety of popular songs, not just the expected rhythm and blues/rock and roll numbers. It may have been Paul McCartney who explicitly composed pastiche songs in these prerock-era pop music traditions, but Lennon was clearly well schooled in them as well.[5]

In the mid-1950s Great Britain was hit by the popular craze of skiffle, a fusion of folksy traditional tunes with Tin Pan Alley sensibilities, played on homemade or inexpensive instruments. The impromptu inventiveness had an appeal for the artistically inclined and attention-seeking young Lennon, and he formed a skiffle group while learning to accompany himself on banjo.

Nearly concurrent was the explosion of American rockabilly, rhythm and blues, and rock and roll that hit Great Britain in full force by 1956. As were many others, Lennon was entranced and excited, and pushed his skiffle organizations to incorporate this new music. Lennon's fascination with and love for the music of Buddy Holly, Chuck Berry, Elvis Presley, and others never left him. In finding them, he had found himself.

BEATLE MOONLIGHTING

Once he found his drive, Lennon was by all accounts relentless. By early spring of 1957, at the age of 16, Lennon had formed his first skiffle band, The Black Jacks. They soon changed their name to The Quarry Men, taking the moniker from the school that Lennon and most of the members were attending. Membership changed fairly regularly, although a standard pool of players seems to have formed, including Paul McCartney, fairly early on. More and more rockabilly and rhythm and blues were played, and the band changed names several times, eventually stabilizing by the fall of 1960 as The Beatles.[6] Just over two years later, in October 1962, the first of their charting hits was released.

With McCartney's assistance and the songwriting of Chuck Berry and Buddy Holly as examples, Lennon began composing songs. Like those two rock and roll pioneers, Lennon and McCartney came up with the music as well as the lyrics. No matter who wrote what or how much, almost all of their professional songwriting collaborations from their teen years until the end of The Beatles are credited to both men equally. Legend has it that this stems from an early agreement between the two while they were in their teens.[7] Some songs were true collaborations, some were the sole effort of one or the other, and it seems an example of every possible variation in between can be ascertained. In the flood of Beatle releases and the sheer amount of work he produced, it is somewhat surprising to discover that Lennon composed songs while a Beatle that the group did not record.

Lennon's most well-known early composition that was not used by The Beatles is "Bad to Me." One of Lennon's pleasanter efforts of the time, it features a spoken-sung opening prologue, a rarity among Lennon's compositions. Also lyrically more sophisticated than most of his early work, the song became a top-10 hit for Billy J. Kramer and the Dakotas in 1963 in the United Kingdom.

One of Lennon's earliest compositions survived in the band's repertoire long enough to be recorded by The Beatles, but only at their failed audition for Decca Records held on January 1, 1962. The song is called "Hello Little Girl," and it was eventually included on the Beatles' *Anthology* collection. This ebullient song with a fast-paced lead vocal was recorded by The Fourmost and was a hit for them in England in 1963.

The lost gem of Lennon's early non-Beatles works is simply titled "I'm in Love." Musically and lyrically more accomplished, the song builds excitement with each strain and verse, shifting meter and rhythm to match the differing lyrical tone of each section. The Fourmost secured this one too, making it a top-20 hit in the United Kingdom.

"One and One Is Two" is certainly arithmetically correct and moves along at a solid pace but has derivative lyrics and a slightly awkward refrain. McCartney is most responsible for this early 1964 effort with some probable input from Lennon, though he later disavowed it.[8] It was never even considered as a possible song for The Beatles, and was even rejected when they first tried to give it away at the height of Beatlemania![9]

"World without Love" was a number-one hit for Peter and Gordon in 1964 and Lennon reputedly made some minor lyrical adjustments, but the song is pretty much McCartney's.[10] Other early Lennon compositions were either eventually turned into numbers for The Beatles or are all but forgotten and now lost.

In the course of The Beatles' recording careers there were several Lennon songs that were either never fully completed, rejected at some point in the process, or abandoned by Lennon himself. Some have been included in The Beatles' *Anthology* CDs; others still exist in the vaults or the hands of audio bootleggers. Because that part of Lennon's career is not relevant to this work, they are not discussed here. However, some compositions of Lennon's done while he was a Beatle but never recorded for release by them, or recorded and unissued at the time of their breakup, were returned to, and therefore will be discussed at the appropriate place in Lennon's post-Beatles chronology.

During his time as a member of The Beatles, Lennon did not really collaborate musically with other recording artists until The Beatles as a functioning unit was coming to an end and Lennon began his personal and artistic partnership with Yoko Ono. There are two brief exceptions to this, and both involve Paul McCartney.

The first also involves another rock group from Great Britain, The Rolling Stones. Members of both groups had known each other for some years, and Lennon and McCartney had given The Rolling Stones a song they had composed called "I Wanna Be Your Man," though The Beatles later recorded and performed it as a vocal feature for Ringo Starr. Supposedly, observing Lennon and McCartney at work on the song had inspired Keith Richards and Mick Jagger to begin composing as well.[11]

In 1967 Lennon and McCartney added harmony vocals to The Rolling Stones' single "We Love You." Even though their voices are easily noticed and the public knew of their contribution at the time, the single peaked at number 50.

Once The Beatles set up Apple Records and began building a stable of artists other than themselves to record for that label, they were involved to varying degrees in the activities of some of their artists. One group Lennon took particular interest in he named Grapefruit, after a book of Ono's. Lennon and McCartney produced a track from their album *Around Grapefruit* titled "Dear Delilah" although Terry Melcher was officially credited. The production is clean and energetic, but nothing out of the ordinary. Oddly, another song on the album, "Lullaby," sounds very much like a Lennon composition, and Lennon must have liked it. When Ono copyrighted a batch of Lennon's home tapes in preparation for the *Lost Lennon Tapes* radio show, she mistakenly, though understandably, included a version of "Lullaby."[12] The group's bass player George Alexander wrote the song. The group had a small hit with "Dear Delilah," but Lennon did not produce another artist besides himself or Ono until Bill Elliot and the Elastic Oz Band in 1971.

The Ballad of John and Yoko, Late 1968 to Early 1970

While it is well known that The Beatles recorded together until early in 1970 and were a contractually bound entity until 1975,[1] various sources have posed the questions of and answers to when, how, and why The Beatles broke up. All agree, however, that it was a slow and fractious process. Some date the band's split as the end of the last tour late in 1966. Others mark the group's dissolution at the death of their manager Brian Epstein in August 1967. Still others select the period when their two-record album *The Beatles* (known as the White Album) was nearing completion and Lennon began his artistic collaborations with his soon-to-be wife, conceptual and performance artist Yoko Ono.

The validity of this interpretation is open to question, but certainly Lennon's creative energies were directed toward non-Beatles projects, and his artistic sensibilities were modified and redirected. It would seem unfair however to blame Ono, as used to be fashionable, for the demise of The Beatles by pulling Lennon away from them. That scenario obscures and ignores other issues impacting the dynamic of The Beatles, such as George Harrison's maturing talent, among many other factors. Just as important is that it ignores the fact that Lennon's impulses were constantly changing, and, if anything, collaborating with Ono refreshed and reinvigorated his work.

Two Virgins

Without the other Beatles, Lennon appeared in a supporting role in the film *How I Won the War* (1967). The film was directed by Richard Lester, who had also directed The Beatles' first two feature films *A Hard Day's Night* and *Help!*

A promotional single was released for *How I Won the War,* which Lennon had no hand in conceiving or executing, although it used a clip of his voice from the film's soundtrack.[2] Discounting that single, the *Two Virgins* album was Lennon's first recorded artistic statement without the involvement of any of the other Beatles. It was also his first of three nonpop music album collaborations with Ono.

The full title of the album is *Unfinished Music No. 1: Two Virgins* and, like the next two experimental collaborations, it invites the listener to cease being a passive consumer, but instead become an active improvisational co-performer, albeit at a technological distance. The recording consists of tape-looped sound collages supported mainly by airy, pulsating percussions at varying speeds; ambient room noise; and brief snatches of dialogue (natural as well as seemingly performance improvised) from Lennon and Ono. The entire proceedings clock in at just under half an hour. Ono's characteristic tremolo wailings are also present throughout. Listeners can add their own sounds, vocal and otherwise, to "finish" the unfinished music.

Lennon had reportedly made similar home recordings previously, and the results of such experimentation had been applied to numerous Beatle recordings from the previous two years. A sample of what these might have been like is the sound collage used for "Jessie's Dream" from The Beatles' *Magical Mystery Tour* television film broadcast near the end of 1967.

A close listen to *Two Virgins* reveals Lennon's natural nonsensical humor popping up at times, his mocking of mundane domestic moments (similar to his books and some of The Beatles' later Christmas fan club recordings), the performing of jangly piano chords (even a bit of a sea shanty) and an early attempt at his increasingly aggressive, yet almost minimalist, feedback guitar playing. The work sets the pattern for much of Lennon and Ono's experimental musical conversations of the next two years. Nothing on the album was particularly new to followers of free form or avant-garde and experimental music and recordings. But the combination of the two artists and Lennon's presence meant that whatever audience the album found would not have been likely to have fully understood the roots of the project, and probably easily ignored it or were just plain baffled by it.

The album gained notoriety not for its recorded content but for its cover, on which Lennon and Ono appeared nude, attempting to convey both a sort of Adam and Eve / childlike innocence with nothing to hide and, perhaps, to symbolize his artistic rebirth through the collaboration. The resulting scandal over the cover ensured that the album was more talked about than listened to, and it was largely and to some degree unfairly dismissed as totally self-indulgent. It remains, though, the least interesting of their three avant-garde albums.

THE ROLLING STONES ROCK AND ROLL CIRCUS

With the White Album released, The Beatles made a promotional film for the single "Hey Jude" / "Revolution." This led to them discussing what would eventually become the *Get Back* sessions. Meanwhile, Lennon and Ono rehearsed and filmed a segment for *The Rolling Stones Rock and Roll Circus,* a concert film made up of various British rock acts performing in a circus setting with the Rolling Stones hosting and capping off the show. Lennon's impromptu band was called The Dirty Mac and included Eric Clapton, who took part in The Beatles' recent recording sessions and who would work with Lennon fairly regularly for the next year.[3]

They ripped through a passionate version of Lennon's "Yer Blues" from the White Album, and then a fast-paced jam featuring Ono, tentatively titled "Her Blues" and later titled "Whole Lotta Yoko."[4] Had the film been released in 1969 as originally planned, it would have furthered Lennon's stance as a performer away from The Beatles, clarified The Beatles' dissolving nature, and showcased Lennon and Ono's artistic partnership for a much larger audience than their joint albums received. However, the film was unreleased for decades, by which point it was a time capsule and curio, though no less welcome for being so.

LIFE WITH THE LIONS

The couple's next collaboration, *Unfinished Music No. 2: Life with the Lions,* is more varied, more successful, and yet slightly more derivative than *Two Virgins* in that it utilizes ideas from the Fluxus art collective of which Yoko had been part. The title makes a pun on the old British radio program *Life with the Lyons* starring performers Ben Lyons and his wife Bebe Daniels, and is a wry commentary on the media circus in which Lennon and Ono found themselves embroiled at the time. The back cover is the now-famous photo of their arrest on drug charges, and the front cover set the tone for the album—Ono is pictured in her hospital bed (shortly after she suffered the first of three miscarriages) with Lennon leaning on cushions at her side on the floor.

The album opens with a live recording titled "Cambridge 1969" documenting Lennon's second professional non-Beatles music performance since their formation. Since the *Rock and Roll Circus* performances of "Yer Blues" and "Whole Lotta Yoko" would remain unreleased for another quarter century, this was the first available on-record public performance of Lennon's free-form guitar playing. It was more assured and developed than it was in its formative stage on *Two Virgins.* The focus, however, is on Ono's vocals; Lennon's work, unexpected and fascinating, remains in support and counterpoint to her efforts. Other musicians join in eventually, and the effect is to clarify Lennon and Ono's work in juxtaposition to them.

"No Bed for Beatle John" follows and is the standout track on the album. It begins quietly as Ono reads / chants / sings newspaper articles detailing her hospitalization and the scandal over *Two Virgins.* Soon, Lennon joins in a whispery semi-falsetto voice performing a news article about his and his first wife Cynthia's divorce. Lennon's voice is in the background of Ono's as a harmonic countermelody of sorts. The simple fun of the appealing idea is countered by the mournful tones of the vocals, and the pair's erratic phrasing that undercuts the rational structure of the news reports. The effect is uneasy and disconcerting; yet, as "unfinished" music, it is assumed that the listener is encouraged to grab some reading material and chant along, perhaps changing the overall effect.

Intriguingly, in a bootleg recording from The Beatles' *Get Back* sessions of January 1969, a couple of months after "No Bed for Beatle John" was recorded, Lennon and the band jam to "Good Rockin' Tonight" singing the lyrics of "I heard the news" while Paul McCartney reads a negative newspaper account of The Beatles' recent exploits. This does not appear to be a conscious development of the idea, but rather both Lennon and McCartney engaging in a little passive-aggressive communication. A humorous variation of the idea is included in the *John Lennon Anthology* set that was released in 1998. Lennon imitates Bob Dylan by reading newspaper passages in a Dylanesque voice while accompanying himself on guitar.

Next is "Baby's Heartbeat," which is a fuzzy-sounding loop of the heartbeat of their unborn and ultimately miscarried child. It becomes trance-like, in an odd parallel to the ending of Lennon's Beatle track "I Want You (She's So Heavy)" released on the *Abbey Road* album five months later. In shocking similarity to that track, it ends startlingly and abruptly. Knowledge of the miscarriage layers this track and the next one, "Two Minutes of Silence," with palpable sorrow.

"Two Minutes of Silence" might more accurately have been titled "Two Minutes of Ambient Sounds Wherever You Are" and has its roots in similar works, notably by Ono's fellow Fluxus member John Cage.[5] But coming as it does after "Baby's Heartbeat," the listener cannot help but contemplate the pain of the expectant parents' loss. Lennon's drive for sheer personal honesty in his artistic endeavors would expand and become clearer in the next year as The Beatles broke up and he began his post-Beatles career. The simple and direct emotional stillness is very powerful, and even more poignant when one considers Ono's public remembrance for Lennon after his killing was a request for 10 minutes of silence.

The album finishes with "Radio Play," which consists of a radio being played as if it were a musical instrument. It is turned on and off, and the tuning dial is spun at random. We hear spoken words, occasional fragments of music, and sometimes just static, whines, and whistles. As with other such Lennon and Ono pieces, background noises can be discerned, adding various layers of sound.

"GIVE PEACE A CHANCE"

At the end of May 1969, The Beatles' single "The Ballad of John and Yoko" was released. The lyric was a short musical account of and Lennon's editorial on the couple's recent newsmaking exploits. Lennon's wish for documenting and explaining his activities had often been veiled in previous Beatles songs. But the group's time in India, coupled with Ono's influence, helped Lennon to become more comfortable with seeing his life, ideas, thoughts, and activities as direct rather than indirect sources for his art. Communicating his current personal emotional and philosophical states became the prime aspect of his artistic agenda, as formatively evidenced by such earlier Lennon Beatles numbers as "All You Need Is Love" and "Revolution." Lennon pursued this not only in his experimental albums with Ono, but, as noted, in his more mainstream songs as well. "The Ballad of John and Yoko" is one of the most explicit examples of this exploration. Interestingly, only two of The Beatles, McCartney and Lennon, play on the track. Despite the lack of airplay—due to the song containing the line, "Christ, you know it ain't easy" in the refrain—the single was a top-10 hit in the United States for the band.

Five weeks after the release of "The Ballad of John and Yoko" came the first non-Beatles single released by a Beatle, which provided further evidence that the group was fracturing and that Lennon's artistic goals were shifting. It was credited as a Lennon-McCartney composition, though McCartney had no hand in its creation. It also had only two Beatles playing on it, this time Lennon and Starr, and was credited to the Plastic Ono Band, the public having never encountered The Dirty Mac. The song was the protest anthem "Give Peace a Chance," purposely designed by Lennon to supplement or even supplant "We Shall Overcome" as a popular song of solidarity and war protest.[6]

The Plastic Ono Band became the moniker for Lennon's musical efforts for almost the next three years and was basically the name of whomever he rounded up to create the group at that particular time. It was not a fixed group, even if Lennon did draw from a pool of regulars. To counter Lennon's frustrations with The Beatles as a near magical entity, he simultaneously declared that the Plastic Ono Band was both a band with no members and a band where all who heard of it were the members; the band was "conceptual." Publicity material for the band included plastic boxes with instruments and recording equipment in them, declaring the packaging and equipment to be the band itself.

"Give Peace a Chance" was composed and recorded in the couple's hotel room in Montreal as they staged a bed-in protest for peace. A crowd of visitors, including several counterculture notables (Timothy Leary, Abbie Hoffman, and Tom Smothers among them), clapped along and sang the chorus while Lennon verbally exhorted them ("Everybody now, c'mon…you won't get it unless you want it!") through the tune. Later, in the studio, Lennon had Starr strengthen the rhythm, sometimes creating a sound eerily similar to a heartbeat, and added some singers to sweeten the chorus.[7]

The calculated simplicity of the song worked and still does. The verses are a quick flurry of multisyllabic terms that "Everybody's talkin' 'bout," which jumble together almost into insensibility, whereupon they are replaced with the simple statement of the chorus, "All we are saying is give peace a chance." The chorus is the message, but that is not all the song has going for it. The humor and cleverness of the song's construction is evident on the verses as Lennon's wordplay reduces the initially serious sounding terms into less and less important topics, sometimes finishing with nonsense and non sequiturs such as "bishops, fishops, rabbis, pop eyes, and bye bye, bye byes." In the live performance of the song a few months later in Toronto, Lennon dismisses the verses' importance. And as a sing-along chant, perhaps this is so. But as a song, the way Lennon says what he does supports and illuminates the message the song seeks to impart. The song ends with Lennon saying "OK, beautiful, yeah!" along with the assembly cheering and applauding.

The flip side is a song featuring Ono's vocals on her own composition, "Remember Love," accompanied only by Lennon's finger-picking guitar work. The song is a yearning number of pure nursery rhyme innocence and simplicity, not at all like the other harsh vocalizations Ono had so far produced.

"Give Peace a Chance" is so well known that it is hard to see it as controversial, yet it was and still has the power to antagonize. Despite the fact that it was the first musical offering of a (more or less) solo Beatle and carried the Lennon-McCartney composition credit, the single was controversial enough in the United States to only briefly make it to number 14 on the pop chart.

WEDDING ALBUM

The third of the couple's nonrock albums was of a piece with the previous two. The packaging was an attempt to include the public in on the wedding, complete with photos, a copy of the wedding certificate, a photo of a piece of wedding cake, and news clippings of their activities. This recording consisted of Lennon and Ono calling out each other's names in various ways (angry, sad, fearful, teasing, etc.) accompanied by their amplified heartbeats for one entire album side, and a sound collage of interviews and mundane snippets (such as ordering room service) from their bed-in titled "Amsterdam" on side two.

The first side, then, expands on the concept of "Baby's Heartbeat" and combines it with the well-known Stan Freberg novelty single from 1951, "John and Marsha." Here, the duo's heartbeats are heard as rhythm background, and Lennon and Ono recite each other's names for the entire side of the album—as long as the technology of the time allowed without a break. In context, it represents the blending and unity of the couple. It sounds as if Lennon is intermittently crunching an apple, which might be seen as both a sly comment on The Beatles production company Apple Records and/or a continuation of the Garden of Eden theme introduced on *Two Virgins*. Or, perhaps he was just hungry.

A section of the piece turned up on Ono's 12-inch promotional single for "Walking on Thin Ice." In addition, Ono later presumably used part of this recording for her song "Never Say Goodbye" from her album *It's Alright* in 1982, as Lennon's voice can be heard screaming "Yoko" on the latter recording.

Side two is an audio impression of the newlyweds' honeymoon event, the bed-in for peace in Amsterdam. Once again, background noises and natural sounds are heard. The recording begins with Ono singing "John John (Let's Hope for Peace)," a more formal live rock version of which was included on their next album. This segues into a part of the tireless interviews they gave during, as they called it, their "advertising campaign for peace" and some of the clearer summations of their message are not surprisingly included here. Lennon can be heard ordering room service and reading the paper to his wife. When a questioner asks about The Beatles' first hit single, "Love Me Do," incorrectly referring to it as "Do You Love Me?" Lennon instantly quips, "Not particularly," in reply.

The ending is a sound collage of the two extemporizing commercial jingles in their advertising campaign for peace and unwinding at the end of the day. Lennon also mockingly performs a few bars of his Beatles composition, "Good Night," which Starr sings on the White Album. Whereas the first side is of novelty interest after more than one listening, the second side succeeds in Ono's and Lennon's goal of creating an immediate, artistic, and communicative documentary impression of their then-current lives. Despite this success, it was to be the last of such experimental recordings released, although another was planned.

A footnote to the album came and went all but unnoticed in 1980 with the release of the couple's *Double Fantasy* album. The *Double Fantasy* cover features a black-and-white photo of Lennon and Ono kissing, a fitting image for that album's theme of couplehood and family. What passed mention was that it was a remake of or a parallel to the interior album cover for *Wedding Album*, which features a similarly posed black-and-white photo of the couple presumably enjoying (or re-creating) their first kiss as husband and wife.

"Cold Turkey"

By the fall of 1969 The Beatles was ostensibly still a functioning unit, yet the group's fragmentation continued as each member found other artistic outlets for his varying interests. As The Beatles completed the *Abbey Road* album, Lennon presented them with his latest song "Cold Turkey." The group rejected it, so Lennon decided to record it as the next release of his Plastic Ono Band.[8] They may have rejected it as a Beatles release, but both George Harrison and Ringo Starr were willing to record it and did so, but

Lennon rejected the effort and re-recorded it with other musicians.[9] *Abbey Road* was then released in October 1969, as was Lennon and Ono's third experimental recorded collaboration, *Wedding Album.*

As discussed previously, *Wedding Album* would prove to be a comparatively minor work, while "Cold Turkey" became a significant marker of Lennon's artistic terrain and growth as The Beatles came to an end and is therefore a significant marker for him as a solo recording artist as well.

Like its predecessor "Give Peace a Chance," "Cold Turkey" was originally credited as a Lennon-McCartney composition (later releases give credit only to Lennon), and its performance was credited as a product of the Plastic Ono Band.[10] And once again, McCartney seems to have had no direct involvement in the song's creation or recording. It would be the last time Lennon would uphold the agreement he and Paul had supposedly made in their youth to share all songwriting credits. McCartney apparently stopped this practice before Lennon when he began composing songs for the film *The Family Way* in 1966. After the film, McCartney went back and forth on his non-Beatles songs, sharing credit with Lennon on two and taking sole credit on four, such as on "Come and Get It" for the group Badfinger in 1969. Interestingly, Lennon did credit McCartney for his similar, though noticeably fewer, non-Beatle compositions until the change on "Cold Turkey."[11]

As Lennon and the Plastic Ono Band released "Cold Turkey," The Beatles released George Harrison's song "Something" as their new single, with Lennon's song "Come Together" on the flip side, both from the *Abbey Road* album. The sensibilities of the two A-sides are quite distinct and partially evidence Lennon's increasing artistic difference from the rest of the group.

"Cold Turkey" shares with Lennon's *Abbey Road* piece "I Want You (She's So Heavy)" a harsh overall sound, straining vocals, and trance-like repetition. In addition, the song's production prefigures the stripped-down minimalist approach that Lennon would employ on his and Ono's *Plastic Ono Band* albums in the coming year.

The song title "Cold Turkey" was a slang term for immediate and complete withdrawal from drugs. The lyrical descriptions of the "thirty-six hours, rollin' in pain" and the self-made hell of rising fevers and bleak, nervous nihilism certainly make the literal point clear. When Lennon's weary, moaning delivery of the simple lyrics are musically coupled with his and Eric Clapton's jarring and rumbling guitar work, the song succeeds as an audio portrait of physical and mental anguish.

Yet, as was not unusual with Lennon, the song goes beyond the literal meaning. Lennon later termed it a song about pain, and was surprised that it was largely banned from radio play in the United States on the grounds that it was about drugs—even though it was antidrugs (or at least, anti–heroin addiction). In fact, the lyrics never mention drugs in general, or any drug in particular, and instead work on the metaphorical level of the pain of total or surprising loss. Something that, as Lennon said about the song in 1972, happens to all of us "one way or another."[12] In that light, the song becomes Lennon's perhaps unconscious statement of anxiety at the apparent dissolution of The Beatles, a major personal and professional support system that he would have to do without.

As if the literal subject matter was not pushing the pop music boundaries enough, the five-minute piece ends with almost 1 minute and 45 seconds of Lennon's screams and moans layered with similarly characterized guitar tones and feedback noises. Where "Give Peace a Chance" drew out its chanting chorus and ends in exultation, "Cold Turkey" draws out tortured moans and ends in exhaustion. The song finishes abruptly with a short series of sounds that are eerily similar to Lennon's groundbreaking work on The Beatles' recordings "Strawberry Fields" and "Revolution #9" as well as his experimental sound collages with Ono. Perhaps this was Lennon's "audio signature." This audio referencing of previous work further implies that "Cold Turkey" recognizes any type of abrupt loss.

The flip side of "Cold Turkey," Ono's "Don't Worry Kyoko," is just as intense, with Lennon and Clapton providing the lilting guitar groove for her vibrant vocalizing and was included as part of Ono's album *Fly* and as such is discussed in that context.

Characteristically, Lennon debuted this strange-sounding (for the era), harsh, and alienating song before its release at a rock and roll festival highlighting 1950s performers, chiding the audience when they did not respond as enthusiastically as he thought they should have. He also used "Cold Turkey" as a joke when he later returned his Member of the British Empire (MBE) award to the British government in protest of (among other things) its support of the United States in Vietnam. He facetiously added that he was also protesting the fact that "Cold Turkey" did not make it into the top 10. It had peaked at number 14 in the United Kingdom and only made it to number 30 in the United States, the pains of drug withdrawal not exactly being acceptable pop music fodder at the time.

The expression of raw emotional pain and angst in "Cold Turkey" would soon be at the core of many of the songs that would make up Lennon's *Plastic Ono Band* album—although that album is significantly more direct, having most of the poetic metaphor absent. In fact, fans and critics alike would soon see such expressions as an integral part of Lennon's strengths as a singer-songwriter. Therefore, the importance of "Cold Turkey" in establishing Lennon as a solo artist and significant creative force separate from The Beatles should not be ignored.

LIVE PEACE IN TORONTO

After the completion of the *Abbey Road* album in late summer 1969, Lennon was basically finished with recording as a Beatle. Although the group would have other recording sessions as Phil Spector worked on the *Get Back* sessions' tapes and turned them into the album *Let It Be,* Lennon did not participate. In fact, Lennon took the unfinished Beatles tracks "What's the New Mary Jane?" and "You Know My Name (Look Up My Number)" and intended to complete them for future release as Plastic Ono Band offerings. McCartney reportedly stopped this, and the former did not see release until the *Anthology 3* collection in 1995, while the latter became the flip side of the "Let It Be" single in March 1970.[13]

In September 1969, Lennon accepted an invitation to attend a rock and roll festival concert in Toronto featuring a few modern groups and such 1950s stalwarts as Jerry Lee Lewis, Little Richard, and others. He quickly formed a version of the Plastic Ono Band again, including Eric Clapton, for the event. The band had no real rehearsals but was able to get through passable if erratic versions of early rock classics such as "Blue Suede Shoes," "Money," and "Dizzy Miss Lizzie." The Beatles, with Lennon performing the lead vocals, had covered the two latter songs. Lennon's combined nervousness and pleasure are evident while the band's roughness is alternately a drawback when they slip out of tune and out of time, and a true joy when the performances of Lennon and Clapton mesh and feed off each other.

Leaving the oldies behind, the band next performs "Yer Blues," which Clapton at least had performed with Lennon before, albeit 10 months earlier. The next number was the debut of Lennon's "Cold Turkey." Although the studio single had been out and on the charts by the time the album of this live concert was released, the song had not yet been recorded when performed here. The performance moves along at a slightly quicker and more lilting pace and is not nearly as harsh as the single became or as it would be in future live performances.

"Give Peace a Chance" follows, with Lennon extemporizing alternate but similar lyrics for the verses, retaining the same thrust and mixing the serious message and humor of the single recording.

Even though contemporary bands were also in performance in addition to the 1950s icons, the event was advertised as a rock and roll revival. In what must have been equal doses of courage and arrogance, the band shifted to featuring Ono and her nonpop performances, expanding on the performance pattern employed for *The Rolling Stones Rock and Roll Circus* almost a year previously. Most might consider this a long way in some respects from Jerry Lee Lewis, but Lennon and Ono saw it differently. She and the band rip into what would become the B-side of "Cold Turkey," "Don't Worry Kyoko." Ono's full-throttle vocals and Lennon and Clapton's hard-core guitar sounds must have been startling to a crowd primed for rockabilly and doo-wop.

The finale of the set is an electrified version of Ono's "John John (Let's Hope for Peace)," an acoustic version of which would be included in the audio collage of "Amsterdam" from *Wedding Album,* as previously mentioned. Like "Cold Turkey," at the time of the concert, a recorded version of the performance had not been released yet. However, it would be issued by the time *Live Peace in Toronto* was released. Lennon and Clapton end up setting their guitars by their amplifiers, thus letting the perpetual feedback end the set as the band left the stage.

An edited version of the performance came out as a record album three months later in December 1969, making it Lennon and Ono's fourth album. Those four albums and the two Plastic Ono Band singles had been released in 13 months, in addition to Lennon's other work, with and without The Beatles. The concert was filmed, but when the documentary was eventually released, the Plastic Ono Band was not included. In 1988, their segment, with a little bit of introductory footage of classic 1950s stars, became its own documentary titled *Sweet Toronto*. As with *The Rolling Stones Rock and Roll Circus* from the previous year, had the band's footage been released as part of the original film, it would have helped to solidify the public's understanding of the end of The Beatles as a living musical entity. Furthermore, it would have highlighted Lennon's distance from them as a separate performer in the public's mind, as well as help answer the perennial "What does he see in Yoko?" question.

On December 15, Lennon and Ono performed with George Harrison, Eric Clapton, and others as the Plastic Ono Supergroup in London at a fundraiser for UNICEF. The group performed superb, hard-edged versions of "Cold Turkey" and "Don't Worry Kyoko" for an audience that, unlike the one in Toronto, at least might have known what to expect. The vibrant performance was recorded and included in their 1972 *Sometime in New York City* double album and Frank Zappa's *Playground Psychotics* almost 20 years later.

"Instant Karma!"

On January 27, 1970, Lennon wrote and recorded the next Plastic Ono Band single, and it was released to the public in less than two weeks, becoming a top-five hit. "Give Peace a Chance" was a more or less an on-the-spot recording, and—although credited to Lennon-McCartney and later overdubbed by Starr—by its nature, it was never considered to be a Beatles recording. "Cold Turkey" initially became the second Plastic Ono Band single by default rather than by design when The Beatles rejected it and Lennon decided to record it anyway. But the third Plastic Ono Band single, "Instant Karma!" was never offered to The Beatles, providing evidence, if any were needed at that late date, that Lennon no longer considered The Beatles his prime artistic outlet, if an artistic outlet for him at all. This and future such releases would credit Lennon and / or Ono along with the Plastic Ono Band until the name was partially abandoned when the couple separated late in 1973, although Lennon jokingly credited some of 1974s *Walls and Bridges* to the Plastic UFOno Band and the Nuclear Ono Band.

The title "Instant Karma!" is also a bit of a joke, because, in traditional thinking, karmic forces might take more than one life time to play out for an individual. Instant karma would indeed be a surprise, and the exclamation point in the title emphasizes the clever nature of Lennon's irony in forcing the listener to ponder just what "instant karma" might be. It also functions as advertising hyperbole, an aspect emphasized in the album artwork for the song in Lennon's 1975 singles collection *Shaved Fish.*

The first verses have a sarcastic tone and berate the listener to "get yourself together...pretty soon you're gonna be dead" and telling the listener "its up to you—yeah, you!" The tone reverses when Lennon seems to mock the listener for thinking he or she is a "superstar" but then he agrees, "Well, right you are!" This leads into the rousing anthem-like repeated chorus of "We all shine on, like the moon and the stars and the sun." Instant karma seems to be a system of positive retribution with "everyone gonna get their share" if they merely recognize their responsibilities to other humans. After implying what proper human behavior ought to be, Lennon then poses the question, "Why in the world are we here, surely not to live in pain and fear?" The answer that we are here to self-actualize through concern for humanity is strongly implied but never stated outright.

Sonically the recording has similarities to "Give Peace a Chance" with its handclapping rhythm and Lennon's chorus-leading vocals. And like "Cold Turkey," it has a simple stripped-down feel despite the jangly rhythmic pianos and echoed mix. There is no piano or guitar solo, but Lennon takes a brief vocal solo of grunts and moans in what may be a joking reference to the lengthy vocal moans and screams of "Cold Turkey." Otherwise, his vocals bite through with a real urgency and sincerity to the performance, despite the 1950s Sun Records–style echo that serves to partly distance and disembody Lennon's vocal presence. The result is that Lennon manages to have it both ways: his voice seems otherworldly, yet tangible. "Cold Turkey" demonstrated Lennon's penchant for taking something personal and expanding its message through metaphor. "Instant Karma! (We All Shine On)" was Lennon providing a chiding though positive and proactive message for humanity. The same artistic drive would be the bedrock of his post-Beatles career.

The single's reverse side, Ono's "Who Has Seen the Wind?" is a low-key, evocative number on which Lennon does not perform.

Lennon had demonstrated his ability to have pop hits without The Beatles. A Beatles compilation album titled *Hey Jude* was released around the time of "Instant Karma!" and The Beatles' *Let It Be* album was issued the following May. By the time it was clear to the public that The Beatles were no longer a functioning unit, Lennon already had the *Live Peace in Toronto* album going gold, and three top-40 hit singles, the most recent ("Instant Karma!") having peaked at number 3.

Gimme Some Truth, 1970–1973

With all The Beatles having finally acknowledged their split in late April 1970, Lennon had already turned his attention to the primal scream therapy of Arthur Janov to help deal with his lingering stress and strain as well as certain addictions, a move that would have a purging effect on his musical and lyrical compositions as the year progressed. Lennon's actions had, to some degree, negatively colored his reputation with the public from his seemingly radical artistic and political endeavors with Ono to the well-publicized public break-up of The Beatles.

JOHN LENNON / PLASTIC ONO BAND

It would not be until December 1970 that Lennon's first "solo" album, *John Lennon / Plastic Ono Band,* would be released. Its uncomplicated and direct sound, gritty frankness, painfully raw emotional content, and moral outrage would become the marker of artistic and personal integrity by which Lennon and other artists making "serious" pop music would be measured. The album stands as a document of Lennon's mental and emotional purgation following the end of The Beatles. For his audience, it is a call to wake up from being narcotized by childhood trauma, parental authority, popular culture, consumer society, and all manner of social, political, and religious institutions. If, during the time the album was recorded, Lennon was strongly influenced by the primal scream therapy practices of Arthur Janov, then *John Lennon / Plastic Ono Band* was the artistic embodiment of his primal scream.

Lennon chose to open the album with the selection he also released as a single, "Mother." The album version opens with four dirge-like bell peals not present on the single release, which also fades out sooner. Lyrically the song is an exorcism of the pain of parental rejection, as Lennon mourns the mother who did not want him and chastises the father who left him, purging the pain by saying "goodbye, goodbye." Percussion from Ringo Starr ticks like a clock, emphasizing the awareness of how the past impinges upon the present, while Lennon's piano hits chords echoing the pealing bells that began the song.

After a third verse in which Lennon warns the next generation not to "do what I have done" (a lyrical nod to the harrowing traditional ballad "House of the Rising Sun"), he begins a series of increasingly agonized laments, shouting repeatedly "mama don't go" and "daddy come home" as if reverting to the anguished, frightened child. Structurally similar to the finale of "Cold Turkey," it is just as emotionally stark and disquieting in its own way, something that could be said of much of the album. To no one's surprise, the barren-sounding, angst-ridden single—backed by one of Ono's better numbers, "Why"—did not break into the top 40.

"Hold On" is a song of affirmation. Lennon does not hide behind an impersonal narrator, but specifically mentions John and Yoko in the lyrics. The first verses allude to the trials and tribulations that the Lennons experienced as John sings of his "fight" and Yoko's "flight." These challenges not only encompass the emotional pain that the Lennons faced in their primal scream therapy, but also the concrete prejudice (racism, sexism, and a public that blamed Ono for taking Lennon away from The Beatles) and opposition (to the causes the duo promoted, such as world peace) that the Lennons faced from the time they became a couple. Lennon reminds his wife and himself that from within they will have the strength to weather the storms.

Lennon then expands this notion to encompass all peoples on earth. He realizes that he and his wife are not the only two who face problems in life. When people of all nations come together and understand they are "one," then they will "see the light." Peace will be more than an imagined dream.

The shimmering guitar work of the song sounds vaguely like parts of Lennon's "Sun King" from *Abbey Road,* but the similarities are superficial. Those who see nothing but bleakness from *Plastic Ono Band* forget the ultimately hopeful messages embedded in some of the tracks, or Lennon's never totally missing humor. Before the verse about the world, the listener hears "Cookie!" in the voice of the Cookie Monster from *Sesame Street.* It is either a complete non sequitur or a clever referential commentary on childhood traumas and adult obsessions.

Continuing in the line of the therapeutic value of self-awareness, Lennon focuses in "I Found Out" on different avenues he tried to find meaning and make peace with himself, only to discover that they all led to dead ends. The title means "I wised up," and the first verse points a finger at hangers-on and others who tried to exploit Lennon and the Beatles for political ends, financial gain, or both. Two years earlier, Lennon and Beatle band mate Paul McCartney flew to New York City and announced the opening of Apple Corps. The two naively encouraged musicians and inventors and those with innovative ideas to approach Apple for funding of their pet projects. Coming to grips with the failure of this tack, Lennon tells these same, and similar, people, "stay away from my door."

In the second verse, he tackles formalized Christianity. Four years earlier, the U.S. media held Lennon over the coals due to his remarks comparing the popularity of the Beatles to Jesus Christ.[1] At a Chicago press conference, he reluctantly apologized. He tacitly withdraws that apology in the second verse as he sings that there will be no Jesus coming "from the sky" to bring salvation. He tells the listener not to expect help to come from some outside source, but rather that one must rely on oneself. For Lennon, this realization frees him. There is no hope to be gleaned from false teachings. He ends the verse singing, "I know I can cry."

The third verse addresses free love and the idea that jumping in and out of bed with a number of partners would bring some kind of meaning and satisfaction. In particular, he addresses men and tells them that sexual prowess will not define their masculinity or who they really are as people.

Lennon makes this verse painfully personal as he closes with the thought that his parents conceived and gave birth to him, but, in the end, they did not want him to be a part of their lives, nor did they want to give of their selves to him. His father went off to sea. His mother chose to let her sister raise him. Agreeing with the pop psychology idea that entertainers seek the love denied them as children, Lennon sings that, because his parents did not want him, they made him "a star," however unintentionally.

Still feeling burned from sitting at the feet of the Maharishi Mahesh Yogi several years earlier, Lennon next casts his critical eye on the promises of Eastern religions. Just as Marx spoke of religion being an opiate for the masses, Lennon asserts that "Hare Krishna" will "keep you occupied with pie in the sky." These teachings will not help the followers come to terms with the issues of everyday life, because they have no special enlightenment of the individual soul. Lennon implicates gurus of any kind, but the listener cannot help thinking that Lennon is visualizing the Maharishi in his lyrics. Lennon had earlier criticized the teacher from Rishikesh in his veiled attack on the guru in the Beatle song "Sexy Sadie" from the White Album. Lennon rejects all leaders who have *the* answer, opting instead to have "found out" for himself.

In the final verse, Lennon deals with drugs and the false high that "dope and cocaine" present. It is an empty place. He again brings up religion, interestingly combining the religions of Christianity and Beatlemania as he sings of "Jesus" and "Paul" in the same line, a typical example of Lennon's punning wordplay, this time to make a serious point. Later, in the album track "God," he sings of how he believes in neither Jesus nor Beatles.

Finally, Lennon tells the listener what he has learned. You have to "feel your own pain." None of the answers he has addressed in the five verses helped him come to terms with his malaise. He had to face what hurt him inside without drugs or religion or fame or good feelings from giving his wealth to good causes or registered charities as buffers, and finds himself better for it.

Lennon's vocals start with sneering and build to a snarl, partnered with a spitting, sputtering guitar sounding like an electric power box shorting out. The guitar solo is only a couple of quickly struck notes repeated a few times, which is yet another example of Lennon's minimalist musical expression. The anger and pain combine until finally Lennon's vocalizing is reduced to a shrill bark, in an approximation of the earlier guitar solo. The track is a particularly strong one in an album of exceptional material.

Lennon then sings of the sleight-of-hand imposed on the masses by the upper class in a song more complex than most listeners consider. In "Working Class Hero," he details how the listener is hegemonically raised to strive for a dream that will always be just out of reach. The "working class hero" is living an illusion. He is "doped with religion" and is told there is "room at the top." Only the bloodthirsty who can learn to "smile as you kill," those whose philosophy is directly opposed to the peace and freedom from hate that Lennon called for and sang about, will get to the mansion on the hillside.

Yet, the refrain declares that a "working class hero is something to be." It seems, though, that Lennon is being sarcastic in the statement. The working-class heroes are merely "fucking peasants" who are manipulated and exploited at every turn by the powers that be.

Using what appear to be his own experiences, Lennon sings of how the masses are molded from the time they come out of the womb to be sheep or followers in the employ of the wealthy. As in "I Found Out," he speaks out of pain. The pain was so great that he became numb to it. Lennon sings, "They hate you if you're clever," which seems to be a direct expression of his youthful troubles in school. The thought carries forward as paralyzing fear until the working-class hero "can't really function."

The only instrument is Lennon's acoustic, steadily-churning guitar, helping the song to capture something of a folk troubadour ambiance. To some, the song seems to have been inspired by the work of Bob Dylan, an ironic observation in view of Lennon's disavowal of "Zimmerman" as a false idol in "God" later in the album. The song was left off many U.S. radio station play lists because twice in the lyrics Lennon employs the adjective "fucking." In the years since Lennon's passing, he has had the "Working Class Hero" mantle placed on him as a positive attribute, a possible misreading of the song. He ends the song by singing, "If you want to be a hero, well just follow me." But in the context of the album, that line is decidedly ironic, as is the entire song. Fans must view Lennon as the "real" working-class hero, who had seen through the manipulation and tried to lift the veil for others. It is part of the odd "martyrdom" layered over Lennon's senseless and brutal killing. One can only wonder what the self-aware and healthily cynical Lennon himself might have said about it all.

At one point Lennon sings about the "folks on the hill," and it is hard not to imagine him singing "fools" instead of "folks" since it would fit and make sense in context. But if he did have "fools" in the lyrics, then the link to Paul McCartney's Beatles song "The Fool on the Hill" would be too distracting from Lennon's message.

In a song that parallels "Hold On," Lennon again sings of himself and his wife, and then casts his net to encompass the world, in "Isolation." A simple piano and drums support Lennon's tentative vocals. An organ then joins in as the vocals become vibrant and wailing. He starts the song by focusing on the relationship between Ono and himself. He observes that people have a perception that, because he is rich and famous, his dream has come true. But, like everyone else, he fears loneliness and "isolation." He notes that Ono and he are trying to make the world a better place, but they continue to face opposition, which leads to another form of isolation.

He does not blame anyone. In a passage inspired by the old rhythm and blues song "I Apologize," Lennon admits that he does not expect anyone to truly understand. After all, everyone has been taught the same, and we are all "victim(s) of the insane." Lennon's hope is that the pervasive fear that isolates people will not cause the end of the world. The song is direct and moving, with Lennon giving an animated and nuanced vocal performance.

A driving rhythmic piano and incessant drumbeat underscore "Remember," a song visiting the memories of childhood with remorse when seen from the adult perspective. The song looks back to childhood events and perspectives with an awareness that has changed their meaning. "Remember today," Lennon sings, as a way to cope with the childhood memories that are now traumatic in hindsight. The first section recalls childhood stories of heroic escape, but the rest of the song indicates there can be no fanciful escape from one's past, but then implies that perhaps escape is not needed after all.

Lennon quotes from the old rhythm and blues classic "Bring It on Home to Me" with the line, "If you ever change your mind about leaving it all behind," but in a vastly different context. Here it is not an invitation to come home to a loved one, but an admonition of such action's impossibility, and a call to face what the present is in an awareness of the past. The chorus then allows for forgiveness, saying, "don't feel sorry" and "don't you worry" about past actions or their consequences. Lennon ends the song with the start of a British nursery rhyme commemorating Guy Fawkes, a conspirator who unsuccessfully tried to cause the death of King James I and the members of a joint session of Parliament on November 5, 1605, by setting off explosives. "Remember,

remember, the fifth of November," Lennon sings, interrupted by the sounds of a quick explosion. It is a stark ending to a surprisingly poignant song, the rupture of childhood trauma echoing in the adult in the form of half-recalled nursery rhymes.

A series of simple cartoon drawings titled "Love is..." was first syndicated in 1970 and may have been part of the inspiration for the lyrical structure of the gentle song "Love." Lennon's hushed voice provides a litany of what love is, ranging from the intriguing "Love is needing, needing to be loved" to the poetic though somewhat perplexing "Love is real, real is love." The near greeting-card simplicity of some of the lyrics runs the risk of being maudlin out of context, but surrounded by the weighty anguish of the rest of the album, this reassuring assessment of the power of love to comfort and shelter keeps it centered in its sincerity and is yet another example of the album's emotional depth and complexity. Even in an ocean of angst, Lennon could find an oasis of hope.

In an interview in 1970 shortly after the album's release, Lennon said that he thought the song might make a good single.[2] Released as a single in England almost two years after Lennon's killing to help promote the *John Lennon Collection* CD, the slightly remixed song made it to number 27 on the British charts 12 years after its debut on this album.[3]

"Well Well Well" is a song of restlessness and uneasiness, and the narrator does not understand why he and his partner feel that way. They enjoy a meal together. The couple walks under the "English sky." They discuss the issues of the day: "revolution" and "women's liberation." Perhaps their pangs of guilt lie in the fact that they can sit and ponder things and take action or not take action since they can do whatever they want with their time and money.

Lennon, Ringo Starr, and Klaus Voorman create a harsh, power-trio sound and Starr's playing is quite effective. Lennon employs crackling guitar through a middle section where he screams the title with real power and abandon. Lennon's work on this cut is of a piece with his playing on Ono's companion album, and these sorts of tracks provide the best evidence for those who wish to argue that the Lennon-Ono collaborations influenced the punk rock sounds emerging later in the decade.

The refrain of "Well Well Well" hints at a self-mocking commentary on the verses, which also include similar stances such as when the protagonists talk of revolution "just like two liberals in the sun." On a composing demo released on *Acoustic*, the lyrics are different. Researchers have said Lennon sings that his love "looks so beautiful I could wee." But Lennon is singing in a slightly nasal voice, some consonants are dropped, and the guitar plays over his voice at points. It is not clear, but he could very well be singing the more conventional word "weep."

"OK?" Lennon asks as "Look at Me" begins, setting the theme for a song that is all about needing to be assured by the self and others. Lennon repeats lines of simple questions and simple phrases in the song. His narrator struggles with his reason for being. He wonders aloud who or what he is "supposed to be." And, building on the being, he ponders what action he should take, and what he should do for his "love." The song does not hint at whether Lennon is singing about who he is and what he should do in his romantic relationship, or if the questions apply more generally to his place in the world. "Please look at me," he sings, as if he will cease to be if not acknowledged. Again, it is reminiscent of a child imploring a disinterested parent for attention.

The song was composed in 1968 and was considered for The Beatles' White Album. It does bear some structural resemblance to "Dear Prudence" and even more to "Julia" from that album, though it is faster paced than either of those songs. Sandwiched between the proto-punk sounds of "Well Well Well" and the lyrical sledgehammer of "God," the song functions as a respite from the album's instrumental and lyrical intensity. Emotionally, though, "Look at Me" is just as strong as any track on the album. The earnest uncertainty and the exposed questions are buoyed along by Lennon's finger-picking styled guitar work. There's a genuine innocence and a fragile honesty to the song that give it an evocative power.

A year after stating that the Beatles' "Ballad of John and Yoko" was a prayer, John Lennon sang, "I don't believe in Jesus." Nor did he believe in God, except as a "concept by which we measure our pain." In the song simply titled "God," Lennon describes God as a concept of the human imagination, and not a concept that would lead to inner peace or transcendence. Rather, God was a rule by which anguish or suffering is measured.

Lennon first connected God, or at least Christianity, and suffering in the Beatles song "Girl." He asks whether the girl was taught as a child that pain leads to pleasure. In the 1970 *Rolling Stone* interview, Lennon stated he was trying to say something in "Girl" about a need to be "tortured" before one can get to heaven.

"God" goes on to become an attack on false prophets, both sacred and secular. The lyrics form a litany that begins with sacred icons (Jesus, Buddha) and turns to popular figures (Elvis, The Beatles). For Lennon, these images are false gods, and the understanding of reality comes from a clear view of the self.

Not only does Lennon refuse faith, but he rejects all systems and institutions. Interestingly, Lennon commented that, at one time, he had intended to leave a section of the song lyricless, so listeners could add to the list on their own. Lennon went on in the song to disavow his belief in "Zimmerman," that is, Bob Dylan. This is puzzling, because Dylan would seem to be the iconic image, and Zimmerman the actual man. In the recording of the song on the posthumous CD collection *Acoustic*, Lennon does sing Dylan and not Zimmerman and in reproductions of his handwritten lyrics, Dylan is listed as well.

Lennon concludes that he only believes in himself, although he immediately enlarges that certainty to encompass Yoko Ono. For him, that is all that is real. Unlike Paul Simon, for Lennon there are no bridges over troubled water that can mediate human pain. After his creed, or noncreed, listing those whom he no longer believes or never believed, the melody shifts and Lennon sings to the listener, who more than likely still embraces the Beatles myth, "The dream is over." He was the "dreamweaver," but he states that he is "reborn." And, he tells listeners to go on without him. For him, there is nothing else, and his listeners have to recognize they are alone as well. Lennon "reborn" is no longer dreaming and no longer taken in by myths, including those partly of his own making.

The album concludes with a brief but powerful song titled "My Mummy's Dead" that couples nursery-rhyme simplicity with stark emotional depth. Lennon sings in a weary and quizzical manner about his mother's death, and the sound fidelity matches that of some of his later posthumously released home demo cassettes. The effect is memorable and chilling. And such is how the album ends, capturing the essence of psychological pain and intimating at its persistence.

YOKO ONO/PLASTIC ONO BAND

Most of Lennon's fans at the time may have been glad that this companion album to *John Lennon/Plastic Ono Band* was not packaged with it as a double record set, but perhaps it should have been, since both are emotional soundscapes. In addition, the albums have similar front and back cover images, and they share the same musicians and same spare style—in sound as well as the exploration of raw emotion.

Lennon's improvisational guitar work and the myriad of sounds he manages to create must have been in his mind when he gave the *Rolling Stone* interview two months after the recordings were made, for he truly does make the guitar "speak" throughout Ono's album.[4] Each track conveys core emotions with minimal or nonexistent lyrical components. The opening cut is a powerful number titled "Why" with searing, cascading guitar work from Lennon matching Ono's vocals as she screams the title word over and over along with nonverbal vocalizations. Firm support from Ringo Starr on drums and Klaus Voorman on bass keeps Lennon and Ono solidly on track. As much as any of Lennon's numbers from his album, this cut embodies slicing pain, and the couple's musical interactions are a marvel to hear, in what is clearly one of their finest joint efforts.

Of course, the inner rage of "Why" would have to be followed by the languid but still tumultuous in its own way "Why Not." Once again Lennon frees his guitar playing and creates a wide variety of accompaniments to Ono's now echoed vocals. Other numbers use the natural sounds of birds and trains to augment the aural approximations of emotional and mental states of being. Each song uses different musical foci, especially rhythmically, to support the emotive content. "Greenfield Morning" and "Touch Me" are the other standout tracks in an album that showcases some of Lennon's most adventurous and inventive guitar playing.

"POWER TO THE PEOPLE"

Not surprisingly, the psychological intensity of "Mother" was not exactly top-40 pop material, and the single only made it to number 43 on the U.S. charts. Lennon then turned back to the more outwardly directed and socially conscious thinking of "Give Peace a Chance" for his next nonalbum single, "Power to the People."

At its heart, the song is another populist anthem, with an overall sound similar to "Instant Karma!" due as much (if not more) to co-producer Phil Spector's return as to Lennon's predilections. A chorus intones the title four times as the sound of marching feet, similar to clapping, opens the recording and sets the rhythm. Lennon's echoed voice takes the lead another four times, helped along by tumbling percussion and Bobby Keyes's aggressive sax playing.

The opening verse references Lennon's Beatle song "Revolution" by nearly repeating the line "Say you want a revolution," while making the important change of replacing "you" with "we." In "Revolution" the opening statement was followed by the tentative "well, you know, we all want to change the world." Here, however, all tentativeness is gone; the line is followed by "we better get it on right away" and a call for listeners to "get into the street."

The generalities continue, as the next verse summons workers to "get all they really own." The final verse is most striking for its feminist stance, declaring that the "woman back home" needs "to be herself so she can free herself." Each verse is broken up by the repeating refrain of the title, which is tripled and faded out at the end.

As generic statements of mass empowerment, the sentiments work, as does the song as an upbeat attempt to straddle counterculture ideals and mainstream disaffections. Simple, direct, and rousing without being vindictive, the song may be little more than sloganeering, but it is not necessarily less of an accomplishment because of it. As Lennon got more specific about his causes in his songwriting over the next year and a half, the success of this song would illustrate just how difficult such an attempt was to properly manage. The song's lack of stridency and ability to be broadly interpreted helped it to the number-11 position on the U.S. charts.

The flip side was an experimental piece by Ono titled "Touch Me" and had been included on her *Plastic Ono Band* album. The track was substituted for the U.S. release when "Open Your Box (Hirake)" was censored in the United Kingdom. "Touch Me" is a gritty effort, with grumbling and staccato guitar work from Lennon under Ono's alternately fractured and wavering vocals. Early on, the piece includes the sound of a tree falling, presumably recorded when no one was there.

THE ELASTIC OZ BAND: "GOD SAVE US" / "DO THE OZ"

Lennon's next single was something of an anomaly in his career. *Oz*, a countercultural underground British newspaper, was in legal trouble with the British government, and Lennon and Ono decided to support the journalists by releasing a single in hopes it would be a fundraiser.

Lennon assembled a band, this time calling it The Elastic Oz Band, and selected Bill Elliot (later vocalist for the group Splinter) to handle the lead vocals for Lennon and Ono's song "God Save Us," oddly using the term "God" in a more conventional sense than in the song "God" on the *Plastic Ono Band* album. Lennon recorded a guide vocal that Elliot copied and, with echo added by Phil Spector, the recording sounds more than a little like Lennon himself. The guide vocal version is included in the *John Lennon Anthology* under the title of "God Save Oz" and seems finished and polished enough to consider it a long-lost Lennon single.

The song resembles Lennon's "Move over Ms. L" from three years later in that it has a fast, rollicking pace helped along by some tight horn work. Lyrically, Lennon and Ono return to the idea behind "Give Peace a Chance," mixing the serious and the absurd. The lyrics primarily list things God should save us from, as well as things we should fight for. On the more serious side, listeners are told they should "fight for children's rights," a fairly radical thought in 1971; on the more absurd side, it is suggested to "fight for Rupert Bear," probably even a more radical stance, if taken literally.

On the flip side, Lennon keeps the vocals, such as they are, for himself and Ono. "Do the Oz" is a methodically paced, experimental number with a heavily echoed Ono going through various vocal pyrotechnics as Lennon shouts, "Do the Oz" and off-kilter "Hokey Pokey"–influenced instructions. The sound is shattering, with a simple chugging, repetitive rhythm pushed along by guitar and electric piano. The use of the word "God" in the title and lyrics may have kept the single from getting much airplay. It is not clear how successful the disc was in raising money for *Oz*, but it did succeed admirably in becoming a Lennon rarity and collectible.

IMAGINE

Lennon's next album was a conscious attempt to create a more palatable and audience-pleasing product than *Plastic Ono Band* had been. Lennon thought that *Plastic Ono Band* was "too real" for most listeners and that *Imagine* conveyed the same message "sugar coated."[5] Phil Spector was brought in to co-produce with Lennon and musicians including George Harrison and two members of the Beatle protégé group Badfinger. The songs cover quite a range, including everything from a charmingly goofy love song for Ono to an extremely vitriolic attack on Paul McCartney. Helped by the instant classic status of the title cut (a number-three hit on its first release in the United States before becoming a perennial favorite), the album is habitually the Lennon album most admired by fans alienated by his *Plastic Ono Band*'s all but unrelentingly stark content.

Even before his murder, the title cut from Lennon's second post-Beatles album, "Imagine," was well on its way to becoming a modern classic of pop music. Lennon even chose to sing it for his appearance at the birthday celebration of media mogul Sir Lew Grade in 1975, which turned out to be Lennon's last public performance. Since his murder, the song has increased in popularity and poignancy and is regularly revived. It is the song most associated with him from his post-Beatles career.

Ono's conceptual art, especially her instruction pieces, has been credited as the inspiration for the song. And if not only understood as a comment on the nature of reality, her oft-quoted remark, "The dream we dream alone is just a dream / The dream we dream together is reality" (used as lyrics to her song "Now or Never"), bears this out. The first step toward change is to imagine something different.

The twist that makes the lyrics of "Imagine" more palatable than the similar sentiments expressed in "God" is the addition of the sweeter instrumental accompaniment along with the lack of specific finger-pointing in the lyric. "Imagine" may be the most subversive pop song recorded to achieve classic status. Lennon marries instrumental music that could have accompanied the sentimental, melodramatic compositions of the prerock era with the idea of a world without religion or civil states. The tension is created by juxtaposing an understated melody with a frank and radical message. The listener is, in a sense, deceived into absorbing the song's message.

Lennon's dream is of a world with no heaven or hell awaiting us. The strong implication is that we must make the best world we can here and now, since this is all there is or will be. But because we are asked merely to imagine—to play a "what if" game—Lennon can escape the harshest criticisms, and the subversive seeds are planted. Those offended by the lyrics are responded to as Lennon's former band mate Ringo Starr did during a television appearance on a Barbara Walters special in 1981. When challenged regarding the song's statements, Starr replied, "He said 'imagine,' that's all. Just imagine it."

The title of the song "Crippled Inside" is a succinct summary of the message of the lyric. Lennon presents another of his psychological explorations. The lyrics complement the subjects Lennon addressed in the previous *Plastic Ono Band* album. The song is about the "masks" or fronts that people put on. No matter what their outward appearance or what bogus activities they participate in, it is what is in the heart that counts. And the lyrics make it sound as though just about everyone is "crippled inside" in one way or another.

The song combines a country and western feel with a little Tin Pan Alley sensibility, creating an ironic contrast with the lyrics. George Harrison provides some exuberant slide guitar work, with Lennon urging him on with a "Take it, cousin!" The piano work by Nicky Hopkins is also notable, bringing a ragtime / early jazz feel to the song. Lennon has to be using satire here, because his singing is vaguely affected as if he is hinting at a Southern U.S. accent without wanting to really do one. The lyrics contain clichés ("a cat has nine lives"), the music is light and bouncy, and all the while he is happily singing about the pervasiveness of emotional disability and the ultimate futility of trying to ignore it. To Lennon, putting on a happy face does not do anything except make one a hypocrite.

While the first verse certainly sets up the song's denunciation of trying to hide one's true self with trappings of success, false piety, or lashing out at others, it may also contain a reference to Lennon's former Beatle band mate Paul McCartney. He addresses someone who "wear[s] a suit," "look[s] quite cute," and "hide[s]...behind a smile." These descriptions can easily apply to Lennon's characterizations of McCartney as seen in a later track, "How Do You Sleep?" from *Imagine*.

His description of the false person in the suit who, in the second verse, also "wear[s] a collar and tie" complements the premise of the mid-1950s popular film *The Man in the Gray Flannel Suit*. People conform to an appearance, but inside they harbor emotions that stifle their potential as well as hurt others. It does not work, Lennon says, because being "crippled inside" is "One thing you can't hide."

Paralleling his earlier attacks on religious hypocrisy, Lennon speaks of churchgoers singing from the hymnal while they are actually crippled inside. He also notes how people compensate for their insecurities by transferring their issues to others through racism and prejudice. For Lennon, there are many methods of masking inner pain, but none of them really work. The song's real strength lies in the humorous approach and performance.

Except for a slightly altered line about dreaming, the confessional ballad "Jealous Guy" had a whole different set of lyrics when Lennon composed it as "Child of Nature" for The Beatles' White Album three years earlier. "Child of Nature" exists in demonstration form, offering some rather dreary and mundane lyrics—such as "I'm just a child of nature, I'm one of nature's children"—that may account for its never being finished as a Beatles track. Turning the song into "Jealous Guy" was not the only legacy of the music, since it matches up very closely with the opening of Lennon's later hit "Whatever Gets You through the Night." The Beatles' opportunity lost became Lennon's positive gain.

Ethereal strings sweep the song along, making it sound more languidly paced than it really is. A piano that combines rhythmic accompaniment with countermelody provides an interesting bridge between the vocals and the strings. Lennon sings both a confessional and an apology about the pain his jealous actions have caused, eventually psychoanalyzing himself by saying he was "swallowing my pain."

The relaxed nature of the piece reaches its apex when Lennon breezily whistles the melody before playfully intoning the warnings of "Watch out" and "Look out," reminding the beloved that he is still "just a jealous guy." This part seems out of place in a song where the narrator is "shivering inside" with a combination of emotional distress and guilt, but perhaps it is meant to be a false bravado in the face of the naked truth being confessed.

Another explanation for the whistle, though mere conjecture, may be the influence of Bing Crosby, of whom Lennon was reputedly a fan.[6] Even the word-play of The Beatles' second hit, "Please Please Me," had been partly inspired by the lyrics of Crosby's 1932 recording "Please," which played on the auditory sameness of the words "please" and "pleas." Imagining an early to mid-1930s Crosby-styled performance of "Jealous Guy" in the mind's ear reveals a striking fit, even down to the patented Crosby whistle so caricatured at the time. Lennon could have been amusing himself by having a clever in-joke on his audience, who perhaps were not as well versed in Crosbyisms as he was.

The band Roxy Music had a hit with their cover version of the song early in 1981 after Lennon's killing, possibly prompting the release of Lennon's original as a single in 1985 in Great Britain, where it reached number 65. In 1988, "Jealous Guy" was released in the United States to promote the *Imagine: John Lennon* soundtrack album and it reached number 80, thereby earning the distinction of being Lennon's last solo top-100 single in the United States for the remainder of the century.

"It's So Hard" is a rumbling funky blues that complains in an oddly cheerful manner about how tough it is to just get by day to day. Lennon's slightly detached-sounding voice provides a litany of common concerns and basic goals from "You gotta love" to "You gotta eat," but he comments that it can be so difficult that he sometimes wants to quit trying. His only salvation lies in the connection he has with his lover. Lennon may be half-punning here, if such a thing is possible, using the phrase "going down" to first mean "giving up" and later as a reference to oral sex.

The legendary saxophonist King Curtis provides a characteristic growling sax counterpoint, later augmented by guitar and strings. The track is enjoyable enough, and makes its simple point quickly without belaboring it.

There are a number of vocations and situations Lennon desires to avoid in "I Don't Want to Be a Soldier." It is not solely an antiwar song—yet that idea should be given the primary emphasis, because, of the many things his narrator does not want to be, soldier is what Lennon chose to incorporate in the title. And, knowing of the Lennons' peace campaign and the heat of the battles going on in Southeast Asia at the time of the song's composition, it is understandable that the song's antiwar components are in the fore.

Lennon's narrator does not want to be a lawyer nor a churchman, in another of his swings at organized formal religions. He uses couplets that do not match—for example, "sailor" and "fly"—and couplets that do—for example, "lawyer" and "lie" (in the stereotypical perception of the occupation). Likely inspired by a traditional and well-known nursery rhyme, he rejects the desire to be "rich" or "poor" or a "thief" or a "failure." The "failure" may relate to the prolonged war in Southeast Asia or any number of other activities.

Lyrically recalling a simple list, the song builds tension as Lennon's voice rises and falls with each item on the list. The simplicity and repetition of the words could be taken as a panicky interior monologue, with the anxiety rising as the list is contemplated. Or, because the early lines refer to "Mama," it is as if a child is pleading with its mother. The production thickens the sound of the song with some solid work from the band, including George Harrison, King Curtis, and Tom Evans and Joey Molland from Badfinger.

A gem of the album, full of clever wordplay, is "Give Me Some Truth," another song Lennon more or less composed while still a Beatle. Over the years, the song has become contemporary again anytime the credibility gap between citizens and governments grows. Written while U.S. forces were mired in Vietnam and Southeast Asia, the song attacks "hypocrites" and "pig-headed politicians" for holding back the truth. The lyric is prophetic in that it was written prior to the Watergate break-in and prior to Lennon's personal, and underhanded, harassment from the Immigration and Naturalization Service.

Lennon's narrator will no longer accept lies from a "son of tricky Dicky." Richard M. Nixon was the president of the United States at the time the lyrics were composed. A critical nickname bestowed on him was "tricky Dick," so Lennon's phrase is a direct reference to the Nixon administration. The offspring of "tricky Dicky" that Lennon sings of is "short-haired" (implying establishment-oriented) and "yellow-bellied." Lennon asserts that conformity is a by-product of cowardice, chauvinism, and paranoia.

Lennon refuses the government's selling of the war. The country's leaders are not going to "mother Hubbard soft soap" him. It is interesting that he uses the image of soap. Lennon also refers to a "pocketful of soap" in the lyrics. When the Lennons explained to the media why they were campaigning for peace with bed-ins and billboards, they stated that they chose to utilize the same effective advertising tools to sell peace that a manufacturer would employ to sell soap.[7]

Even though performed with contempt and rage, Lennon's wordplay in "Give Me Some Truth" is akin to his vocal delivery on "Give Peace a Chance." He similarly mashes images together in this *Imagine* track: "schizophrenic, ego-centric, paranoiac, prima-donnas" as if spewing them out in anger. A prominent, broiling guitar approximates the seething character of the lyrics. After a brief guitar break from George Harrison that bites and barks the notes, and after more ingenious word combinations, Lennon closes the song very simply by demanding the truth over and over again.

"Oh My Love" is a love song written by Lennon and Ono and also dates from his time with The Beatles. Calming yet simultaneously mournful, Lennon sings of the clarity that results when one is renewed by romantic love. There is a clearer view of one's surroundings and of one's purpose. There is self-realization. The song conjures an interesting image of the mind feeling. How does a mind feel? He goes on to say he feels "sorrow," which is comprehensible, but then he closes the thought with "I feel the dreams." So, there is yet another question for the listener to ponder: how does one feel a dream?

The lyrics also talk about seeing the wind. These contributions would seem more Ono than Lennon, but such was their cross-pollination by then that this is not a certainty. When Lennon sings that "Everything is clear in our world" the song momentarily sounds like the lyrical passage, "Nothing's gonna change my world," from his Beatles recording "Across the Universe." Once again Lennon has sequenced a gentle song of questioning innocence between two songs of frustration and pervasive anger.

"How Do You Sleep?" is Lennon's bald tirade against former songwriting and artistic partner Paul McCartney. Lennon claimed he was responding to previous musical salvos from McCartney, especially from McCartney's second post-Beatles album *Ram*.[8] Lennon saw the album's song "Too Many People" as an attack on himself and Ono, with such lyrics as "Too many people preaching practices" referring to the couple's activism. In the same song, McCartney sings about someone spoiling their lucky break, which Lennon took to mean McCartney blamed him for the end of The Beatles. *Ram*'s song "Three Legs" was interpreted as attacking the trio of Lennon, Harrison, and Starr, claiming that a dog with three legs cannot run. A photograph on the cover shows two beetles copulating, and, of course, "getting screwed" in popular slang can refer to sexual intercourse as well as to being taken advantage of unfairly.

Lennon's song opens with sounds of the band settling down, a short parody of the beginning of "Sgt. Pepper's Lonely Hearts Club Band," also referenced in the first line of the song. Lennon rasps and hisses the lyrics with real vitriol. If McCartney's assaults were veiled, Lennon's are blunt. Swelling strings and a bubbling electric piano give the track a festering energy. For all the talk of Lennon's anger that the song has generated, few comment that the song is helped along to no small degree by the aggressive slide guitar of George Harrison. Lennon was apparently not the only former Beatle peeved with McCartney at the time.

Lennon attacks McCartney's character and his profession as a recording artist. The lyrics include a number of specific references to McCartney. Lennon sings, "The only thing you done was yesterday," which refers to McCartney's early Beatles number-one hit "Yesterday" and also suggests that McCartney's best work was in the past. The next line includes the phrase "you're just another day." Again, Lennon asserts that the creative spark has gone from his old band mate, but the line also refers to McCartney's easygoing charting ballad "Another Day." Lennon describes this song—as well as the remainder of McCartney's contemporary output—as "Muzak." At the time, Muzak was a purveyor of syrupy, string-heavy, slow and mid-tempo instrumental music. Office-based businesses and hotels were among the subscribers to the service, and, as such, it was referred to as insubstantial "elevator music."

Lennon's lyrics speak of McCartney's "pretty face." From the time The Beatles arrived on U.S. shores in 1964, McCartney was known as the cute Beatle. In the first verse, Lennon states, "Those freaks was right" when rumors abounded that Paul "was dead." The leader of The Beatles suggests that the "Paul is dead" rumors were prophetic. As far as Lennon is concerned, musically and artistically McCartney is deceased.

Lennon's lyrics also describe McCartney's marriage relationship with Linda Eastman. He suggests that McCartney "jump[s]" at the moment his "momma" speaks—an ironic comment in view of his own reactions to criticisms of his relationship with Ono. Finally, Lennon, in frustration, wonders how, after their long songwriting and musical partnership, McCartney's work reveals no evidence that he "learned something." To Lennon, the collaborations were for naught.

In a song that hearkens back to the thoughts Lennon wrestled with on his previous album, *Plastic Ono Band,* "How?" focuses on three personal subjects. In a song full of questions, Lennon asks about moving ahead with one's life; the place of feelings; and offering love. This is a song about self-doubt, as Lennon sings about his uncertainties regarding love and life. Early in the song, Lennon lists personal issues regarding his emotional, mental, and spiritual state of being and consciousness.

In the first verse, which asks about moving forward, Lennon speaks of the insecurity that comes with taking risks or stepping out. In the second verse, he suggests that he does not know how to get in touch with his feelings because he does not "know how to feel." Sadly, he confesses, this is because "my feelings have always been denied." "How can I give love," he asks, "when love is something I ain't never had?" As noted earlier, his father abandoned Lennon for the sea, and his mother was tragically killed during the singer's teenage years.

In the chorus, repeated twice in the recorded performance, Lennon suggests that he has the choice of either facing adversity or giving up. The chorus does not provide an answer to the song's titular query. It merely states that life is sometimes tough and that we must carry on somehow. Perhaps there are no answers to the "how?" questions. The final verse is a mirror image of the first, except that Lennon expands its purview from his individual concern to the corporate "we." As in "Hold On" and "Isolation" from the *Plastic Ono Band* album, he expands the embrace of his lyric beyond himself and his situation to that of the world at large. We all have similar issues. That is part of what makes us one.

"Oh Yoko!" is an unabashed paean of love and devotion to Lennon's soul mate, Yoko Ono, gleefully parading to a near manic conclusion. Rolling piano and jangling rhythm provide the effervescent atmosphere that permeates the cut. The chorus stretches out the words "My love will turn you on" as if the joy cannot be contained in a normal-paced rhythm. A brief harmonica solo is so peppy it almost loses control, prefiguring the end of the song, when it does. The band fades out and the harmonica continues playing frantically in its happy abandon.

The words are a catalog of locations and situations implying the omnipresence of Ono, either literally or figuratively in the singer's heart. Lennon's later song "Dear Yoko" from *Double Fantasy* in 1980 reversed the omnipresence of Ono, discussing how much her absence was felt. No matter where he is, in a bath, in front of the mirror, in a dream, or in a cloud, his thoughts turn to his wife. Five times he repeats the phrase "I call your name," attesting to the power of voicing a name aloud (as noted in certain spiritual teachings), as well as reflecting the title of the Beatlemania era song he wrote called "I Call Your Name." The song underscores the premise of the British group The Troggs' hit from three years earlier, "Love Is All Around."

The track's infectious character and unabashed silliness in comparison to most of Lennon's generally serious, frequently solemn, and sometimes dour output of the prior two years made it surprisingly popular, especially in the face of the incessant Ono-bashing that plagued the couple. Lennon was encouraged to release the song as a single but declined.[9]

Lennon was successful in his attempt to create an album of artistic achievement and expression that would also appeal to large audiences, and *Imagine* was a commercial and critical success. The mistiming of his next single, and his move toward radical activism and overt issue-oriented songs in the next year, would dissipate the efforts he had made at solidifying his popularity after The Beatles' breakup. While Lennon was always creating interesting music and lyrics, they were not always well received by the public or by the critical establishment, as the next year would demonstrate.

"HAPPY XMAS (WAR IS OVER)"

Counting "God Save Us," Lennon had already released three singles in 1971. Motivated by a similar desire to create a new holiday standard as he had tried to create a new protest standard in "Give Peace a Chance," Lennon came up with his fourth single of the year. His timing was a bit off, however, and the single, originally on holiday-appropriate green vinyl, was released too late in the season and as a result failed to chart.[10] "Happy Xmas (War Is Over)" did become a hit the next year in the United Kingdom, and again charted after his homicide.[11] Although not the standard Lennon hoped it might become, the song does turn up regularly in the holiday season's musical mix. It would be his last single that did not come from an album released during his lifetime, though the flip side of 1975s "Stand by Me" from the *Rock 'N' Roll* album, titled "Move over Ms. L," was also a nonalbum cut.

The song combines elements of Lennon's previous singles. The "war is over if you want it" backing chant is reminiscent of both "Give Peace a Chance" and a combination of "We all shine on" from "Instant Karma!" and the titular refrain from "Power to the People." And, like the lyrics to "Instant Karma!" Lennon both prods and challenges listeners before providing reassurance. His testy opening statement, "So this is Christmas, and what have you done?" is soon followed by Ono leading a chorus singing the slightly disconcerting "A very merry Christmas and a happy New Year, let's hope it's a good one without any fear." The next verse follows the pattern by reminding listeners of how it is Christmas for both weak and strong, rich and poor, black and white, yellow and red—while urging us to recall that, for many, "the road is so long" and for all to "stop all the fights."

The emotion in Lennon's voice almost becomes pleading and the chorus swells and, as in George Harrison's "My Sweet Lord," the infectious chant soon has listeners singing along almost unaware of what they are saying, be it "Hare Rama" or "war is over." As the chorus shouts multiple rounds of "Happy Christmas," Lennon ends the song with everyone cheerfully applauding as he had ended "Give Peace a Chance." This loud communal response at the finish is the opposite of how the track begins with both Lennon and Ono whispering a personal message to their children Julian and Kyoko. Further, it parallels the song's message of expanding the sense of family celebration the holiday engenders to include not only a concern for the state of humanity, but a call to do something about that concern in the coming year.

The B-side is an engagingly simple work by Ono named "Listen, The Snow Is Falling." The song begins with the crunching sound of a person walking through snow as the wind whistles by. Sleigh bells are heard as Ono sings of several places being covered by the falling snow, beginning with physical locations such as "between Trafalgar Square" and moving to poetic locations such as "your head and my mind" before returning to the physical again. Descending sounds replicate the falling of the snow, countered by a gently ascending guitar riff. Later in the piece, a few measures sound similar to Lennon's work on The Beatles' "Sun King" from the *Abbey Road* album before the song returns to the sound of footsteps, wind, and Ono's urgent whispering of "listen!" as the song fades out. It is one of her best conventional recordings and indicates her early abilities to skillfully fuse her poetic and conceptual imagery with the format of mainstream pop songs, a talent she would continue to develop with increasing success.

FLY

Lennon also worked on Ono's next album, a two-record set called *Fly*. It contains some of the duo's experimental music, including works for their films' soundtracks, more or less making up one disc, and a series of tracks similar to those on Ono's *Plastic Ono Band* album on the second disc. At least two tracks include essential work from Lennon, and both were flip sides to his earlier singles.

As discussed previously, "Open Your Box" (also known as "Hirake") was the original B-side for "Power to the People." The track was banned from radio broadcast for the supposedly suggestive lyrics "open your legs ... open your box" whereas the intent was ultimately to open people's hearts and minds. The song was remixed for reissue in the United Kingdom and replaced on the B-side of the "Power to the People" single by "Touch Me" for its U.S. release. Moderately paced and with a chugging, splintery rhythm, "Open Your Box" looks forward to the similar though smoother sounds Ono and Lennon would employ on future numbers, even as late as the work for *Double Fantasy*. In a joke, Ono has "Toilet Piece"—the sound of a flushing toilet—follow the abrupt end of the track.

The standout inclusion on *Fly*, however, is "Don't Worry Kyoko," finally on an album over a year after its release as the B-side to "Cold Turkey." The guitars of Lennon and Eric Clapton alternate between a lilting semi-slide and sniping bites while the slowly varying drum work of Starr keeps the underlying tension mounting. Ono's vocal line is one of her most effective, and the recording is still an amazing achievement decades later.

"Midsummer New York," both musically and in Ono's vocal interpretation, is a rocking Elvis Presley parody, although lyrically it describes the physical and psychological effects of a nightmarish panic attack. The song also shows that Ono was absorbing Lennon's lessons in the school of rock as readily as he was absorbing her schooling in the avant-garde. The ironic ballad "Mrs. Lennon" also has an intriguing counterpoint between its lyrics of anxiousness at Ono losing her identity in Lennon's shadow and the overall plaintive lovesong sound of the track, which is helped considerably by Lennon's simple and evocative faux classical piano playing.

Of interest is that one of the engineers on this album, Jack Douglas, who would help engineer David Peel's *The Pope Smokes Dope* (also produced by Lennon and Ono), later became the co-producer with Lennon and Ono for the recording sessions that produced the *Double Fantasy* album, as well as Ono's "Walking on Thin Ice" single and Lennon's unfinished cuts from the *Milk and Honey* album.

DAVID PEEL: *THE POPE SMOKES DOPE*

Late in 1971, Lennon and Ono took up residence in New York. Their previous activities had introduced them to various counterculture and underground personalities, and this continued and intensified. One such person they met was activist and street musician David Peel. Lennon was impressed with Peel's sense of melody and his folksy sing-along approach to protest message songs. It probably helped that Peel had a strong sense of the absurd that found humorous expression in most of his work. Lennon and Ono were enthralled enough to produce and appear on an album for Peel called *The Pope Smokes Dope*—but the depth of their direct artistic input is not clear, and it may have been minimal.

As with Lennon's other work from this time, both the strengths and the weaknesses of this album relate to it being a bit of a time capsule, as titles such as "Everybody's Smoking Marijuana" and "Chicago Conspiracy" demonstrate. The songs on the album are sonically blended, sometimes musically, but often with the sounds of a crowd applauding and reacting to the performance. The attempt is to capture the urgent energy and immediacy of the street performance experience, and it largely succeeds.

The album also exhibits a free-spirited sense of fun, with Peel's off-kilter and earthy humor in full evidence, notably on the title song that is introduced with some audio-vérité from a Lennon interview. Peel's absurd humor and the joyful hippie ambiance of the album make it difficult to judge how serious the cover's proclamation of "The Rock Liberation Front" (RLF) and its call for subversive action against media sellouts really is, although previous works of the RLF indicate it was serious indeed. Lennon had engaged in press releases and open letters that espoused the radical cause of the RLF with harsh solemnity.[12]

One song of particular interest is "The Ballad of New York City (John Lennon–Yoko Ono)." It is a rollicking performance that also begins with a segment from an interview with Lennon and Ono and lyrically states why Lennon and Ono have found the perfect home in New York, with Lennon providing a dobro accompaniment on the cut. They must have agreed with Peel's sentiments, and the song makes an interesting companion piece to the contemporaneous *Elephant's Memory*'s "Local Plastic Ono Band" as well as Lennon's "New York City."

Its recording time is not clear, but an unreleased nine-and-a-half-minute opus titled "America," featuring vocals by Peel and Ono, may date from this period—however, some of Ono's vocals may have been mixed in from her previous recordings. Since Peel guests on a vocal of the Elephant's Memory album Lennon and Ono produced later in the year, it may have been recorded then, or perhaps when Ono was recording her solo album *Approximately Infinite Universe*. Like those albums, the track is reputedly produced by Lennon and Ono and may have Lennon playing or singing on it, although, if so, he is not readily evident. It is a captivating fusing of Ono's vocal pyrotechnics with Peel's chant-like intoning of the title and a litany of locations, events, and attitudes dealing with the United States. They are backed by a hypnotic pulsing rhythm with flute and voices provided by what might be Elephant's Memory, alone or augmented, and finishing with what sounds like tribal bongos with a drill sergeant leading a platoon through a call and response on a double-time march. As one of the more successful of such recordings, it ought to be legally released.

SOMETIME IN NEW YORK CITY

Released in June 1972, nine months after the commercial and artistic success of *Imagine, Sometime in New York City* became Lennon's most lambasted and least successful album. It is the most sustained version of Lennon's drive to create musical news reports and commentaries in quickly released songs, a drive that began in earnest with The Beatles' "Revolution," the flip side of "Hey Jude," and continued through his early solo work culminating here in this album-length effort. As such, it has the strengths and weaknesses expected of a more-or-less spur-of-the-moment opinion-editorial. At the time of its release, many reviewers disliked it for its lack of subtlety as much as for its opinions. As might be expected, more recently it has taken on the sheen of a time capsule of the period and, to a limited degree, has been somewhat redeemed as a result.

The album cover is a mock-up of the front page of the *New York Times,* with the song lyrics listed as if they are the news articles. As originally released, a second disc comprised two live appearances. One performance was as the Plastic Ono Supergroup in 1969 to support UNICEF; the other was as the Plastic Ono Mothers and was a 1971 appearance with Frank Zappa and The Mothers of Invention. Zappa did not release his mastered and edited version of the show until over a decade after Lennon's shooting, calling the CD *Playground Psychotics.*

Ono had moved into combining her experimental compositions with more conventional pop-oriented songwriting, and, even though the couple duet and support each other on the various tracks and even share songwriting credit on most of the cuts, the album somewhat alternates between songs that feature Lennon and songs that feature Ono. This foreshadows the more intensified application of this approach eight years later for the *Double Fantasy* album and its posthumously completed and released companion album *Milk and Honey.*

Another change from their previous work is that on the *Sometime in New York City* album the Plastic Ono Band is now formed around a rough and ready bar band called Elephant's Memory. The group had enjoyed moderate success for almost four years by the time Lennon and Ono began working with them. Fueled perhaps by the desire for a "real band" in the wake of their acoustic appearances in Detroit and Harlem in December the previous year, Lennon and Ono would work with Elephant's Memory as their backing band throughout 1972, including the recorded concert performances released in 1986 as the *Live in New York City* album and video.

The release of the *Sometime in New York City* album had been preceded by the Lennon / Ono single "Woman Is the Nigger of the World" / "Sisters, O Sisters" the previous April. Both songs are on the album, and "Woman Is the Nigger of the World" is the first cut. The song is an accusatory feminist plea, employing racial metaphor to highlight the severity of the social injustice to which women are subjected. Lennon had previously employed a shocking metaphor for a song title with "Happiness Is a Warm Gun" from The Beatles' White Album. In keeping with Lennon's artistic aim of the directness and immediacy of a news report, the ironic humor of the earlier song is absent here. The recording contains one of Lennon's most subtly nuanced vocal performances and intriguing productions and is one of his most unjustly overlooked recording efforts.

If a bit radical for the time, the feminist message may have been relatively palatable. But the use of the epithet "nigger" in the title all but ensured that the song would receive limited airplay. In fact, AM radio banned the song for its potentially inflammatory use of the term. The song did garner some limited FM airplay, albeit usually late at night on college and underground radio stations.

Certainly Lennon had been in the United States long enough to know how incendiary the term was and could have predicted the response. So the fact that he released the song as a single nonetheless shows his commitment to the ideas expressed in the song, even at the risk of damaging his career. Before Lennon performed it on television's *The Dick Cavett Show* in May, Cavett was forced by the ABC network to warn the public in advance, even after Lennon had explained the song's meaning and intent. Lennon's stance and metaphoric use of the word "nigger" was understood and supported by the leader of the Congressional Black Caucus, as well as by *Ebony* magazine.[13] Having stood his ground, Lennon had to be content with the single reaching only number 57 on the charts.

The catalyst for the song was an interview comment made by Ono in 1969 that became the title.[14] She receives co-credit for the work, although that seems to be her only contribution. Part of the negative reaction to the song might have stemmed from Lennon's poetic license: the lyrics state what "woman is," not that "woman is treated as if she is." The metaphor gives the message its plaintive power and a sense of real indignation that would be lacking if it were instead a simile, but it may have confused those who failed to listen closely. A deeper critique is that, to a certain degree, the song reifies the concept of "nigger" in order to make the metaphor work. Those wishing to disavow the "reality" implied by the term are forced to think of the song's title statement as a metaphor based on an admittedly spurious socially constructed concept; mental gymnastics that most were not accustomed to having to perform in dealing with a pop song.

The recording begins with a jarring jump into the moderately paced and comparatively simple melody bolstered by the successful application of a

Spector-style "wall of sound" provided by Elephant's Memory and a decid-edly Beatlesesque string section, somewhat reminiscent of Lennon's use of strings on "I Am the Walrus" from The Beatles' *Magical Mystery Tour* soundtrack. The abrupt beginning immediately smoothes as Lennon's soft but firm and slightly echoed vocal announces the title followed by the affir-mation "yes she is" and encouragement for the listener to "think about it" before repeating the opening statement. This somewhat parallels his open-ing to *Plastic Ono Band*'s "God," in which he vocally underlines the shock-ing opening statement by saying he will repeat it and then does so.

Lennon implicates the listener, and by extension the male-dominated social system, in the hypocritical treatment of women by detailing the acts and attitudes "we" have engaged in. Double standards, familial pressures, sexual stereotyping, institutionalized sexism, and mass media images are all exempli-fied and decried. With each line, Lennon's voice becomes slightly stronger, more plaintive, more accusatory, and more outraged. Lennon's deceptively natural-sounding vocal work includes numerous shouts of exhortation to the listener. He also stretches out certain terms into long calls and moans, while chopping up other words into approximations of sobbing. Before the second instrumental break, Lennon encourages the band to "hit it!"

The low strings form the broiling bottom sound of the song, somehow without making it seem as though there is anything solid there; again, very similar to the use of strings on "I Am the Walrus." At the same time, the rough-edged sound of Elephant's Memory builds tension against the methodical pacing of the song. Instrumental solo breaks, first from saxo-phone, and later from saxophone and guitar, punch through the existing musical tension only to build the tension further. The swelling strings strain and crash against Elephant's Memory, and Lennon's pleading vocals result-ing in some concrete sonic fury without sounding cluttered. This works quite well in supporting the intellectual and emotive impact of the lyrics and Len-non's passionate vocalizing.

Lennon then implores listeners to "do something" about the situation, after proclaiming that woman is "the slave to the slave." Finally, he cries out for a response of agreement, calling for believers in the injustices dealt woman to at least "scream about it" before he himself screams the closing line over and over as the ascending low strings and screeching high strings and guitars blanket and propel the vocals with wave after wave of sound.

It is a tour de force performance both instrumentally and especially vocally, matched by the stacked and layered yet discomforting and ironically ephem-eral sound of the production. It remains one of Lennon's genuine, though largely unacknowledged, masterpieces.

Ono's cheerful feminist anthem "Sisters, O Sisters" opens with a spoken joke as Ono chides the "male chauvinist pig engineer" and Lennon offers a comically sneered "right on, sister!" in support. The song has a nice shuffle to it as Ono sings encouragement directed to a female audience about women's power to change the world for the better. Elephant's Memory is particularly spry here, with a momentum-gathering middle-eight section.

"Sisters, O Sisters" is followed by a dramatic song about the conditions at New York's Attica correctional facility and the aftermath of a deadly riot the prisoners engaged in during September 1971 as a result of those conditions with the opening line of "What a waste of human power." Both Lennon and Ono share songwriting credit as well as the lead vocal, a duet. A couple of lines outline the situation in brief terms, clearly expecting that listeners know the basic story. The lyrics quickly universalize the event, declaring, "We're all mates with Attica State," and calling for the freedom of "all prisoners everywhere," echoing Henry David Thoreau's idea that in an unjust system, only the just would be imprisoned. The sloganeering path continues with the lyrics calling for all to join the revolution for human rights, eventually reaching a low point with the rather diffused plea to "free us all from endless night." The song tries to decry the events at Attica on one hand, and use them as a springboard for related commentaries on the other. Rather than building, the song loses focus. At least musically the song has a nice groove, helped by Lennon's ringing guitar, which is used as a sort of instrumental response to the vocals as he had done in "Cold Turkey."

But the next track, "Born in a Prison," does make good poetic use of the prison metaphor. The excellent saxophone work of Stan Bronstein ties the verses together, with the chorus a harmonized duet of poetic statements from Lennon and Ono, such as "Wood becomes a flute when it's loved." The verses decry the human condition of being bounded by unjust social constrictions that literally and figuratively stifle the individual and, by extension, society itself. Not only one of the better tracks on the album, it is one of Ono's better tracks from this phase of her career.

"New York City" is the album's primary rocker and probably could have been a solid-selling single if released as such. The fast-paced song is directly autobiographical and a close relative to The Beatles' "The Ballad of John and Yoko." The number recounts the goings on of Lennon and Ono, such as meeting up with countercultural figures, while commenting on their immigration problems. To the government's attempts to force him and Ono out, Lennon reminds the elected officials and bureaucrats, "The Statue of Liberty said 'come.'"

Both David Peel ("The Ballad of New York City [John Lennon–Yoko Ono]") and Elephant's Memory ("Local Plastic Ono Band") had songs about Lennon and Ono on their albums contemporary with this, and Elephant's Memory had a couple of seriously rocking numbers as well, the aptly named "Power Boogie" and "Liberation Special." In a sense, "New York City" combines those efforts. Elephant's Memory boogies in solid support of Lennon's energetic singing, and both vocalist and band seem reluctant to let loose of the groove. Lennon seems to relish the band's drive and momentum. He urges them on several occasions with shouts and comments. It is easily the most enjoyable and brisk track on the album.

The killing of Irish Catholic protestors by British soldiers prompted the angry "Sunday Bloody Sunday." Lennon's rage is palpable, and the recording has a suitably chaotic and rambunctious sound, but the song does not quite succeed. The lyrics start off with some nice rhetorical spins and a modicum of insight, but after the guitar break they lose centering and all that remains is the anger, thus drifting into lyrical hyperbole. Lennon also inexplicably pronounces "learn" as "loyn" in the second verse, forcing him to then pronounce "turn" and "burn" in a similar fashion so that they rhyme, which detracts from Lennon's message. The wailing of guitar and saxophone support a mix of Ono's emotionally appropriate vocal screeching and Lennon's yells and calls of "do it!" as the song begins to fade out and then returns, as if reminding listeners that the tragedy continues even when not the focus of attention and it will not go away on its own.

"The Luck of the Irish" is more general and more successful. A listing of innocent Irish clichés and idyllic stereotypes in the chorus sung by Ono is cleverly countered with the harsh contemporary political realities and historical summations sung by Lennon in the introduction and verses. This is all set up with the sardonic irony of the opening couplets that play off the usually bromidic phrase of the "luck of the Irish," indicating that any luck the Irish have had has been bad—so bad that "you'd wish you was English instead."

The contrasting irony continues with a pleasant lilting rhythm and a flute providing fills and a near countermelody in support of Lennon's singing of "pain and death." Lennon continues characterizing the then-current events as rape and genocide while singing in pleasant, soft tones. The idea of a dark humor approach is clever, and the song, as sociopolitical polemic, succeeds. Interestingly, at the same time as Lennon and Ono created these songs and recordings, Lennon's former artistic partner Paul McCartney, inspired by the same events, wrote and recorded "Give Ireland Back to the Irish," enjoying a number-21 hit with it.

Lennon's song in support of activist John Sinclair, at the time serving a 10-year prison sentence for the sale of two marijuana cigarettes, is simply called "John Sinclair." Here the lyrical statements and musical statements mesh to form a strong song that communicates its point of view and message with directness and simplicity. Lennon asks rhetorical questions to good effect in the lyrics, from the opening "won't you care for John Sinclair?" to the later "what else can the bastards do?" referring to the corrupt and unjust system as well as particular individuals.

Lennon compares the severity of Sinclair's crime with the reputed immoral, unethical, and criminal actions of others and then asks, "was he jailed for what he done, or representin' everyone?" The flowing questions and explanatory statements of the lyrics stream by to the sounds of Lennon's exemplarily played bluesy slide guitar that rolls and tumbles the song along with urgent tension, but no stress. "They gave him ten for two," Lennon repeats. He then pushes to the finale with "we gotta set him free!" with the word "gotta" earnestly repeated several times.

Lennon performed the song on television and at a rally to support Sinclair's release, and Sinclair was in fact set free less than three months after the album came out.

A song about activist Angela Davis was far less successful. Lennon and Ono again duet more or less equally on the vocals, and instrumentally the song has some vibrant orchestral string work in addition to fine guitar and organ moments. But the lyrics do not really add up to much more than generic platitudes such as "the world watches you" before veering into unintentional self-parody with such absurdities as "they gave you coffee, they gave you tea, they gave you everything but equality." The point may be that the power structure and social institutions deal in surface niceties but not in actual substance, but neither Lennon nor Ono seem to have been particularly inspired here.

The album ends with another strong Ono track, "We're All Water," the refrain having been adapted from one of her poems. Ono describes the essential oneness of humanity by listing a series of supposed similarities between seemingly disparate celebrities, historical figures, and locations. For instance, her opening line indicates that there may not be much difference between Chairman Mao and Richard Nixon if we "strip them naked," or between "Manson and the Pope" if we "press their smiles" in a later passage. Another line was adapted from her book *Grapefruit,* where she suggested counting the windows of certain buildings. Here she says there may not be much difference between the White House and the Hall of People if we count their windows.

The refrain happily states, "we're all water" and that someday "we'll evaporate together." The band keeps the staccato beat going as Ono engages in her familiar vocal escalations while asking, "what's the difference?" and soon replying, "there's no difference!" The track is one of the better transferences of her conceptual art instructions into song lyrics, and the high-energy performance of the band adds immensely to the appeal of her playful yet serious lyrics and delivery.

LIVE JAM

The original issue of *Sometime in New York City* included a bonus disc entitled *Live Jam.* The first three numbers are from the aptly named Plastic Ono Supergroup (including George Harrison) for the live show from December 1969.

The first numbers performed are "Cold Turkey" and "Don't Worry Kyoko." Although released only three months after the debut of both at the Toronto Rock and Roll Revival Festival, the readings are noticeably different. "Cold Turkey" now has the raw intensity of the single release, and the band's performance builds the tension the song needs rather than lilting along as it did in the Toronto show. Ono's number is a stunning masterwork complete with her vocals bouncing through a call and response with the horn section and a hyped-up finale that even Ono has trouble sustaining.

The remainder of the *Live Jam* album is taken from a 1971 guest appearance the couple did at the Fillmore East with Frank Zappa and the Mothers of Invention. Lennon is featured on an old rhythm and blues number, "Well (Baby Please Don't Go)." Considering the few live appearances Lennon made, this performance is a real gem. Lennon must have liked it, because he recorded this song during his *Imagine* sessions a few months later, though it was not released until the *John Lennon Anthology* collection in 1998. The live version is a strong and welcome vocal performance with full-throttle support from Zappa on guitar and the Mothers.

The rest of the album consists of a lengthy jam featuring Ono. The jam loses momentum at some points but manages to recover and contains some good work from all three principals. The nature of the jam made it possible for Lennon to divide the performance into different numbers, although it is not always clear why the divisions occur where they do. Two decades later, Zappa released his own version on the double CD set *Playground Psychotics*. The differences in song divisions may be minor, but Zappa's mix is superior in sound quality and in the intuitive sense of where the jam changes. Perhaps Ono was tacitly acknowledging this when she remixed and remastered the *Sometime in New York City* album for CD release in 2005 and omitted the jam entirely, replacing it with the holiday single of "Happy Xmas (War Is Over)" / "Listen, The Snow Is Falling." The omission means that the only available digital version of that portion of the concert is Zappa's.

THE ELEPHANT'S MEMORY BAND: *ELEPHANT'S MEMORY*

Lennon and Ono produced and played on this album for their backing band. Lennon is on 6 of the 10 cuts, playing guitar and singing on 2 cuts, playing electric piano on 1, and adding vocals to 3 others. Ono vocalizes on 4 of the cuts with Lennon.

Lennon historian John Robertson relates that Lennon worked on composing but then abandoned a song about classic rockers Chuck Berry and Bo Diddley.[15] Abandoned or not, just such a song titled "Chuck 'n' Bo" closes the first side of the album. Perhaps Lennon was running through this number just for the fun of it and Robertson or his sources thought it was an abandoned composition of Lennon's. In any event, it pastiches the famous characteristic musical riffs and rhythms of the two men and tells an amusing story of a concert situation in which Diddley and Berry demonstrate the invigorating freedom of rock and roll music, a concept close to Lennon's heart. In the midst of the political turmoil of Lennon's activities in 1972, it is interesting to speculate that he might have contributed to this semi-nostalgic rocker that touts the liberation of the musical form itself, with no overt messages or specific slogans. Both Berry and Diddley were at the 1969 Toronto Rock and Roll Revival Festival, so perhaps the song was inspired by something Lennon observed there, though he receives no songwriting credit for the song.

Both "Liberation Special" and "Power Boogie" are solid rockers, with Lennon adding to the drive of "Power Boogie." Each is also somewhat reminiscent of Lennon's "New York City." In addition, Lennon's electric piano contributions to "Wind Ridge" are quite appropriate and fill out the song with real flourish. The album ends with a droll number called "Local Plastic Ono Band," in which Elephant's Memory good-naturedly jokes about their status as Lennon and Ono's backup group. The lyrics playfully imply that the notoriety may be both helpful and a hindrance to their career.

APPROXIMATELY INFINITE UNIVERSE

Ono helped to open Lennon to more experimental composing and to thinking more seriously of himself as an artist with a particular role in society. And at the same time, his influence had been prompting her to make more forays into conventional pop music songwriting. As the year closed, Ono and Lennon worked on and completed this double album set of pop songs, Ono style, with Elephant's Memory backing her up as they had done on Lennon and Ono's *Sometime in New York City*.

Lennon co-produced the album with Ono and can be heard both vocally and instrumentally on many of the tracks. His genuinely exuberant happy cheering on "What a Mess" and his vocal fills on "I Wish I Knew" are welcome additions to those numbers, but his most significant vocal contribution to the album is on Ono's remarkable and plaintive song of female forgiveness and understanding for the sins of male sexism, "I Want My Love To Rest Tonight." Late in the song it features backing and harmony vocals by Lennon. The male and female voices sharing equally in the mix complement the ideals of the song beautifully, and though the heartfelt lyrics become melodically cumbersome and distracting for no discernable reason, the song is still one of true emotive power.

Lennon's instrumental contributions are strongest on a handful of numbers, including "Kite Song," where he provides a growling guitar undercurrent that anchors Ono's account of a disturbing dream. No less impressive is his guitar work on "Move on Fast," a straight-ahead rocker that hits the ground running and never lets up. Lennon then revisits some guitar playing reminiscent of "Cold Turkey" on "Peter the Dealer." The guitar lines on "Yang Yang"—presumably performed by both Lennon and Elephant's Memory member Wayne "Tex" Gabriel—are appropriately forceful in one of Ono's better songs about social and internal revolution, and their interconnections.

What You Got, 1973–1975

Radio airplay banning and its controversial nature helped keep "Woman Is the Nigger of the World" from rising higher than number 57 on the charts, and Lennon did not release any other single from the *Sometime in New York City* album, despite the obvious choice of "New York City." The general public's as well as Lennon's fan base's lack of appreciation for Ono's work (making up a significant part of the album), the extreme countercultural, politicized content, the slightly higher cost for the "free" live disc, and the lack of a top-40 hit single caused the album to be a comparative commercial flop, especially in the wake of the much-praised and high-selling *Imagine* album. This occurred despite the fact that the duo, backed by Elephant's Memory, promoted the material on *The Mike Douglas Show, The Dick Cavett Show,* and *The Jerry Lewis MDA Labor Day Telethon* broadcast. In addition, the two One to One charity concerts were also filmed and broadcast, and later edited into the posthumously released *Live in New York City* album and video tape.

By the end of the summer of 1972, Lennon's immigration troubles had deepened, consuming much of his time.[1] In October 1968, he and Ono were arrested for possession of cannabis resin, pled guilty, and paid a fine. Later, this was used to declare Lennon an undesirable alien in the United States and therefore deportable. Lennon's high-profile, countercultural actions got him noticed, and evidence shows he was in fact targeted by government agencies and officials for expulsion for those very reasons, with the drug charge being merely an excuse. The harassment slowed down after Richard Nixon's reelection as president, but did not really abate until Nixon resigned from the presidency in August 1974. Soon after Lennon and Ono's son Sean was born in October 1975, the U.S. government officially ended its harassment of Lennon. However, it was not until July 1976 that Lennon was granted full and permanent status as a resident alien, with the option to earn citizenship five years later in 1981.

He and Ono cut back on their overt political activities and rhetoric as well as their public appearances. While the couple finished both the Elephant's Memory and Ono's albums, Lennon seems to have hit a period of creative and personal malaise that began in the fall of 1972 and lasted until the start of 1974. That malaise may have contributed to his and Ono's separation in the early fall of 1973 that continued until early 1975. Lennon later termed the malaise and separation his "lost weekend," and, while it clearly had its personal and professional rough spots, it did not keep Lennon from working and ultimately creating some of his best recordings.[2]

RINGO STARR: "I'M THE GREATEST"

Lennon's former Beatle band mate Ringo Starr had produced two nonrock albums and two nonalbum hit singles since The Beatles' breakup. Both singles had employed fellow former Beatle George Harrison, who had also played on Lennon's *Imagine* album. At the time, Starr and Harrison shared to some degree Lennon's frustrations with Paul McCartney, which was so fiercely exhibited in *Imagine*'s "How Do You Sleep?" discussed in chapter 3. One of Starr's charting singles, "Back Off Boogaloo," had been about McCartney; the term "Boogaloo" was an insider code word for McCartney, and the lyrics obviously related to him.[3] Freudians may want to note that the promotional film Starr made for the song at the time shows him amiably contending with Frankenstein's monster. Also, one of Starr's B-sides, "Early 1970," expressed his uncertain relationship with McCartney while asserting the dependability of his relationships with Lennon and especially Harrison.

By the time Starr decided to do his first rock-pop album, relationships among the former Beatles were on the mend, and Starr asked each of them to contribute something to the record. Harrison collaborated with Starr on four songs, McCartney on two, and Lennon one. Lennon's contribution was performing on his composition "I'm the Greatest," and it includes a sardonic take on the Beatles' experience.

The song became a sequel of sorts to The Beatles' "With a Little Help from My Friends" as Starr once again sings that "my name is Billy Shears" while crowd noises cheer him on. Lennon's lyrics compare The Beatles to a circus by stating, "I was in the greatest show on earth," but then deflate the importance of that remark immediately by adding the pithy "for what it was worth." Klaus Voorman handled the bass, with Harrison on guitar, Starr on percussion and lead vocals, and Lennon on piano and backing vocals. The collaboration on "I'm the Greatest" was the closest thing to a Beatles reunion during Lennon's life time, and, though not a monumental work, its humor and sense of fun recapture some of the true joy at the core of much of The Beatles' best work.

The *John Lennon Anthology* contains a portion of Lennon's run through with Starr, Harrison, and Voorman to rehearse them for the recording of the track and to provide Starr with a guide vocal. What is most noticeable is how assured Lennon is in directing the band and finding the feel he wants. Also striking is how, even in rehearsal, the tone of the song seems harsher. Starr's shouting of "I'm the greatest, and you better believe it baby!" is inherently affable and comical in a manner that Lennon's obviously tongue-in-cheek delivery of a similar phrase cannot quite match.

FEELING THE SPACE

Before Lennon began work on his next album, *Mind Games,* Ono had started on her next album, titled *Feeling the Space*. The production of the albums overlapped, and both were released in November 1973. The album remains one of Ono's best and most accessible records.

Lennon contributed guitar work on "She Hits Back," a percolating track that musically sounds like it could have come from the *Double Fantasy* sessions. "Woman Power" showcases another especially gritty guitar line and rhythm solo from Lennon that closely prefigures his work on the "Walking on Thin Ice" single released shortly after his murder. These tracks are surprisingly similar to work that they did seven years later. It is as if Lennon and Ono picked up in 1980 where they left off in 1973.

Lennon's final contribution is to "Men, Men, Men," where Ono satirically engages in a comical reverse sexism. A condescending lecture on the nature of and value of men while reducing them to sexual playthings ends with Ono telling "honeyjuice" that he can "come out of your box now," to which we hear Lennon subserviently reply, "Yes, dear."

MIND GAMES

The *Mind Games* album was welcomed as a sort of recovery from the agit-prop of the previous year's releases. Lennon later dismissed it as hackwork, and fans considered it a definite cut below *Imagine*. Time has been good to it, however, and, although it largely fails as a unified effort, certain individual songs have justifiably earned their spots in Lennon's pantheon.

The title cut, which was also a single release, sets the tone and informs the underlying theme for the album, a theme sometimes hard to discern as much of a unifying force. Sonically lush, Lennon's transformed and muted slide guitar work ably stands in for an orchestra and is countered by a churning rhythmic accompaniment that adds a feeling of earnestness to the lyrical pleas.

The sound is reminiscent of "Being for the Benefit of Mr. Kite" from The Beatles' *Sgt. Pepper's Lonely Hearts Club Band* album, and a similar approach would again be used on *Double Fantasy*'s "Watching the Wheels."

Lennon started "Mind Games" in 1970 as another of his pop anthems under the title of the then-popular slogan "make love, not war" and as an abandoned 1950s-style melodramatic rocker called "I Promise."[4] Portions of both appear on the *John Lennon Anthology*. However, enough time had passed that he decided the "make love, not war" phrase was dated and would appear passé at best or might be seen as unintentional self-parody. Clearly, the phrase would have been the refrain, and its ghost can be heard as the song fades out, with Lennon adding an apologetic "I know, you've heard it before." A consciousness-raising book with the song's eventual title was also an early inspiration for the song, but no less so was Ono's conceptual art. In fact, Lennon sings that "yes is the answer," a direct reference to an installation of Ono's at the Indica Gallery, where the couple first met. Lennon frequently told the story of climbing up a ladder, grabbing a magnifying glass hanging by a string from the ceiling, and using it to read the word "yes" on a small piece of paper attached to the ceiling.[5] Lennon was impressed by the message of positive acceptance he inferred from the word, and, in later years, he and Ono would express their belief in positive thinking and imagery as tools for social change.

Lennon's lyrics express that view on "Mind Games" and are sharp and spirited, with his cheeky sense of humor evident throughout. The combination of the solemn message delivered by a tongue-in-cheek cleverness is Lennon at his best—a big improvement from the somber sloganeering of the previous year's output. The song could be seen as both the last hurrah of the flower children and the opening salvo of new ageism. Lennon's humorous catalog of pop mysticisms runs the gamut of references, including mantras, Druids, magic, the Holy Grail, the (instant?) karmic wheel, image projection through space and time, ritual dancing, and soul power. These are all part of the mind games. However they think of it, he calls on people to be "mind guerillas" for the "absolute elsewhere." The vagueness is clarified when he tells listeners that it all comes down to love, which is ultimately "the answer." This insight, combining the power of the mental outlook and the power of love, makes "Mind Games" of a piece with Lennon's previous hopeful paeans, stretching back at least to The Beatles' "The Word" and including such songs as "All You Need Is Love," "Instant Karma!," "Love," and "Imagine."

A taut number, the appropriately titled "Tight A$" cannot help but remind listeners of "That's Alright, Mama" or other similar rockabilly numbers that surely inspired Lennon in his younger years. The song prances along with jubilant energy, and Lennon seems to be having fun, cutting loose with shouts of joy several times in the song.

The title is inexplicable word play on "tight as" and "tight ass" compounded by the dollar sign. The lyrics do not offer much of an explanation, as clichés such as "if you can't stand the heat you better get back in the shade" are tossed in with surprising similes such as "as tight as a dope fiend's fix." Rhyming words provide shifts into harmless nonsense that sound like they probably mean something but have rushed past by the time the listener realizes they do not, such as "got it made" becoming "got it laid."

The band captures the feel of country swing that informs much of classic rockabilly, helped along considerably by the steel guitar playing of "Sneaky" Pete Kleinow. There is not any emotional investigation to be had here, and certainly no overt political commentary. The song is a rejuvenating slice of simple rock, and it feels as good to the listener as it must have to Lennon.

"Aisumasen (I'm Sorry)" is definitely another matter, as Lennon apologizes to his wife by name in this mid-paced ballad. This is the first release in which Lennon uses Japanese words in the lyrics, and they are a tribute to Yoko Ono's heritage. Most of the lyric is in English with the Japanese phrases sprinkled throughout the song. As in "Oh Yoko!" from the *Imagine* album, Lennon notes that calling out her name makes a difference in his life. It is a cure for melancholy.

Lennon had begun work on the song two years earlier, with the lyrics telling the loved one to "call my name," the song's original title, for assurance and comfort. "I'll ease your pain" was the line instead of "aisumasen." The song might have worked better with that perspective, but the roles were reversed when Lennon returned to the song, and the direct address of Ono was added as well. Interestingly, by the time the album was released, the couple had separated. Lennon might really have had something for which he needed to apologize.

The second verse, in which he uses the word "pain" three times, casts a look back at the primal scream therapy that informed his *Plastic Ono Band* album. Lennon sings of how hard it is to "feel your own pain" when the hurts of the past rise to the surface, a phrase he had employed in the earlier album's "I Found Out."

A sterling guitar solo continues to plead the case, ending somewhat abruptly, as the lightly hypnotic flow of the supporting instrumental passage locks on one note and fades. The hypnotic flow is no accident and in some ways bears a sonic similarity to Lennon's late-era Beatles song "I Want You (She's So Heavy)" from *Abbey Road*, also inspired by Ono. "Aisumasen" has a rhythmic current not unlike a slowed down, semi-acoustic version of the earlier song. The abrupt ending of "Aisumasen" sounds as if the apology has been rejected and there is no point in continuing. Despite the slightly unnerving abjectness of the song's tone, it is one of the stronger cuts on the album and would likely have been even stronger had Lennon kept the original lyrical point of view.

Uninspired and uninspiring couplets of images that complement or contrast one another make up the lyrical structure of the love song "One Day (At a Time)." Lennon combines "weakness" and "strength," "together" and "apart," "apple" and "tree," and "door" and "key" along with other images in the song that celebrate his relationship with his "woman." In the final verse, he repeats four of the image couplings to summarily close the song.

The underpinning motto of the Alcoholics Anonymous support group has been "one day at a time" for many years. For a while, it seemed to be the most popular automobile bumper sticker. Lennon asserts that the same motto is useful for a romantic relationship, but comparing a romantic unity to a method for surviving the debilitating effects of drug/alcohol addiction is a rather unnerving choice.

The production seems to try too hard, not succeeding in supporting or complementing the song but working as if to cover up its shortcomings and failings. Lennon sings in an oddly chosen, whispery falsetto that reinforces the tentative nature of the lyrics. This is clearly what he was going for, but what is not so clear is why. One almost wishes that he were being ironic and mocking rather than straightforward. Keyboard and saxophone join in but do not salvage a rather vapid effort. Strangely, Elton John covered the song with Lennon on guitar for the flip side of John's remake of Lennon's Beatles classic "Lucy in the Sky with Diamonds" the next year. Oddly, John managed to match Lennon's cloying performance. Odder still, a rehearsal recording of the song on the *John Lennon Anthology* is not sung in the annoying falsetto, and, while the song's other weaknesses are still evident, it is far easier to take at face value than the final version.

"Bring on the Lucie (Freda Peeple)" is an anti-authoritarian/antiwar song directed at world leaders who send their sons and daughters off to fight. Lennon seems to be rallying the band to battle as he calls them "over the hill" before the great slide guitar work begins that anchors and buttresses the sinuous rhythm of the song. Lennon's vocals are emotive and powerful, light years beyond the insipid performance of the previous number. The first verse seems to be an address to a gathering of diplomats, such as might be found at the United Nations, perhaps from the delegates of Nutopia. He understands that this is the group that makes "all our decisions" and has the power to change the world. Lennon does not care what countries they hail from or what flag they wave. He wants them to act in unity to let the people go. In the chorus, he asks the decision makers to "free the people" from the chains of war and strife. Lennon encourages listeners to voice the appeal as a "prayer." Again, he underlines the power inherent in voicing a need out loud, "let's shout it aloud," he sings.

As in "Give Me Some Truth" from *Imagine,* Lennon rejects the "game" played by politicians. He compares politicians to Satan by labeling them by the biblical number of the beast/antichrist ("666 is your name"); additionally, others report that Lennon took to referring to Richard Nixon as 666. Lennon offers an image of the diplomatic masturbation that occurs when world leaders confer. He warns them that a new world is coming ("your time is up"). Like a new Moses, Lennon is telling the powers that be to let the people go.

In the final verse, Lennon offers a harrowing image of what these diplomats have done to the people they represent. Those gathered at the conference table "slip and slide...on the blood of" those they have "killed." The killers are caught with their hands in the "kill" rather than the "till." There are no victors—and there will not be until the killing is stopped, as Lennon sings in the final chorus.

"Stop the killing" he urges, while the vocal chorus still chants, "free the people." Like the previous year's "John Sinclair," where Lennon repeated "gotta" with increasing intensity to the glissandos of the slide guitar, he now repeats "do it" to a similar accompaniment with the same effect. Despite the unexplained title of "Bring on the Lucie," only sung as the song fades out, this is one of the best tracks on a very erratic album.

If Lennon meant to use the concept of mind games to unify the album, he did so only by implication and inference, such as in the previous song, and not through any overt application. One of the few times the mind games motif is explicit and might work as part of a unifying theme or principle for the album is with the cut "Nutopian International Anthem." The original album cover explained that Nutopia was a conceptual state of no location or laws "other than cosmic." Lennon and Ono had declared the state of "New Utopia" earlier in the year, on April Fool's Day. The anthem also exists as a concept only, represented here by a few seconds of silence. Presumably, the listener should think about the anthem, or the state of Nutopia, during those seconds and those thoughts are, then, the anthem itself. A few seconds of silence being a relatively common occurrence, the number has the potential to be Lennon's most often performed composition, albeit unintentionally and likely without garnering royalties. Mind games indeed.

"Intuition" is another insubstantial effort that never comes alive. Lennon sings about the power of trusting his instincts "in order to survive" but does not seem to have much to say about it beyond his basic belief in them. The song tries for an upbeat feel to parallel the positive message but, while competent, lacks any genuine verve.

The first verse relies on formulaic truisms, claiming his intuitions "take me for a ride" through the "game of life." Lennon has to "struggle in the night" until the "magic of the music seems to light the way." It is not quite clear what his intuitions have to do with those situations, though it is implied that they help him cope. The second verse is a little better for avoiding the overly commonplace phrases, but an unintentional admission may come when Lennon remarks that he sometimes will "lose communication with nothing left to say." That may have been the case here, but he decided to go ahead and say it anyway. The performance is good but nothing special; the material is lackluster and sinks the song.

"Out the Blue" is much better, a moving piece about the awe of finding true love unexpectedly. The song begins with a simple, melancholic, acoustic, finger-picking guitar introduction and a restrained Lennon vocal. The song then shifts to a happier country blues sound declaring the inevitability of "two minds, one destiny," which is intensified by a gospel chorus. The sound swells and continues to build throughout the song, as Lennon's voice gets stronger and more assured as well, finally demonstrating a sort of joyful contentment with love having come "out the blue."

The lyrics have intriguing passages, such as when the love "blew away life's misery" and brought "life's energy." Lennon sings that all his life has been "a long slow knife" in one of his more poetic images of emotional anguish. A fine honky-tonk–styled piano solo leads to the somewhat obscure line "Like a UFO you came to me," but the song survives it, delivering a more satisfying emotional impact than might be supposed.

"Only People" presents a more optimistic view than "Bring on the Lucie (Freda People)." Lennon says that the masses can "change the world." He is rallying the "million heads" to communicate their desire for peace to those who have the power to make it happen. There is hope for change if people will walk "side by side" and communicate the wishes of the common folk. The future looks bright, as long as we can avoid a "pig brother scene." That is, there is hope as long as protesters do not get their "million heads" bashed in with nightsticks, as occurred at a number of demonstrations in the late 1960s and early 1970s.

This rollicking number that captures a celebratory and positive mood was inspired by an aphoristic line of Ono's, the deceptively simple observation that "only people change the world." A buoyant pace is kept spinning by both mellotron and acoustic piano with some charging but not oppressive work from the percussion and rhythm guitar. Lennon might have been attempting to recapture a bit of the anthem-like magic of "Power to the People" with this track, and, if so, he managed to succeed. A rallying call to keep up the good fight, the song makes up in assured energy what it lacks in profundity.

Once again the lyrics have some clichéd phrases that to a small degree weaken the song's force and message. But this time they also further the sense of democratized unity and, therefore, do not seem to be empty of meaning in the song's context. In addition, Lennon alters some of them. For instance, having your cake and eating it too becomes "bake the cake and eat it too." This song fades out, indicating that the struggle to change the world continues.

"I Know (I Know)" and "You Are Here" are songs of love written by Lennon for his spouse. The nurture, growth, and maturation of love are the subjects of "I Know (I Know)." Lennon's narrator realizes that the romantic relationship with his love is a living thing as time goes by. As the couple works at getting to know each other more, their love grows. As they see how each views the other, they understand how they need to change to grow closer.

The song stands out as lyrically superior to and expressing a more complex maturity than most of the songs on the album. The song's repetitive title highlights the fact that the lyrics indicate that knowing the self creates a deeper knowledge of the other, and vice versa. Lennon admits his past failures regarding his love, but states his increasing understanding and growing awareness of what he has done in the past and what should be done in the future. Twice Lennon sings, "Today I love you more than yesterday," a variation on Spiral Starecase's number-12 hit of 1969, "More Today than Yesterday." The song has an unexpected ending, as Lennon intones, "No more cryin'" four times. The line could be imploring the wronged loved one to stop crying, or to promise the self and/or beloved that there will be no more need for tears. It is a potent ending that heightens the song's power.

"You Are Here" is more precise in its lyric about the story of John and Yoko. He marvels at how two people from "distant lands"—specifically "Liverpool" and "Tokyo"—have found each other. And it does not matter whether they are geographically together, because, as Lennon sings, "Wherever you are, you are here." She is always in his heart.

"Nine!" Lennon's multitracked and warped voice says as an invocation as the song opens, citing the number he believed had mystical meaning and significance for him. The song drifts pleasantly along as a steel guitar gives it an alternately South Seas and then country and western ambiance. A strong female vocal chorus lends substance and auditory depth to the recording, as Lennon's soft vocals dreamily glide through the song.

A rehearsal take of "You Are Here" on the *John Lennon Anthology* is missing the steel guitar and vocal chorus, throwing the emphasis to the shimmering mellotron and giving the song a more ethereal quality. The rehearsal recording also has an additional verse not included in the final version—a shame, because Lennon sings of the wonder of the unity encompassing the "mystical to magical," which would have been a nice addition to the song. Further, he sings the more provocative "Love has opened up my mind" and "blown right through" instead of "opened up my eyes," as he sings on the finished track.

"Meat City," a rave up number, ends the inconsistent album with a gleefully tongue-in-cheek romp. The song has no deep meaning but demonstrates that Lennon could still fashion a perfectly fine rocker if he wanted. Lennon wails a drawn out "well!" in classic rockabilly style, thus starting the song with a solid punch, but the track has an aggressively funky riff and does not attempt a rockabilly style as "Tight A$" had. Lennon invents his own amusing street vernacular in the lyrics with his characteristic playfulness, singing at one point about "chickensuckin' mothertruckin' meat city shookdown U.S.A." with whatever meaning there is being derived from the attitude of his delivery.

Lennon employs a little backward recording technique on the album, something he had used sporadically since The Beatles' "Rain" in 1966. The first usage comes about 30 seconds into the song after Lennon sings, "Just gotta get me some rock and roll." A squeaky vocal sound is heard that when played backward sounds like "fuck a pig." At the time, "pig" was a common derogatory term for the police. Because nothing else in the song has anything to do with law enforcement or figures of authority, the phrase is likely just Lennon simultaneously exercising his freedom to be both vulgar and nonsensical. The next time he sings the "just gotta get me some rock and roll" line it is followed by backward instrumentals and no vocals. The third time through, the listener encounters a buzzing guitar that could be either backward or not.

The 2002 CD reissue of the *Mind Games* album includes a composing demo of Lennon working on "Meat City." Two minutes into it, repeating the start-stop staccato riff that so solidly propels the song, Lennon begins a wordless vocal melody, repeating it. It would turn up as a countermelody in "Steel and Glass" on the following year's *Walls and Bridges* album.

Mind Games is a frustrating album because the more intriguing efforts do not sustain themselves. Good tracks musically or in production either make no attempt at lyrical substance or fall into the vacuous or the mundane. And the more prosaic music numbers have moments of lyrical cleverness or insight. And yet there are a few tracks where it all comes together and works. Lennon was entering a period of personal distress, but with an increase in both productivity and artistic accomplishment. *Mind Games,* because of its hit-or-miss content on the whole, would continue to be viewed as second-tier Lennon.

COLLABORATIONS I

The first few months of Lennon's "lost weekend" may have been sporadically productive at best, but at least the core of the future *Rock 'N' Roll* album was created, as well as the groundwork for some of the *Walls and Bridges* album. Most interesting, however, was the burst of collaborations Lennon engaged in once Spector was all but out of the picture and Lennon started work in earnest. The recording sessions for *Walls and Bridges* were sandwiched in between these collaborations. Most of Lennon's previous post-Beatles work in supporting roles or collaborations had been in service to Yoko Ono's recordings, and they include some of his most innovative creations. His efforts with David Peel and The Elephant's Memory Band from 1972 stand out as being the notable exceptions. All of his collaborations, with Ono and otherwise, are intriguing in their own right. But the ones from this time period also indicate a regrettably underdeveloped and potentially fruitful aspect of Lennon's professional career.

Johnny Winter: "Rock and Roll People"

During the *Mind Games* sessions, Lennon had produced a simple, straight-ahead rocker, complete with a light dose of his rambling wordplay, called "Rock and Roll People," but he decided it did not fit the album. Lennon shared the work with rockin' bluesman Johnny Winter, and a version of the song turned up on Winter's album *John Dawson Winter III,* released late in 1974. As might be expected, Winter makes the most of the hard-driving beat to crank out some solid bluesy guitar lines and infuses the less-than-stellar lyrics with a more sincere interpretation than they may warrant. In short, he manages to spin, if not gold, at least something solid and shiny out of Lennon's high-grade straw. Lennon's version was finally released on the posthumous *Menlove Ave.* album and is discussed in chapter 6.

Mick Jagger: "Too Many Cooks"

Late in 1973, the erratic *Oldies but Goldies* recording sessions helmed by Phil Spector (that eventually formed the basis of Lennon's 1975 album *Rock 'N' Roll*) were unraveling in a haze of confusion and alcohol. At that time, "Too Many Cooks," a cover of a rhythm and blues/soul tune, was recorded with Lennon producing in Spector's absence. In addition to Mick Jagger's lead vocals, the all-star band reportedly includes Lennon, Ringo Starr, John Entwistle, Keith Moon, Harry Nilsson, and the session musicians who were already working with Lennon. At times the Spectorish wall of sound can be a bit overbearing, but the cut has a rollicking feel and manages to find its groove early on, and then proceeds to make the most of it. Lennon broadcast the recording when he appeared on a radio show in San Francisco in October 1974. The song title has proven to be somewhat ironic because the recording has never been legally released (as of 2007), reputedly due to trouble in working through contract legalities regarding the artists involved. Had the song been released at the time, it would have been Jagger's first recorded lead vocal away from The Rolling Stones, a feat he did not attempt successfully until a dozen years later in 1985.

Harry Nilsson: Pussy Cats

With the *Oldies but Goldies* sessions having collapsed from the combined assault of Lennon's drunken indifference and Spector's escalating eccentricities, Lennon and Harry Nilsson decided to make an album together. It would be Nilsson's album, with Lennon producing, and would eventually be released as *Pussy Cats.*

Lennon assembled an all-star group to support Nilsson, including such luminaries as Ringo Starr, Keith Moon, Bobby Keyes, and an array of noted session musicians, several of whom supported Lennon on his *Walls and Bridges* album recorded soon after *Pussy Cats.* Lennon and Nilsson both had a hand in arrangements, and one Lennon song, "Mucho Mungo," was blended into a medley with "Mt. Elga." Somewhat surprisingly, Lennon is not credited with performing vocally or instrumentally on any of the numbers. The album did not produce a hit single despite four attempts and, as a result, charted no higher than a disappointing number 60 on the U.S. charts.

The Spector influence on Lennon is quite evident on some of the songs' arrangements and production, and perhaps in the choice of the cover material attempted as well. The album opens with a too-slowly-paced "Many Rivers to Cross," featuring clever vocals from Nilsson that must be an homage to, or a friendly parody of, his producer. In fact, Lennon recorded a home demo of it a couple of years later. The orchestration has some nice low string work, but the part the high strings are playing Lennon would take and adapt into "#9 Dream" on his next album.

"Save the Last Dance for Me" also suffers from a ponderous pace that attempts to give weight to a song that does not really warrant it and is a misfire as a result despite a grand and emotional vocal reading by Nilsson. Lennon's composition "Mucho Mungo" is pleasant enough, though slight and possibly unfinished, and, outside of rehearsal demos, he never recorded it himself. It is fused into a medley with a Nilsson arrangement of "Mt. Elga." "Loop de Loop" falters, and "Rock Around the Clock" tries for a party atmosphere, much like Lennon's Spector-produced "Since My Baby Left Me," recorded before the beginning of the *Pussy Cats* sessions but not released until 1986's *Menlove Ave*. Also, similar to Lennon's effort, the engaging vocals carry it, but it does not quite capture any genuine celebratory feel.

The other cuts are decidedly better, playing more to Nilsson's strengths. The album lacks any substantial unity but does have some superior moments, notably "Old Forgotten Soldier" and "Black Sails." In "Black Sails," Nilsson makes a vocal quote from Carly Simon's 1972 hit "You're So Vain." This is of interest because on Lennon's next project, which immediately followed *Pussy Cats*, Lennon utilizes quotes both musical and lyrical from his previous works and those of others. Lennon was on the verge of restoring his pop music Midas touch, finding hits in collaboration with Elton John, David Bowie, Ringo Starr, and on his own. Sadly, it did not work here, and the album remains a near-miss despite some shining moments.

WALLS AND BRIDGES

Spurred by his work with Harry Nilsson, Lennon turned his efforts to an album of his own, using some of the musicians he and Nilsson had been working with as the core of his band.[6] With Nilsson and Elton John as guest stars, the album went to number one and produced two top-10 hits, including Lennon's only post-Beatles number one during his life time.

The distraught emotions present in the album likely stem from his separation from Ono and concerns about the status of his career future as well. The recording evidences Lennon's multiple talents as a singer-songwriter, producer-arranger, and musician in full force. The album is lush and romantic when it needs to be, edgy and snarling when it wants to be, and evocative and wistful when it wishes to be. Best of all, Lennon's humor comes through playfully as he references his and others' past works musically and lyrically to some degree in every track.

Those who want to see Lennon as a boundary-obliterating pop artist prefer his *Plastic Ono Band* for its angst, honesty, and numerous profundities growing out of stark simplicities. Others who are put off by the grating, often bleak, harshness of *John Lennon/Plastic Ono Band* will name the *Imagine* album as Lennon's supreme statement, easily the equal of his achievements with The Beatles. Yet *Walls and Bridges* has gained its proponents over the years. The crispness of the production, the successful application of a wide range of musical styles, and the intelligence and humor of the lyrics all mark the album as a significant effort. It could be that in this, of all his post-Beatles album-length efforts, Lennon came closest to sustaining the magical balance of creating adventurous popular music that worked not only in form but in content, while communicating to his audience in ways both intellectual and emotional, as well as immediate and lasting.

The album begins with a languid, funky number, "Going Down on Love." The song expresses a defiant sort of helplessness, as Lennon sings about a love "precious and rare" that "disappears in thin air." The singer will "pay the price" for past abuses by suffering through the rejection and loneliness of the present. The title refers to the emotional abyss that sinks the loser, "going down" means "giving up." Yet Lennon's playful humor surfaces when he sings, "Got to get down" to a funky beat as if feeling the rhythm at a spiritual level, before adding "down on my knees" as if to plead his case. In fact, the phrase, in the context of the title, has another level of meaning since it implies a sexual component that never materializes in the song, thereby presenting another Lennon joke as both the romance and sexual liaison are denied.

Though lyrically bleak, the song glides between a leisurely pace with flowing horn work and some jumpy funk rhythms with bongos and tight, sputtering horns. The contrast provides a feeling of nervous energy, appropriate to the anxious but somehow resigned mood. Lennon quotes his past work and that of others throughout the album, and on this song he quotes his classic Beatles recording "Help!" In the same melody as that song, but at a slower pace, Lennon sings "Somebody please, please help me" very much as he had in the earlier recording.

Elton John's vocals are so prevalent on "Whatever Gets You through the Night" that it almost feels like cheating to call this Lennon's first solo number-one single since the demise of The Beatles. Lennon continues the clever musical and lyrical echoing and borrowing that permeate this album by copying himself again. The melody that accompanies the title line is the same as the opening of the line to *Imagine*'s "Jealous Guy," as Lennon himself recognizes in a composing tape included in the *John Lennon Anthology*. A lengthier version of the rehearsal appeared on *The Lost Lennon Tapes*.

"Whatever Gets You through the Night" is a jovial, high-energy rocker that keeps moving from verse to chorus with a rollicking saxophone solo line and handclaps. Elton John's keyboard work underpins the track, sounding in the same vein as his keyboard playing on his own energetic hit single "Honky

Cat" from two years earlier. Lennon can be heard, though not always understood, happily making comments in the midst of the instrumental passages, including an opening remark that sounds vaguely like he is jokingly swearing, though it is really unintelligible. At other points he shouts "hear me woman!" and "take it easy, woman!" which are more discernable and make sense in connection to the lyrics.

The lyrics are somewhat comically aphoristic, with such phrases as "don't need a watch to waste your time" and "don't need a gun to blow your mind" while more poetic and Ono-like is the statement "don't need a sword to cut through flowers." The song's chorus is one of pleading assurance, asking for trust and proclaiming "I won't do you no harm," thus serving as an excellent outgrowth of the verses' confident fortune-cookie affirmations. Positive, infectious, and rocking all the way, the recording restored Lennon's pop magic and helped propel the album to number one.

A writing collaboration with Harry Nilsson produced "Old Dirt Road," and Nilsson is credited vocally on the recording but is indistinguishable. He later recorded his own version. Mournful and relaxed, the song has a slight country and western feel, but it is not emphasized much and retains much of a generic ballad feel. The slight song is all tone and mood, with lyrics that do not make much literal sense but somehow sound right on an intuitive level.

The road is seen as a temporary anchor in a world where things are in a state of indeterminate flux; a place where life is like "trying to shovel smoke with a pitchfork in the wind," a line reputedly provided by Nilsson. Even the road is in danger of being covered by a mudslide, and all we can do is "keep on keepin' on" despite life's vagaries. On this cut, Lennon quotes from the song "Cool Water." A traveler on the old dirt road encounters a person "lazy bonin'," who says the only thing needed is "cool, clear, water" just as it is sung in the perennial country and western/folk favorite, which was a hit for The Sons of the Pioneers in 1947–1948.

Opening up with an odd, warped-sounding count of "one," echoing Lennon's shout of "Nine!" from his previous album, "What You Got" is a solid, mid-paced, blues-tinged rocker with more than a little Latin funk thrown in for good measure. Lennon takes the old saying "you don't know what you have until you lose it" as the core and tosses a few other standard sayings into the lyrics. The result is that the clichés take on an air of desperation; the singer is trying to convince himself and find solace, however temporary, in those old sayings. The clichés alternate between the self-recrimination of the title and self-reassurance such as "you gotta hang on in." The taut rush of the song implies that the singer is trying to run away from himself and is supported by the line "I've just got to run away" before he shouts "it's such a drag to face another day."

One chorus quotes Little Richard's "Rip It Up" with "Well, it's Saturday night and I just gotta rip it up." Here it is not a call for exuberant celebration, but a statement of hopeless anxiety, with the singer not knowing what else to do or where to turn. "Give me one more chance," he screams, as the energy of the song propels the plea forward, but it remains unanswered.

The emotional panic gives way to recognition and resignation in "Bless You," one of Lennon's strongest and most unique love songs. A rippling electric piano and gently cascading melody provide a floating effect to the slightly jazzy music. The singer blesses the loved one, "wherever you are" and calls the separated couple "restless spirits" that are still "in each other's heart." The refrain reaffirms that the relationship may be repaired and continue because outsiders do not comprehend the depth of the couple's connection.

The second verse blesses the new lover of the beloved "whoever you are," and asks for the new lover to be "warm and kind hearted" while warning that the old love will remain "now and forever." There is no return to the chorus, and the song bubbles along for a few bars before ending on a slightly ominous-sounding chord, giving the song a final feeling of disquiet and unease in place of the hopeful outlook expressed by the chorus after the first verse.

Lennon's vocal performance is at once weary and earnest without being cloying or overly dramatic. He wonderfully conveys the sense of having all but given up, only holding out hope for reconciliation in the chorus. The song's second verse is not the sort of thing often heard in any genre of music, and lifts the song out of the very good into the extraordinary. The song could easily slip into the maudlin, but the tone is exemplary with a grand fusion of effervescent instrumentals, yearning lyrics, and an emotionally real performance.

The uneasy ending of "Bless You" leads into the mournful howling of a wolf that opens "Scared." The guitar picks up the howling sound and turns it into a bending counterpoint that continues throughout the recording. Strip the track of its production consisting of layered horns and the wolf howl guitar, and its harrowing core is as brutal as anything on *John Lennon/Plastic Ono Band*. But with those instruments in the mix, they paint the picture of a confusing emotional maelstrom rather than exposed pain.

The simple admission "I'm scared, so scared" is soon explained. Life is "what it is" and must be dealt with, but the price may be too high because what little he has gained continues to "slip away." "Scared" turns into "scarred" for the second verse, where all Lennon says he has been able to do is "manage to survive." The frustration is all self-directed as Lennon sings about his shortcomings. He will "sing out about love and peace" but he will not face the "red raw meat" of his hatred and jealousy.

The last verse declares "I'm tired," qualifying it with "tired of being alone with no place to call my own." But the feeling is much closer to one of existential angst, being scared of the present and future, scarred by the past, and tired of life's battles. The trudging rhythm continues as the song fades out, implying that the battles will continue.

Lennon's second single release from the album, "#9 Dream," was a languorous account of a dream state, sharing something with his previous songs "I'm Only

Sleeping" and "I'm So Tired" from his Beatles years. Sonically it bears some closeness to "I Am the Walrus" as well. Built around the melody of the orchestration used for "Many Rivers to Cross" on the Harry Nilsson *Pussy Cats* album produced by Lennon, and actually inspired by a dream, the song has an airy majesty that is hard to define other than to say it is dreamlike fantasy.

A few bars of the opening guitar work, like other moments from Jesse "Ed" Davis on this album, are graceful and reminiscent of George Harrison—intentionally, according to some sources.[7] Perhaps sleep and dreams are respites from the pains expressed in "Scared." Lennon sings of "magic in the air," and that accurately describes the orchestration's otherworldly sound here. Lennon's vocals are appropriately hushed and tentative, even asking whether it was "just a dream" after all before surrendering the effort to understand with relaxed acceptance. Lennon sings of "heat whispered trees," "a river of sound," and other images worthy of "Lucy in the Sky with Diamonds" before the chorus of the perplexing but somehow reassuring "Ah, bawakawa pousse pousse" first interrupts and then later finalizes the reveries. This connects with Lennon's earlier blending of gibberish and real non-English language words in The Beatles song "Sun King" from *Abbey Road* in 1969.

Twice in the song, Lennon's vocal intensity builds ("hear—hear—hear" and "feel—feel—feel") and then lets the tension evaporate into the chorus. This is followed by a break in the rhythm as if the dreamer almost awoke before falling back into the dream state. Lennon's lover at the time, May Pang, can be heard whispering "John" when he sings that he heard somebody calling his name in the dream. Later she can be heard saying his name backward, whereas some have said she is saying "Hare Krishna, George" on behalf of John to George Harrison.[8] It sounds like "nhoJ" to the hearer though. With the remastered CD release in 2005, some fans accused Ono of replacing Pang's voice with her own but there seems to be no evidence for the accusation; it might stem from the promotion film made for DVD release in which Ono's image is present at that point in the song, not Pang's.[9] The single was a top-10 follow-up to "Whatever Gets You through the Night," peaking, as it surely had to, at number 9.

The shock of new love is the topic of "Surprise Surprise (Sweet Bird of Paradox)," a song reportedly written in praise of Lennon's off-and-on lover for the last seven years of his life, May Pang. This is not the dawning realization that love was meant to be as in *Mind Games*' "Out the Blue," but sudden astonishment at self-centered lust ("She makes me sweat and forget who I am") giving way to love ("I need her," "I love her").

The pleasure of the realization is expressed in the jubilant and near-fractured structure of the lyrics as well as the buoyant music. Lennon uses marginally connected phrases to approximate the excitement that causes the thoughts to leap ahead of themselves, and their expression to be disrupted as a result. "Natural high...butterfly," he says, trying to describe his feelings, and later "just like a willow tree...a breath of spring." "A bird of paradise," he puns, followed by "sunrise in her eyes."

When he sings, "I need her," he sounds surprised at the realization, wondering how long his feelings and/or the relationship can go on. Finally, he crosses into the manic repeating of "I love her" in a higher and higher pitch until he is in falsetto shouting "Sweet-sweet, sweet-sweet love!" over and over as the song fades. This is another joke and borrowing from his past, as the phrase follows the melody and rhythm of "Beep-beep, beep-beep, yeah!" from the ending of The Beatles' "Drive My Car." The song is primarily McCartney's composition, but Lennon made contributions to the song, so it is not clear whether he is quoting himself or his former Beatle collaborator.

From the manic, the album shifts to the poisonous rage of "Steel and Glass," a companion to "How Do You Sleep?" from *Imagine*. Both songs attack someone Lennon depended on and felt betrayed by—McCartney in the earlier track and The Beatles' and Lennon's one-time manager Allen Klein in "Steel and Glass." Neither man is named directly, but the clues are not difficult to follow if one is familiar with Lennon's history. The songs are similar in tone and structure, even to some degree in arrangement with strident strings stretching over choppy horns on the later track instead of George Harrison's gliding guitar as in the first.

Lennon spitefully mocks his target by asking, "how does it feel to be off the wall?" "You can't pull strings if your hands are tied," he sneers, before saying that Klein leaves his smell "like an alley cat." The song may have made Lennon feel better, but aside from showing that getting on Lennon's bad side was still a dangerous place to be if you were concerned about your public image, the song is only of interest for its similarity to the McCartney attack and as part of Lennon's personal history. Lennon's only clever insult is to say "your mind is capped." One of his more inexplicable corporate insults did not make it to the final version, but exists in the rehearsal on *Menlove Ave*. Lennon berates Klein for standing there with his "Mickey Duck" and his "Donald Fuck."

Discounting the posthumously released and fragmentary composition demo of "It's Real," "Beef Jerky" is the only Lennon instrumental from his post-Beatle years. The basic riff came from Lennon's composing variations on *Mind Games'* "Tight A$" and "Meat City," as a rehearsal tape broadcast on *The Lost Lennon Tapes* demonstrated. The track acknowledges that it is inspired by soul music and rhythm and blues by being credited to "Booker Table and the Maitre D's," a telling homage to the group Booker T. and the MG's. The track is a brass-laden rocker that moves through rhythmic variations and distinctive horn riffs with aplomb and ease. Lennon and Jesse "Ed" Davis have the lead focus on guitars, but the horn section is equally predominant. The cut is fine in and of itself but is even better in an album sequence, where it provides a palette cleanser after the previous venom of "Steel and Glass" and in preparation for the next tune—the sullen "Nobody Loves You (When You're Down and Out)."

Lennon was likely joking when he said "Nobody Loves You (When You're Down and Out)" was a prefabricated arrangement for Frank Sinatra, but Sinatra might have done a fine version nonetheless. The song captures the essence of a three o'clock in the morning, bleary-eyed, self-pitying, booze-drenched interior monologue. There's a certain bravado and grandeur here that makes the weary emptiness of the verses and the impotent rage of the refrains eloquent and poignant despite the patchy string of variant familiar phrases.

For the second time in the album, we are given a clichéd phrase to examine in the title, and again listeners confront emotional pain and despair that words fail to describe; the vacuous cliché must suffice because nothing else remains. Lennon's voice is hoarse and the slight echo has a hollow tone, giving a distanced and alienated ambiance to his lethargic (but not dull) vocal performance. Strings and horns are heavy and descend onto notes with a weighty thud, imparting the song with a thick musical overcast that is not dispelled by the guitar solo that almost sounds like the howling wolf from "Scared" has returned.

The singer laments that "it's all showbiz" as a cynical response to being asked whether he loves someone. He claims he has revealed it all and has nothing to hide; yet it apparently was not enough. The world-weary singer has "been across the water now, so many times" yet still has not found the answers to life's questions: "Everytime I put my finger on it, it slips away." The statements maintain their cynical self-pity with "I'll scratch your back and you knife mine," along with "everybody loves you when you're six foot in the ground." The observation is left to stand as Lennon follows it up with the emotionless whistle of a short countermelody as the song fades out, leaving a bleak and desolate aftertaste.

Certainly Lennon had done songs of despair and desperation before, but nothing quite like this. This is a defeated perspective, a near surrender after trying everything and running out of ideas and options. The little sparks of humor are quite bitter, and the riling up during refrains are shouts of frustration, not defiance. In context, the final whistle is a dirge.

Unlike his *Plastic Ono Band,* however, the album does not end on a bleak note. The last track on *Walls and Bridges,* "Ya Ya," is a throwaway track consisting of a few seconds of Lennon busking his way through a section of the rock and roll classic with his son Julian accompanying him perfunctorily on drums. It has been speculated that perhaps Lennon hoped its inclusion would satisfy the legal demands from his suit over plagiarizing Chuck Berry since the same company owned the copyright for this song. The number, however, feels tacked on as an odd afterthought, even less justifiable as a coda than "Her Majesty" from The Beatles' *Abbey Road* or "Maggie Mae" from *Let It Be.* Comparing it with the integral and summarizing nature of "My Mummy's Dead" from his *Plastic Ono Band* album highlights just how different the albums are and how ranging Lennon's artistic predilections had become. Of marginal interest is that a version of the song from the early 1960s recorded in Hamburg by Tony Sheridan and The Beat Brothers was often included on album collections of the recordings Sheridan had done with The Beatles as his backing group. Sometimes The Beatles were credited as The Beat Brothers, and there was originally confusion as to which tracks they, as a group or as individuals, may have played on. None of them contributed to Sheridan's version of "Ya Ya," however. Lennon redid the song properly for his *Rock 'N' Roll* album.

COLLABORATIONS II

With the *Walls and Bridges* sessions over, Lennon continued his productive and creative streak with more collaborative efforts. He then returned to the *Oldies but Goldies* project before finishing another collaboration, this one with David Bowie.

In the 16 months of his "lost weekend," Lennon created his most commercially successful album, which was his only number-one album without The Beatles during his life time, and included a number-one single and another top-10 hit. And another album he recorded during this time produced a top-20 hit. He also helped both Elton John and David Bowie with two tracks each, with John and Bowie each getting a number-one hit for his and their efforts. He assisted Ringo Starr on three tracks, providing Starr with a top-10 hit. In addition, he produced an entire album with Harry Nilsson and tangentially guided Johnny Winter and Keith Moon through one track each. Lennon may have felt lost and spiritually desolate, but he was at or near the top of his game in both sheer volume of creativity, and in terms of high quality as well. That combination marks a phase in his career comparable only to his artistic output at the height of Beatlemania.

Keith Moon: "Move over Ms. L"

A situation similar to what had occurred with Lennon's "Rock and Roll People" and Johnny Winter during the *Mind Games* sessions repeated itself with Keith Moon, the drummer for The Who, during the *Walls and Bridges* sessions, with the fast-paced nonsensical number "Move over Ms. L." Lennon worked on the song and eventually considered it for inclusion on *Walls and Bridges*, but he was not satisfied with the results and it did not make the cut. Keith Moon was in attendance for some of the *Oldies but Goldies* and *Pussy Cats* sessions and picked up the song, performing a version on his *Two Sides of the Moon* album, released early in 1975. (He also took the opportunity to perform an interesting cover of Lennon's Beatles track "In My Life.")

In Moon's version of "Move over Ms. L," the horn section riffs are a little different than in Lennon's, but the overall arrangement is much the same. The recording makes the most musically of Moon's limited vocal abilities. At the time of Moon's recording of the song, Lennon had not released his version, but he eventually did so as the B-side to "Stand by Me" in March 1975.

Ringo Starr: "Goodnight Vienna," "Only You," and "All by Myself"

Upon completion of his work on *Walls and Bridges,* Lennon sat in on three numbers for Ringo Starr's upcoming album, one of them being Lennon's own composition, "Goodnight Vienna," a nonsensical Liverpool slang expression for bemused surprise that became the title of Starr's album as well.

The most interesting musical aspects of the piece are the chorus breaks, partly made up of brief sections where there is a shift in the back beat for a few measures creating a mixed-meter feel before resuming the original rhythm. The lyrics are yet another quasi–stream-of-consciousness flow of disconnected images and free-flying similes ("felt like an Arab who was dancing through Zion") that have no real meaning, finally resolving in the phrase "it's all got down to Goodnight Vienna" before the chorus break and the ambiguously exhorted phrase of "Get it up!"

As previously with "I'm the Greatest," Lennon rehearsed the band and provided Starr with a guide vocal, and his performance seems good enough, given the nature of the song, to have been released on its own. Like the earlier collaboration, Lennon's version was included on the *John Lennon Anthology.*

"Only You" was a relaxed cover of the often-recorded ballad popularized most successfully by The Platters. Lennon thought it a good idea for Starr to attempt such numbers in general, but especially in view of Starr's earlier hit with a remake of "You're Sixteen." Perhaps Lennon's temporarily abandoned *Oldies but Goldies* project was in his thoughts as well. In any event, Lennon proved correct, and the recording became a top-10 hit for Starr. Hearing Lennon's studio guide recording (*John Lennon Anthology* again, though, surprisingly, a slightly clearer mix was on *The Lost Lennon Tapes* radio series) makes his rhythm guitar work on the song more noticeable and demonstrates that Lennon used almost the exact same guitar rhythm line for his remake of "Stand by Me," recorded two months later. With "Only You" having done better on the charts than "Stand by Me," perhaps Lennon should have kept the idea for himself.

"All by Myself" is not the American standard by Irving Berlin, nor is it the rock power ballad of Eric Carmen, but a composition of Vini Poncia and Starr's on which Lennon plays guitar with Alvin Robinson. The recording is a pleasant mid-paced rocker, with nothing distinct, notable, or even particularly noticeable about Lennon's contribution. The only evidence he is on the track comes from his credit in the album's liner notes.

Elton John: "Lucy in the Sky with Diamonds" and "One Day (At a Time)"

Returning the favor of Elton's John's guest work on *Walls and Bridges,* Lennon worked on Elton John's nonalbum single of two of Lennon's compositions, "Lucy in the Sky with Diamonds" and "One Day (At a Time)." The single became a huge hit, making it to number one early in 1975. The version is not a strict duplication of the original but still manages to capture its mood, though more dreamy than psychedelic this time. Lennon plays guitar and also appears vocally on the chorus, rasping out the song's title in an aggressive manner.

Several times in later interviews, Lennon noted his love of reggae and his attempts from early Beatles' tunes to his post-Beatles career to attempt to slip reggae sections into his recordings. A bouncy countermelody takes center stage at one point before returning to the verse and then a chorus break that must have been suggested by Lennon, since the chorus turns into a reggae shuffle for several bars. The song goes on too long, as in the complete version the ending cranks up a bit and takes about a minute and 40 seconds to fade, running a total of six minutes. However, since Lennon so infrequently revisited his Beatle-era works, it remains an intriguing example of his refusal to see his previous work as sacrosanct, at least in terms of remakes.

The version of "One Day (At a Time)" is a fairly close arrangement to Lennon's original from the *Mind Games* album. But Elton John's performance emphasizes the saccharine qualities of the song, and it comes across as annoyingly cloy when it is not bland. Or he could be joking, but it is not possible to tell for sure. Lennon is on the track as well but, like the previously mentioned Starr track "All by Myself," cannot really be picked out vocally or instrumentally.

ROCK 'N' ROLL

The film *American Graffiti* (1972) had been a surprise hit, and its soundtrack of pre-Beatles rock and pop (the film was set in 1962) spurred a small revival of interest in such songs. That, coupled with Lennon's love of the era, prompted him to contemplate an album of rock and roll/rhythm and blues covers. At the same time, music publisher Morris Levy won a lawsuit about Lennon's "over borrowing" from Chuck Berry's "You Can't Catch Me" for his Beatles song "Come Together" on *Abbey Road*, forcing Lennon to agree to record at least three songs owned by Levy's company, ostensibly on Lennon's next album.[10] Lennon decided to turn himself over to Phil Spector as producer, not with Spector working under him as previously, but with Spector completely in charge. The idea of Lennon romping through some prime rock and roll/rhythm and blues classics sounded irresistible, and the project was tentatively called *Oldies but Goldies* (jokingly called *Oldies but Mouldies* by the participants), and sessions convened in October 1973 as his *Mind Games* album was released.

By all reports, the sessions were a disaster almost from the start. Spector's idea of making each number a miniature symphony, layered to create his patented "wall of sound," simply could not work for every selection and, more often than not, drained the primal vitality out of the songs. What was left was a lethargic, droning husk devoid of any spark or energy. Lennon was reportedly no help at all, as his interest quickly waned and he began drinking heavily. Outtakes reveal Lennon and Spector sniping at and baiting each other when Lennon is not rambling on the edge of embarrassing drunken incoherency. Almost three months of steady work had produced only a handful of tracks before both men cracked under the strain and the project was temporarily abandoned. Spector promptly disappeared with the recordings and Lennon soon moved on, pulling himself together to produce *Pussy Cats* with Harry Nilsson.

Later in 1974, after *Walls and Bridges* was released and Morris Levy did not see the three agreed-upon songs included in the album, he met with Lennon to press the issue of the settlement. Lennon's successful collaborations with Elton John and Ringo Starr were completed, and he had gained control of the recordings from the October to December 1973 sessions helmed by Spector. Lennon decided he had barely half an album of salvageable material, and even those numbers needed new vocal tracks. He hastily reconvened several of the musicians he had used on *Walls and Bridges* and set to work repairing what he could of the Spector recordings and coming up with new material.

Once finished, he gave copies of the tapes to Levy, who prepared them and released them as a special television offer called *Roots: John Lennon Sings the Great Rock and Roll Hits.* Apparently, what Lennon had thought was talk of an idea, Levy had thought was a gentleman's agreement verbal contract to proceed. Lennon sued to stop further sales and rushed his own version out. Two songs, "Angel Baby" and "Be My Baby," made Levy's *Roots* collection but not Lennon's *Rock 'N' Roll.* The running times of some of the songs were also a little longer on *Roots,* not being faded out at the same point. In addition, two other songs from the Spector sessions, "Since My Baby Left Me" and "To Know Her Is To Love Her," were passed over by both collections but were later included on the *Menlove Ave.* album along with a Lennon-Spector original composition, "Here We Go Again."

The album starts with a rave-up version of the Gene Vincent classic "Be Bop-A-Lula" that bounces along nicely and features a vocal that sounds like Lennon is enjoying himself. The production is perhaps a bit too smooth for rockabilly purists, a problem with much of the album in general, but remains engaging nonetheless. If only the entire album were this effortless at capturing the joy and excitement the original recordings must have instilled in Lennon, it would be the classic it should have been.

Since the album was hurried into release, there was no advance single to help promote the record, as was Lennon's usual custom. This time, a single— "Stand by Me"—came out three weeks *after* the album was issued. In a move to try and make up for the tardy release, in addition to increasing notice and sales, the flip side was not another rock and roll oldie from the album, but a track composed by Lennon and not included on any Lennon album to that date, "Move over Ms. L."

"Stand by Me" is one of the stronger numbers on the album. Lennon kicks it off with an acoustic guitar line that is suspiciously similar to the one he used when recording "Only You" for Starr a couple of months previously. The song builds wonderfully as electric guitar and then acoustic piano slowly trickle in before the rest of the band, including a full horn section, descends on the first chorus. The number stands out, however, due to Lennon's masterful vocal interpretation as it moves from simple declaration, through tentative pleading, to earnest shouting, finally trailing off in semi-uncertainty.

A different, though just as sterling, performance was given by Lennon when he was filmed performing the song for the television show *The Old Grey Whistle Test* about five months after recording the track. Lennon is again clearly enjoying himself and manages to slip in a greeting to his son Julian and others back in Great Britain, makes fun of how many times he has to sing the title line, and sings the opening lyrics from "Unchained Melody" over the start of the guitar solo, thereby pointing out the songs' similarity. Lennon's joy is palpable and infectious without spoiling the emotional mood of the song.

Lennon had attempted "Move over Ms. L" during the sessions for *Walls and Bridges* but never tackled it to his approval. Reconvening the same musicians for this album and cranking them through the rock and roll oldies must have made him think they had developed the feel for it and they attempted it again, this time getting it to Lennon's satisfaction.

The song is another fast-paced rocker with Lennon's characteristic wordplay and mixed clichéd phrases strung together in near non sequitur runs spouted over the driving rhythm. One clichéd phrase, "they're starving back in China," turned up on his song "Nobody Told Me," recorded in 1980 and released after his murder. Other lyrical observations that hurtle by include the seemingly censorable paradox that "you can't get head in a head shop" and what in 1975 would be the broadcast-halting observation that "your jeans are full of crap." Verses aside, the chorus is reputedly a nod to Ono, as Lennon sings the title coupled with "you know I wish you well."

Lennon gives a full-throttle vocal performance, sometimes belting out the lyrics, stretching notes into lengthy screams, and exhorting the band several times with shouts of "whoo-ooo-hoo!" "hey-hey!" "alright!" and "that's right!" Closer listening, though, reveals that some of those may be redubbed into the mix—but no matter, partially artificial or not, it remains a lively performance that boosts the recording into being of more than marginal interest.

The *John Lennon Anthology* has a slightly looser version, without the horn section and overdubs, but with Lennon's exuberance intact. Bootlegs from the earlier attempts during the *Walls and Bridges* sessions are also available.

The medley of "Ready Teddy/Rip It Up" lasts only a few seconds more than a minute and a half, but Lennon's throaty vocals and a great horn section work to make it one of the most successful tracks on the album, and the production succeeds in staying out of the way. There should have been more numbers like this on the collection.

Chuck Berry's "You Can't Catch Me" was the song that was the impetus for the oldies collection, since Lennon used it as partial inspiration for "Come Together" on the *Abbey Road* album. This is a product of the Spector sessions, and, although it goes on a bit too long with its repetitive riffs, it is not too bad. Then again, it is not particularly noteworthy either.

Lennon's take on "Ain't That a Shame" is another winner along the lines of "Be Bop-A-Lula." Once again the arrangement is fairly straightforward and Lennon's gritty vocals with a touch of echo keep the song rocking. There is a certain slickness here that is possibly a bit "too good" for some tastes, but, all in all, this is another excellent track.

In "Do You Want To Dance?" Lennon's love of reggae shows up again in the arrangement for this favorite that was often covered. In fact, a cover hit of the song by Bette Midler had made the top 20 as relatively recently as 1973. The reggae idea does not quite come off as well as it might, but Lennon at least gets points for trying. All but buried in the mix are amusing vocal asides from Lennon, including him answering the titular question with "I'm not quite sure!"

"Sweet Little Sixteen" is another one of the Spector tracks, somewhat weakened by a puzzling choice in the arrangement that has pauses between some of the vocal lines, causing a lessening of the momentum the song tries to build lyrically. And, again, the repetitive horn lines do not find much of a groove or lay a foundation but instead emphasize the faults of the questionable arrangement by becoming monotonous.

"Slippin' and Slidin'" is a standout track in every way, with the band (especially the horn section) roaring from the first bar and Lennon in fine form throughout. Good as it is, Lennon topped it later in the year when he performed it for *The Old Grey Whistle Test*. Lennon is absolutely bursting with joy in the broadcast performance; relaxed, joking, and in full command. At one point he remarks that the band is a "lovely little group" and quite amusingly pretends embarrassment at messing up the timing of the ending. The rendition is simply wonderful.

An energized version of Buddy Holly's classic "Peggy Sue" follows, complete with hiccups, and the slightly affected vocal makes this one of the more enjoyable entries of the collection. "Look out!" an excited Lennon warns before the band launches into the section of well-known guitar break. The cut is brisk and clean without being antiseptic and hence a superior effort.

Lennon's voice is partially obscured by the chorus early in the medley of "Bring It on Home to Me/Send Me Some Lovin'," almost as if he were just another chorus member and not the lead, hampering the song to some degree. But by the time of the transition to "Send Me Some Lovin'," he sings solo and lifts the song out of the ordinary into a couple of minutes of heart-felt enthusiasm. If the first part of the track were as impressive, this would be one of the better cuts.

A grumbling, fuzzed guitar line anchors Lennon's front-and-center double-tracked vocals on "Bony Moronie." Lennon shouts and chomps his way through the number, with some nice comments during the fade out. Once again, though, the slightly plodding Spector production pulls things down and takes the edge off a good number. Lennon certainly tries, though, and almost salvages the track with his grating (in a good way) vocals.

Lennon threw away a performance of "Ya Ya" as a sop to Levy on *Walls and Bridges,* but here he does it for real—more or less. Lennon tries to inject a little energy, urging the band to "boogie down one time" and adds a yelp for good measure, but the track never really takes off. There does not seem to have been much to work with at the start. The aforementioned Tony Sheridan version has more life.

"Just Because" is surely the best of the Spector tracks, but, like the others, Lennon had to redo his vocals to make it releasable. Everything works on this recording, from the solid low horns, through the choppy rhythm section, to the erratically noodling keyboard. Of special enjoyment are Lennon's vocals that range from the appropriately histrionic to the almost absurdist spoken passages. After debating how old he might have been when the song came out (never getting it right, for those who are curious), Lennon turns in one of the best vocals in an album often salvaged by his vocal performances. A nearly ridiculous recitation passage includes Lennon saying good-bye to his love because the last time he saw her she was "wearing a man's clothes." He declares that he is not prejudiced but that he "had problems with the zipper." Or at least that is what it sounds like he's saying. After that, he tells us "there's two basses in this, an' I hope you appreciate it."

Outtakes of Spector versions of this are painful to listen to, as Lennon drunkenly fumes and sputters his way through the song out of tune, missing entrances, and spouting profanities. On the 2004 CD reissue, Ono includes a snippet of one of these performances where Lennon says hello to his former Beatle band mates.

And so the marginally frustrating album ends. The overly thick and some-times ponderous production gets in the way of the spirited performances enough times to keep this from being the superb album fans expected. But more than half the tracks hold up well enough to make it enjoyable, if all the more frustrating for the remainder that do not quite live up to their promise. Considering the circumstances of its creation, the fact that the album was not totally abandoned or sapped of all drive is something of an achievement in itself.

Also included on the 2004 CD reissue are versions of "Angel Baby," "To Know Her Is To Love Her," and "Since My Baby Left Me"—but not

"Be My Baby," thus oddly keeping the CD from being complete by not encompassing all of the legally released *Rock 'N' Roll/Roots* tracks. The first two songs are the same as on *Menlove Ave.* (all three are discussed in chapter 6 in the section about that album), but "Since My Baby Left Me" is not the same take, running almost a minute longer. Lennon's performance is more assured on this version, but the chorus is less controlled with the harmonies and "response" to Lennon's "call" faltering quite a few times.

David Bowie: "Across the Universe" and "Fame"

Riding high on the success of *Walls and Bridges* and having completed the revived *Rock 'N' Roll* sessions, Lennon accepted an offer from David Bowie to join him to work on a cover version of Lennon's comparatively (and unjustly) obscure (at the time) Beatles track "Across the Universe." Bowie drops the "Jai Guru Deva Om" part of the refrain and overdubs himself in a typically histrionic performance as Lennon adds some restrained guitar. The sessions took place while Lennon's collaboration with Elton John on his Beatles classic "Lucy in the Sky with Diamonds" was topping the charts.

During a rehearsal jam, the duo, with guitarist Carlos Alomar (who later sang in the chorus for Lennon and Ono's *Milk and Honey* album), eventually developed the song "Fame," which became a number-one hit for Bowie in the summer of 1975. A semi-funk riff percolates throughout the song and bears similarities to Lennon's work with Ono in late 1972 and early 1973 (such as "She Hits Back") while looking ahead to sounds employed on various tracks of *Double Fantasy*. Guitarist Earl Slick is on the cut, and he became one of the guitarists for Lennon and Ono's *Double Fantasy* album sessions.

The lyrics describe several vagaries associated with fame—some serious, some mocking, and some absurd. The title is shouted out at various intervals, with the tone usually bent, overlapping, and echoed until finally its speed is distorted in a downward-toned cascade. It might be Lennon's voice that can barely be picked out of the mix on a couple of the shouted "is it any wonder?" moments, but with the inclusion of other voices (including Fanny co-founder and bassist Jean Millington) and electronic alterations, it is impossible to discern his other recorded contributions. The best guess is that Lennon contributed some of the higher-pitched vocal sounds.

Lennon performs "Yer Blues" with The Dirty Mac in *The Rolling Stones Rock and Roll Circus*, his first formal musical appearance without The Beatles. Courtesy of Photofest.

Lennon readies himself to perform "Instant Karma!" on Britain's *Top of the Pops* television series. Courtesy of Photofest.

Lennon records the vocals to "How?" during the sessions that produced the *Imagine* album. Courtesy of Photofest.

Lennon performs during the One to One shows in 1972, his only full-length concert performances post-Beatles. Courtesy of Photofest.

5

Cleanup Time, 1975–1980

By the beginning of summer 1975 Lennon was allowing his career to wind down. Over the next year he signed no new recording contracts and all but stopped giving interviews. His wife was pregnant; he either had met his performing and recording obligations or had specific plans in the works to do so; his public appearances became fewer and fewer; and, at long last, his immigration struggles were beginning to break in his favor. His second child, another son, was born in October 1975, and he was granted permanent residency status in July 1976.

For the next four years, Lennon was mostly out of the public eye. Lennon (and, for that matter, Ono) produced nothing professionally during this time. After his shooting, posthumous releases of home recordings and writings evidenced that Lennon sporadically composed songs, recorded himself for his own amusement, and concocted surreal and comic sound collages and narratives during this period. This runs counter to interviews he gave during the last months of his life, in which he declared he did not so much as touch his guitar for five years.[1] Despite his remarks to the contrary, Lennon did compose and polish new material during his self-imposed professional exile. Some of the songs were finished, and others were not. A few were cannibalized for other compositions and the remaining shells abandoned. Perhaps he meant his remarks to be taken in a purely professional capacity. In any event, some (but not all) of the more superior recordings he made during these years were included in *The Lost Lennon Tapes* radio series and have been issued on CD.

In a 1977 interview in Japan, Lennon confirmed that he was taking time off until his son Sean was about five years old, at which point he was considering returning in some capacity to the public eye.[2] That proved to be the case, for in late summer 1980, Lennon began recording polished demos of new material and some of the songs he had been toying with over the last five years. Ono joined in, and by August they were in a professional studio, making what would become the *Double Fantasy* album.

SHAVED FISH

October 1975 saw Lennon's 35th birthday coinciding with the birth of his second son and the only release of a "greatest hits" album collection that Lennon himself compiled. It is credited to "John Lennon: Plastic Ono Band." The collection is somewhat inexplicably titled *Shaved Fish*, which is perhaps intended to comment on the "commercial product" as implied by the artwork on the back of the album cover, which depicts a partially opened tin of fish on shaved ice. The front cover is equally intriguing, with sketches to convey the meaning of each of the songs included.

The strength of the collection resides in the fact that, at the time of release, it was the only collection of Lennon's nonalbum singles as well as his controversial singles that had smaller sales. All of Lennon's album singles up to that time, with the exception of "Stand by Me," are included. Lennon eschews strict chronological order and bookends the collection with different (though both incomplete) performances of "Give Peace a Chance." He begins the record with the first minute of the single and ends the collection with a chorus sequence from the performance at the One to One concert. In later interviews, Lennon said he wanted to be sure the lesser-selling singles were not forgotten and properly archived, and the best way to ensure that was to produce this album.[3] There would not be another Lennon album for five years.

A FINAL COLLABORATION: RINGO STARR'S "COOKIN' (IN THE KITCHEN OF LOVE)"

Once again Starr called and Lennon answered. An April 1976 session to record "Cookin' (In the Kitchen of Love)" was Lennon's first time in a professional recording studio since his collaboration with David Bowie in January 1975 and would be Lennon's last until the *Double Fantasy* sessions began in August 1980. The resulting song is a slight, innocuous rock-pop tune that harmlessly bounces along to its somewhat forced party atmosphere conclusion. Ono later incorporated the song into the musical play about Lennon's life that she mounted in 2004 to 2005.

In 1980, Lennon again came to Starr's aid as Starr began preparations for what would be his *Stop and Smell the Roses* album of 1981. Lennon was reportedly turning a handful of his incomplete compositions into possible numbers for Starr, including "I'm Stepping Out" and a song called "Life

Begins at 40."[4] Only home demos of the latter song exist because Lennon never recorded a studio version of the song. Some accounts contend that it, like "I'm the Greatest," would be another Billy Shears song, while Internet rumors indicated that it might have been under consideration for completion by the surviving Beatles for the mid-1990s *Anthology* collection.[5]

PRESENT IN ABSENTIA

Lennon may not have been producing any new recordings for public consumption, but that did not mean he was totally out of the public or industry consciousness by a long shot. Every time a former Beatle released an album, Lennon was mentioned, and his and George Harrison's lack of new material was regularly addressed in trade journals and fan magazines. Harrison had a more than two-year gap between albums, having released nothing between *Thirty Three & 1/3* in November 1976 and *George Harrison* in February 1979. During the dry period of no albums of new material from Lennon from February 1975 to October 1980, McCartney released five albums, Starr three, and Harrison three even with his hiatus. So, approximately every six months, there was a new album release, and the resulting publicity, from a former Beatle. In addition, repackaged Beatles materials were released with regularity, and even "new" Beatles material kept Lennon, to some degree at least, in the public eye, if inadvertently. Although an analysis is beyond the purview of this work, the Beatles' releases bear mentioning in that context.

The repackaging of Beatles materials was indeed fairly common, but the release of legal, previously unheard material was rare. In 1977, two different collections of The Beatles performing live were released. The first was arguably the more interesting, because the recording predated their complete rise to fame but postdated Ringo Starr's entry into the band. It was *The Beatles Live! At the Star Club*. The sound quality was poor, but the release included several songs never otherwise recorded by the Beatles, and it is fascinating to hear them. Lennon jokes with and taunts the audience and is in fine form on several numbers.

Live at the Hollywood Bowl came out a few months later and was an album culled from the group's performances at that famous venue in 1964 and 1965 by their producer George Martin and made to sound like one show. The screams of Beatlemania take a while to get used to, but eventually the band can be enjoyed. Lennon's humorous remarks are part of the album's highlights, and it is certainly an auditory time capsule of historic interest in addition to fun listening. It has not been issued on CD, and arguably another blending of the concerts should be attempted for a proper CD release.

The next year saw EMI release a box set of The Beatles' entire catalog with a bonus album of, and called, *Rarities*. The album was then released in 1979 on its own but exists in two very different versions. The British version consists of obscure Beatle B-sides and singles that never made it on to any album collection. Even by the late 1970s, there were still several such tracks in the group's catalog. Releasing "new" material was complicated because different countries had released different collections of these recordings, so some were available on an album in some nations but not in others. There was no universally consistent release of this material. It was not until 1988 that official album releases of all of this material finally came out as two albums with the punning titles of *Past Masters* Volumes One and Two.

The *Rarities* album released in the United States was rather more esoteric. This was not an album of missing B-sides, but true obscurities. Listeners were treated to such tracks as "Penny Lane" with a bit more piccolo trumpet solo, "I Am the Walrus" with an extra beat or two of strings, and a mono version of a recording commonly known only in stereo or vice versa. Sometimes only hardcore Beatlemaniacs could tell the variant version from the classic, and many of them did not care to make the effort. If the group's albums were not considered such sacrosanct entities, such rarities would have made good bonus cuts on future reissues. As it was, several of the variants from this version of the *Rarities* album found their way into the Beatles' *Anthology* collections.

DOUBLE FANTASY: A HEART PLAY

In the summer of 1980, Lennon sailed with a small crew from Newport, Rhode Island, to Bermuda. The island proved to be fertile ground for Lennon's creativity. He finished composing a slew of songs, several he had been working on sporadically for years, and was motivated to record again. Upon returning to New York, Lennon and Ono booked time during August and September at The Hit Factory recording studio in Manhattan and began laying down tracks. The couple gathered a group of veteran studio musicians, including guitarist Hugh McCracken (who had played on Paul McCartney's *Ram* album); drummer Andy Newmark; and guitarist Earl Slick, who participated in the Lennon–David Bowie "Fame" sessions five years earlier. Jack Douglas, who achieved great success producing Aerosmith and Cheap Trick in the 1970s, was called in to co-produce with Lennon and Ono. Years earlier, Douglas had been an assistant engineer for the *Imagine* sessions.

Despite the insecurities associated with not being in the studio for almost half a decade, the recorded results have a relaxed feel, in part because Lennon was not under contract to any record company. At the time, media mogul David Geffen was starting up a new label, Geffen Records. Geffen had already lured Elton John from MCA and former disco diva Donna Summer from the Casablanca label. The Lennons would prove the hat trick. Geffen sold the Lennons on his label because of its small, intimate environment and, more convincingly, because he did not ask to hear the new product before signing them. He also had the savvy to approach Yoko Ono.[6] The couple signed with

Geffen in late September, paving the way for John Lennon's first release of newly composed material in six years.

The album was *Double Fantasy*. The title has several meanings. The Double Fantasy is a flower that was blooming in Bermuda during Lennon's visit in July 1980. The title also refers to the close working and intimate relationship between Lennon and Ono. Kishin Shinoyama's black-and-white head-shot cover photo of the Lennons in the midst of an eyes-closed, gentle kiss underscores the duo's relationship. The photo also references the interior cover photo of the couple's *Wedding Album,* issued 11 years earlier, which displayed a black-and-white photo of the couple caught up in a kiss.

The title also relates to the concept and sequencing of the album, which is a dialogue between two equal artists. The final product is generally sequenced to alternate between tracks composed and sung by Lennon with those composed and sung by Ono. The dialogue aspect is most evident in the tracks "I'm Losing You" and "I'm Moving On," which are discussed in more detail below.

The album begins simply with the gentle hitting of a bell in the first measures of "(Just Like) Starting Over." Lennon talk-sings the introduction at a slow tempo in his trademark ballad voice, making it into a recitative song opening, a technique he used for "Listen," "Bad to Me," and "If I Fell" 17 years earlier. The recording picks up its tempo and morphs into a mid-tempo rock song that vocally conjures up 1950s rock singers Eddie Cochran, Gene Vincent, and Buddy Holly and adds a touch of 1960s girl-group singers in the background vocals. Lennon jokingly named his vocalizing style here as that of "Elvis Orbison."[7] With echo added to his vocal, Lennon brings up the vocal styling of his youth. Whereas the lyrics are overtly about a renewed love ("we both are falling in love again"), the song is also the duo's pronouncement that Lennon and his music were back.

"(Just Like) Starting Over" was the first single released from *Double Fantasy*. The recording was number one on the *Billboard* charts for five weeks, but not until after his murder. Lennon appears to have always been enamored of song titles that included parenthetical phrases going back to the rhythm and blues and soul songs of the early 1960s, and they flood his entire catalog. With The Beatles, he had composed many songs with such titles, including "Norwegian Wood (This Bird Has Flown)," "I Want You (She's So Heavy)," and "You Know My Name (Look Up My Number)." His post-Beatles work included "Bring on the Lucie (Freda People)," "I Know (I Know)," "Instant Karma! (We All Shine On)," and several others. He did it again with this track, except that the parenthetical aspect came first this time.

As noted earlier, the album alternates between Lennon tracks and Ono tracks. The first Ono effort on the album is "Kiss Kiss Kiss." The music track has elements of the punk rock aesthetic with martial drum rolls added. The recording reveals the influences that Ono's earlier work had on the music and vocal styling of Blondie, The Slits, Nina Hagen, the B-52s, and other punk and new wave outfits of the era. Ono's style, if not herself, now had a following. The lyrics have an erotic tone. She sings "touch me" and "shaking inside" in the same line. In the last half of the song, she adds her spoken voice that, mixed at the same volume, competes with and alternates with her singing of the lyrics. Ono's voice-over builds toward an orgasmic climax calling "faster!" and "harder!" in Japanese, and Lennon's screeching guitar work matches her and urges her on.

In the closing lines of the song, Ono sings of the "faint sound of the childhood bell ringing." This ties in with the bell that opened the record in "(Just Like) Starting Over" and provides closure for the opening couplet. This was the flip side of "(Just Like) Starting Over" and certainly showed a different side of relationships. Where Lennon's song was praise to the joys of renewing romance at middle age, Ono's captured the still potent desire of sexual yearning and need.

Lennon's "Cleanup Time" has the feel of the Stax and Atlantic label's soul records of the mid-1960s. This is particularly evident in the horn charts that embellish the recording. Lennon's lyric makes a direct reference to the lifestyle the Lennons were living at the Dakota in Manhattan over the previous five years. He sings, "The queen is…counting out the money." Yoko Ono handled the couple's business affairs and made shrewd investments during the time Lennon was taking care of their young son Sean. Beatle fans couldn't help but notice the lyrical referencing to Lennon's White Album song "Cry Baby Cry," where he also sings about the actions of a king and queen in their domestic habitat for part of the song.

Right after the line about the "queen," Lennon sings, the "king is in the kitchen making bread." Again, this follows the story of how the Lennons were living. John Lennon was so proud of his first loaf of baked bread that he took a Polaroid photo of his creation. Lennon's lyrics speak of the home as the "center" and of being "absolutely free." He had no recording obligations and he was enjoying life.

This is hinted at in Shinoyama's unpretentious back cover photo of the couple in the city they loved. Dressed in black, they both look across the street toward Central Park. Each is focused on the same object. The city shows its blemishes. The street in front of them is filled with an asphalt patch. The trash can on the curb just behind them is full. The couple is one element of the hustle and bustle of Manhattan. Traffic moves briskly in both directions, and pedestrians occupy the same sidewalk off of which the pair just stepped.

Ono's "Give Me Something" again offers a punk aesthetic. Barely over a minute and a half, it races through a listing of things and activities that are cold (eyes, bed) and hard (voice, feelings), and she growls in frustration, saying "give me something!" that is neither cold nor hard. She then offers her "heart beat and a bit of tear and flesh" in exchange. The track ends quite abruptly, leaving a moment of silence before the most interesting couplet of *Double Fantasy*.

With the big drum sound that would come to define recordings later in the 1980s, Lennon offers the darkest song of the album in the mid-tempo track "I'm Losing You." Though not as stark as the songs of the *Plastic Ono Band* era, the guitar line and the drums create a tense atmosphere that underscores the relationship tensions that are covered in the lyrics. The narrator went for comfort in the room of a "stranger" and wonders why, or it could be that the narrator is so alienated that he sees his or the lover's room as now belonging to a stranger. In the "valley of indecision," the lines of communication have been cut. He sings of forgiveness or the lack thereof ("do you still have to carry that cross?"). The narrator is repentant, but still his relationship is "slipping away."

The song is Lennon's toughest on the album, but it could have been even tougher. Early on in the *Double Fantasy* session, two members of Cheap Trick (Rick Nielsen, Bun E. Carlos) and one from King Crimson (Tony Levin) came into the studio to record the track with Lennon. A take was released on the *John Lennon Anthology* in 1998. The take is quite good and, without the production gloss of the album, it roars while not sounding incomplete, making it an obvious highlight of the 1998 collection. Leaked news that Lennon had recorded with members of Cheap Trick spurred rumors that he and Ono were going to tour with Cheap Trick as their band, similar to how they had adopted Elephant's Memory eight years earlier, a fascinating idea that was probably never under serious consideration—although Cheap Trick's 1982 song hit "If You Want My Love" certainly sounds more than a little Lennon-esque in spots, indicating that it might have been a successful collaboration.

The underlying music and rhythm remain the same as the track segues into Ono's "I'm Moving On." This is the sequel or the rest of the story to Lennon's "I'm Losing You." The album's subtitle "A Heart Play" is most apparent in the juxtaposition of these tracks. Ono's narrator tells Lennon's narrator to "save (his) sweet talk." She accuses him of being false and will have nothing of his "window smile." She does not want to be intimate with him ("don't stick your finger in my pie"). "I'm Moving On" is an explanatory rebuff to "I'm Losing You." Ono ends her performance with painful vocal sounds that give the impression that she has been strangled by the relationship. The previous song had ended with similar sounds from Lennon's guitar (and an almost hidden Morse code message). The narrator wants to break it off but, as in complicated love entanglements, cannot break it off without much grief.

From the dark tension of these two tracks, the move shifts dramatically with Lennon's ballad paean to his young son Sean. The song "Beautiful Boy (Darling Boy)" has become one of Lennon's higher-profile compositions since the time of his passing. The song was used to great effect in the film *Mr. Holland's Opus* in the reconciliation scene between the music teacher protagonist and his deaf son. And one line from the song, "Life is what happens to you when you're busy making other plans," has become a greeting card and calendar quote staple.

"Beautiful Boy (Darling Boy)" is a lullaby. The relationship of the album to its creation in Bermuda is evident in the music and lyric of the track. The instrumental parts of the track are highlighted by steel drum played by Robert Greenidge. In 1998, Sean Lennon's first solo album recording, *Into the Sun,* had a number on it called "Sean's Song" that used similar ocean sounds and kettle drums in parts of its production.

The lyrics speak of the narrator "out on the ocean sailing away" thinking of when his son will "come of age." (This alludes to the opposite relationship Lennon had with his father, Alfred, who worked on merchant ships for long stretches of time but likely did not spend his free moments thinking of the welfare of his son. John Lennon asserts that things will be different for Sean and him.) Lennon's five years with his son at and around the Dakota, and away from the music business, are evident in the lyric and gentle instrumental backing.

One bittersweet element when listening to the track is the thought that Lennon never performed a song with a similar sentiment for his first son, Julian. Lennon's song "Good Night" from The Beatles' White Album was a lullaby for Julian, but Ringo Starr sang it, and Julian is never named as Sean is in "Beautiful Boy (Darling Boy)." Rather, the mantle to do so was assumed by Lennon's Beatle band mate Paul McCartney, who was inspired to write "Hey Jude" for the young Julian Lennon.

Breaking the alternating sequencing by not moving into what sounds like Ono's response song "Beautiful Boys," the centerpiece of the album opens side two of the original disc. "Watching the Wheels" begins with a quiet, elegant piano figure. The lyrical premise of the song complements an open letter that the Lennons published as full-page advertisements in 1979 in newspapers in New York, London, and Tokyo. In the letter, the couple attempted to justify their activities outside the media spotlight.[8] Lennon's lyrics to "Watching the Wheels" offer similar sentiments. The song's narrator is content observing "shadows on the wall." He offers the quizzical concern of those the Lennons tried to address with their open letter by singing their question, "Don't you miss the big time?"

In the chorus, Lennon uses the image of a merry-go-round as an allegory for the life of the celebrity superstar he experienced. Beatlemania and the pressures of recording obligations with the group and in his solo career had the artist going around in circles. The backing musicians create a sound akin to a carousel pump organ to complement the chorus's underscoring lyrics and it is also reminiscent of the backing sounds to "Mind Games" and "Being for the Benefit of Mr. Kite."

"Watching the Wheels" was the third single release from *Double Fantasy.* It reached number 10 in the United States and was the first single by Lennon that was not selected by him. With the strength of the performance and its location at the head of an album side, it would be difficult to imagine that Lennon would not have picked the track as a single had he lived.

Ono's "I'm Your Angel" turns the clock back to the big bands of the 1930s and 1940s with a dominant clarinet in the mix. Ono plays the big band vocalist, even singing lyrics from the "moon-June-spoon" school: "I'm in your pocket, you're in my locket." Lennon contributes several lines of whistling the melody to the song, adding an informal, carefree touch to the bandstand arrangement and vocal styling. It is as if the traditional pop styling works to underscore the traditional aspects of romantic love with a slightly-embarrassed-at-it-all ironic twist. Ono faced a lawsuit due to the similarities between this work and the 1920s Eddie Cantor hit that became a standard, "Making Whoopee."[9]

The opening guitar chords of "Woman" announce Lennon's ballad of love. In form, the track hearkens back to Lennon's White Album–era ballads, such as "Julia" and "Dear Prudence." In fact, in later interviews Lennon sometimes called it "the Beatles' track."[10] Though more polished than those White Album tracks (such as in the added background vocals), "Woman" has a similar feel in its structure and lead vocal. In the lyric, Lennon writes of the "little child inside the man." This is interesting because John Lennon often referred to Yoko Ono as "Mother." The printed lyrics on the inner sleeve also note one line as "I never mean(t) to cause you sorrow or pain." Even when Lennon sings "meant" in the recorded performance, suggesting that the problems are in the past, the printed lyric more realistically notes that romantic relationships always present further unseen challenges that will arise.

Like Otis Redding ("[Sittin' On] The Dock of the Bay") and Sam Cooke ("A Change Is Gonna Come") before him, artists who had best-sellers with ballads shortly after suffering untimely deaths, Lennon had a hit record with "Woman," released a month after his death. The single, the last track Lennon handpicked to be a single release, was number two on the *Billboard* charts for three weeks.

Lennon's masterful track is followed by one of Ono's most unsettling, "Beautiful Boys," which is a companion piece to both previous Lennon tracks. The opening verses are directed at her son ("don't be afraid to cry") and then at her husband ("your mind has changed the world") directly, just as Lennon's track had been directed to Sean. She then directs the chorus to all men as "Woman" has been directed to all women. Backward noises and other sounds create an uneasy atmosphere as Ono encourages men not to be afraid to "go to hell and back" in their life's journey. Where Lennon's songs had been songs of reassurance and acceptance, Ono's response is a challenge to accept that a well-lived life will have heartbreak and danger.

Taking a musical cue from Buddy Holly's recording of "Rave On" for the opening and maintaining a Holly-like vocal style throughout, Lennon's response to Ono's admonitions is to express his joy at her mere presence in "Dear Yoko." Full of the lighthearted giddiness of "Oh Yoko!" from the *Imagine* album nine years earlier but without the manic quality, the track uses Caribbean rhythms to create the playful mood, a clue to Lennon's environment during its composition. The song bounces along with occasionally fresh-sounding lyrics such as Lennon's observation that "there's a hole where you're supposed to be" when Ono is absent. In a demonstration recording, Lennon sings "the gods have really smiled upon our love," but, on the album, perhaps as a nod to Ono's influence in broadening his outlook, he sounds as though he sings "the goddess really smiled upon our love"—though it could be "gods 've" after all.

Ono's response to Lennon's praise is a vaguely sinister-sounding number called "Every Man Has a Woman Who Loves Him." The tune has something of a reggae feel and talks about the preordained nature of soul mates but says that one may not find his or her soul mate "in this lifetime." There is also some hesitancy expressed in acquiescing to the inevitability of the relationship as Ono sings, "Why do I run, when I know you're the one?" Lennon sings a backing lead on this; four years after his death, a version of him singing lead and Ono backing was released and it is discussed later. In 2004, Ono had a dance-mix hit with a remixed version of the song with lyrical alterations to allow for same-sex unions.

The album ends with Ono's gospel-tinged ballad that declares "Hard Times Are Over." Lennon sings along, with the couple joined by a chorus that swells with pounding piano and wailing sax. It gives the song a sweeping majestic, but maintains a loose feel. This feel complements the lyrics that declare that hard times are over, but then add that they are only over "for a while."

The twentieth anniversary CD reissue of *Double Fantasy* from 2000 included a snippet of the dialogue called "Central Park Stroll" culled from a longer piece used in the introduction to Yoko Ono's 1981 version of "It Happened." The A-side of that release, Ono's masterwork "Walking on Thin Ice" (discussed later), was also included. Most welcome, however, was the inclusion of a home demonstration recording of Lennon performing a song he composed called "Help Me To Help Myself" previously only heard on a *Lost Lennon Tapes* broadcast.

The demo is very clear sounding and of much better quality than other demo releases by Lennon. He plays piano in a 1950s gospel-influenced ballad style after first commenting about the sticky pedals of the piano. The piece has a vague musical semblance to his song "I Know (I Know)" from the *Mind Games* album. He sings of trying hard to stay alive despite the "angel of destruction" hounding him. He sings of how "deep inside" he was "never satisfied," and finally he prays, "Help me now, help me Lord." His request has some self-reliance though, since he only asks for help in order to help himself.

When he hits a wrong-sounding chord, Lennon asks in a mocking voice, "I say, I say! That's how you're going to do it, is it? OK" and then plays the chords to a proper ending. The song is short and needs something more, but what is there is quite good, and, again, the potential for a captivating spiritual is present.

Bootleg versions abound of Lennon alone and with his Beatle band mates, and an interesting one exists from the *Double Fantasy* sessions of August 18, 1980.[11] Lennon's flowing sense of the ridiculous is seen to good advantage during a rehearsal of "(Just Like) Starting Over." Lennon jokes around with his lyrics explaining how easy it will be to renew the couple's love by singing "Just take your clothes off honey, and stick your nose in money." When he gets to the point where he should ask, "Why don't we take off, alone?" he instead queries "Why don't we do it in the road?" and laughs at his reference to Paul McCartney's song from The Beatles' White Album. The best joke, however, is when he sings that the private getaway will consist of "just you, me, and the cook, and the servants too." Lennon then stops the number, saying the performance takes "too much energy!"

The same rehearsal session includes Lennon and the band running through several 1950s-era rock oldies, including a couple that Lennon had performed on his *Rock 'N' Roll* album. The band keeps slipping into McCartney's Beatle track "She's a Woman" and Lennon plays along with more parody lyrics ("My love don't buy me pickles"), but he reminds the musicians that the 1950s are his era.

Most of the numbers attempted are fragmentary and not taken as a serious performance. The band is just unwinding and having fun. The exception is a medley of "Dream Lover" and "Stay." The band is on course and Lennon delivers a rousing vocal. He does make a small but noteworthy change in the song, however. He alters the lyrics of his answer to "Dream lover, where are you?" from the standard well-known response to the censorable "up my ass and in my flue" or "up my ass and in the stew" each time the refrain comes up.

Double Fantasy was the number-one album on *Billboard*'s charts for eight weeks and remained in the Top 200 album charts for a year and a half. No one knows whether the album would have been as successful if the tragedy of Lennon's killing had not occurred. Reviews were mixed when the album arrived on the shelves and Lennon was still alive. Critics and fans had not expected most of Lennon's output to consist of compositions extolling the virtues of domesticity. And those who had ignored Ono's musical development—and that would have been the majority—were not prepared for her edgy authority. With his murder, the album and its songs took on a whole new meaning. Lennon's musical peers also honored him with a Grammy Award for his and Ono's return to recording as a team. The National Academy of Recording Arts and Sciences voted *Double Fantasy* the Album of the Year for 1981.

I Don't Wanna Face It, 1981–1988

POSTHUMOUS RELEASES, 1981–1984

Lennon had planned on releasing "Woman" as his next single, so it was no surprise when it came out as his first posthumous release early in 1981.[1] Nor was it surprising that in the first few years after his murder there were issued several tribute songs dedicated to Lennon as well as the release of some first-rate recordings of live and studio Lennon tracks. In a horrible irony, Lennon was a more active public figure in the four years following his killing than he was in the four years that preceded it.

"Walking on Thin Ice"

This is the song Lennon was working on in the last hours of his life, and it ended up being a dance-track hit single for Ono. It is a wonderful showcase for Ono musically and lyrically, notably her oblique but disturbing poetic imagery such as "when our hearts return to ashes, we'll be just a story." A middle narrated section tells of a woman who tried to walk across a supposedly frozen lake that was "as big as the ocean" and is sandwiched between Ono's barking and vibrating vocals. At one point she sounds as though she is vomiting, which then segues into casual humming. Lennon opens the song with a backward guitar screech and is in rare form, banging out jarring chords and providing his ultimate minimalist solo to perfection as well as other eerie and seemingly random and sometimes backward tones. The end result is one of their best collaborations.

The record was released as a special single two months after Lennon's killing, with a snippet of the couple talking as they strolled through Central

Park introducing one of Ono's mid-1970s songs, "It Happened," on the flip side. An even briefer snippet was included as an extra on a CD reissue of *Double Fantasy.*

"Whatever Gets You through the Night"/ "Lucy in the Sky with Diamonds"/"I Saw Her Standing There"

March 1981 saw the release of this memorial maxi-single, which contains Lennon's November 28, 1974, surprise concert appearance with Elton John. The crowd sounds wildly appreciative on Lennon's introduction, and the band performs a version of "Whatever Gets You through the Night" that may be a bit too loose, but more than makes up for it with genuine energy. Lennon's part of the co-lead vocals is more discernable here than on the studio recording.

Elton John then introduces his new single, his cover of Lennon's Beatles composition "Lucy in the Sky with Diamonds." Lennon helps out vocally, sometimes with solo lead on the chorus. The reggae section is not pulled off quite as successfully as it is on the studio recording and the hallucinatory mood of the song is hard to capture and maintain in a live setting, but the band does as well as any could.

The finale is a rousing version of "I Saw Her Standing There," complete with Lennon's admission that it was from "an old estranged fiancé of mine called Paul." This part of Lennon's guest performance had been previously released early in 1975 as the flip side to Elton John's hit single "Philadelphia Freedom." Both men give high-spirited, full-throated vocal efforts, with Lennon urging "Boogie, baby!" at the start of the guitar solo. The raucous fun of the number was ably captured, providing a fitting end to Lennon's guest appearance.

The John Lennon Collection

Two years after his killing, this second "best of" collection of Lennon material was released. The set consists mostly of single releases, but oddly includes six of his seven *Double Fantasy* numbers. Almost as puzzling, "Love" from *John Lennon/Plastic Ono Band* is included and was released as a single to help promote this collection; it did not chart in the United States but did in Great Britain. "Jealous Guy" from *Imagine* is also included, and, interestingly, it became a minor hit when released as a single three years later in the United Kingdom in 1985 and another three years after that in the United States in 1988.[2]

To this collection's merit (and unlike the *Shaved Fish* collection), "Stand by Me" is included, as well as the entirety of "Give Peace a Chance." At the time, vinyl releases were still the industry mainstay, but CDs were present, often sporting "extra" cuts. On this collection, the extras were the inclusions of "Cold Turkey" and, for the first time on any album, the flip side of "Stand by Me," which was "Move over Ms. L." The latter made certain that the CD was the obvious choice for fans and completists alike.

During this time, a disc of The Beatles' 1962 Decca records audition recordings was released. The release featured the only recording of Lennon performing his early composition "Hello Little Girl" in addition to several rock and roll classics.

Heart Play: An Unfinished Dialogue

Released at the third anniversary of Lennon's shooting, *Heart Play: An Unfinished Dialogue* is edited from publicity interviews the couple gave to *Playboy* magazine during the time of *Double Fantasy*. The "unfinished" part of the album title may hearken back to the music of the three experimental albums, while obviously referencing Lennon's unfinished efforts in the form of an artistic conversation with his fans. The cover features Lennon and Ono lovingly looking at each other across a breakfast table, their relationship being yet another "unfinished dialogue."

Much of the album was painful listening in 1983, since it ironically features Lennon discussing his plans and ideas and what he sees for the future as he reflects upon his approaching middle age. One of the most difficult parts to listen to occurs when Lennon expresses his inability to fathom why it is in history that people who have espoused peaceful solutions have died violently. The record is neither a sound collage nor experimental effort, but it does seem calculated to lay the promotional groundwork for the John and Yoko album *Milk and Honey* that Ono released the following month. Lennon is heard saying that his new album (*Double Fantasy*) had been conceived as part of a two-volume work and that the work was more or less a sort of musical dialogue. Because *A Heart Play* is the subtitle attached to *Milk and Honey,* the implication was clear that the forthcoming album was supposed to be the one Lennon was discussing, especially in view of the fact that *Double Fantasy* had the same subtitle. Despite this attempt to weave the albums together, one would search in vain for any reference to Lennon and Ono's *Heart Play Trilogy.*

Whatever the agenda behind its creation, the album provides a nice last verbal testament for Lennon fans. He is relaxed, responsive, focused, and self-aware. The range of topics, his hopeful outlook, personal philosophy, and keen observations make this a neglected gem. Collectors and fans might appreciate having a more complete set of the interviews available, perhaps as a podcast, as was done with the 1970 *Rolling Stone* interviews in 2005–2006.

Milk and Honey: A Heart Play

Billed as a sequel or continuation of sorts to *Double Fantasy* upon its release in January 1984, *Milk and Honey* was presumed to be the album Lennon was working on when he was shot to death. The front cover is similar to *Double Fantasy,* being another close-up of Lennon and Ono about to kiss, or just having kissed. But the album is not exactly a true sequel. A follow-up album was planned and announced, but nothing of Lennon's was as yet formally recorded for it, and it is not clear how much of Ono's material had been. Lennon's songs were jaunty but basically unpolished studio run-throughs of five of his songs in varying stages of completion and were, in fact, recorded at the start of the *Double Fantasy* sessions before the album's final tracks were finished. They were ultimately not completed and not considered for inclusion on *Double Fantasy*, leading to the speculation that Lennon may have had them in mind for future work or may have just been getting himself back into performing mode while getting the musicians comfortable working together. In addition, another Lennon song on the album, "Grow Old with Me," is from a home demonstration or demo recording, paired with Ono's "Let Me Count the Ways." Both songs were reputedly set for inclusion in *Milk and Honey* but were never recorded in the studio.

Sources vary on which, if any, of Ono's materials for *Milk and Honey* were recorded during Lennon's life time and, therefore, with the possibility of his creative input to them or of his performing on the tracks. It is entirely likely that all were recorded after Lennon's killing. One source cites "Don't Be Scared" as being recorded on August 9, 1980, and on the *Onobox* collection, Lennon can be heard saying, "you listening, mother?" before the song begins as if we are hearing a playback.[3] However, also from *Onobox*, he can be heard saying, "good night Sean, see you in the morning" at the end of "You're the One," which is listed as having been recorded in 1983, after Lennon's murder. Most probably, though, Ono's contributions were recorded during or soon after the sessions for her 1982 solo album *It's Alright* since band personnel from that album are listed as playing on *Milk and Honey*.

According to the *Onobox* booklet, the remaining three Ono songs were composed and recorded in 1980 but were copyrighted in either 1982 or 1983, as was "Don't Be Scared." Of course, the version of "Don't Be Scared" on *Milk and Honey* is therefore likely not the version recorded in 1980, but a later recording of the song. What listeners are left with is uncertainty. Perhaps two of the cuts—the studio recording of "Don't Be Scared" and the demo-sounding "Let Me Count the Ways"—were known to Lennon, and he may have co-produced and played guitar on the former. And, just as likely, "You're the One," despite Lennon's voice at the end, was not recorded during his life.

In addition, Jack Douglas, the co-producer of *Double Fantasy*, does not get any credit for *Milk and Honey*. Jon Smith, an engineer who worked on "Walking on Thin Ice," is credited in the same capacity for the *Milk and Honey* album. Is it possible that the three remaining Ono cuts ("Sleepless Night," "O'Sanity," and "Your Hands") were recorded in October and November 1980, after *Double Fantasy* but before "Walking on Thin Ice"? It seems perhaps even Ono's "Walking on Thin Ice" was a candidate for the next album, after its inclusion in the Ono EP the couple was preparing.

Lennon was composing other material in the last months of his life, and he had a backlog of songs to develop if he so chose. Whether he would have returned to any of the unpolished songs that make up his contributions to *Milk and Honey* and what he might have done with them if he had is unknowable.

Predictably, the album does not hold together despite Ono's attempt to reapply the *Double Fantasy* formula. There was no overdubbing of Lennon's material nor any attempt to make it blend into Ono's work. For that matter, Ono's songs, though complete, are also not layered with natural sounds, noises, orchestra, or horns as some of the tracks on *Double Fantasy* are. The sounds and studio layering that ultimately give *Double Fantasy* its extra depth and dimension are not present. What Lennon might have done with the tracks is open to conjecture, but there is no reason to believe that he would have released them as they were.

Clearly, Ono was in a "damned if she did and damned if she did not" situation and opted for the latter. The rough edges of Lennon's recordings are no surprise given their rehearsal status. The production and polish of *Double Fantasy* is part of what unifies it beyond its theme, and it is interesting, though not necessarily useful, to consider what *Milk and Honey* might have been if it had been treated in a similar fashion. If minimal overdubbing and polishing had been added, the album as a whole would be a more unified statement and the stronger companion to *Double Fantasy* as it purported to be. Although most listeners are glad to hear Lennon rough and ready, it makes for a disjointed-sounding album. Perhaps his songs should have been "finished" to better match the tone and polish of Ono's work. Or perhaps she should have kept her efforts in an even more raw state, similar to his, and tried to fit the results into some sort of works-in-progress artistic concept. As it is, as an album, the work fails; Lennon and Ono's works stand far better as independent tracks, as evidenced by the fact that three of Lennon's efforts made it onto the charts as hit singles.

The album begins with the first song the band attempted to record in August 1980, appropriately called "I'm Stepping Out."[4] Lennon introduces the proceedings with a joking introduction that, "this here is the story about a househusband" who has been "screwin' around with the kids and watchin' *Sesame Street*" to the point of "goin' crazy." So now the protagonist happily prepares to go out for a night to "do the city."

As on other tracks in this collection, Lennon is clearly taking the band through their paces here, verbally cueing them ("one more," "hold it down") and offering encouragement ("boogie!"). His directions here and elsewhere on the album are no different from his directing style during the rehearsals and guide vocal takes discussed elsewhere. Such evidence suggests that he had no trouble getting back to professional work.

"I'm Stepping Out" moves along well, especially with the rhythm of the chorus conveying the idea of more energy being held at bay, as Lennon merely repeats the title with intensifying musical variations. Another part of the chorus helps explain the need to step out, proclaiming, "if it don't feel right, don't do it," and advising that "you can't go pleasing everyone." There's no malice in this observation, as Lennon blithely advises that the listener just leave a phone message telling those who want the listener to do something that does not feel right to "screw it." The verses tell the story of the protagonist's state of mind with some precise images, such as the opening "blues around my head." Lennon's compact lyrical structure continues with a few home details, singing, for example, that "the cats have all been blessed."

Other, subsequently released versions of the song contain an additional verse about a doctor who steps out dancing for the odd reason of sweetening up his breath. The shift to a verse about someone other than the narrator and the offbeat explanation for his behavior was wisely eliminated during rehearsals. This was the third single released from the album and became a small hit, making it to number 55 in the United States.

Ono's "Sleepless Night" follows, as if the man's having stepped out for the night has put the woman into a state of frustration, sexual and otherwise. The song gulps along as the singer continues in a state of emotional and physical unease, broken up by a bit of sexual humor.

"I Don't Wanna Face It" is the real rocker on the album and a standout track in all respects. The song has several blistering guitar passages supporting much of it, similar to Lennon's late 1960s or early 1970s rumbling volcano sounds during his minimalist phase. This alternates with a catchy rhythmic riff that kicks the song off after Lennon's characteristically free-form count in of "Un, deux, ein, zwei, hickle-pickle" and returns a few times throughout the number. This song finds its slot from the first note and successfully gallops with it to the end.

What the words refuse to face is the sense of self and responsibility in relationship to the rest of humanity. Once again Lennon's lyrical control is firm, as he looks into the mirror and dialogues with himself about these issues. Lennon blends clichés with sharp descriptions and ironic juxtapositions, such as "lookin' for oblivion with one eye on the hall of fame" and a saying he may have found in the work of cartoonist Charles M. Schulz: "You wanna save humanity, but it's people that you just can't stand." Schulz's character Linus had made the same observation in a *Peanuts* daily cartoon strip years before Lennon used the line.

The introspective lecture contains obvious references to Lennon himself as a seeker of "peace and love" and the leader of a "big ol' band," a possible reference to The Beatles. The singer further chides himself for looking for a "world of truth" while always refusing to see himself for what he really is. There is a final hopeful assurance, though, as the last lyric of the last verse states that the promised land can be seen and the singer is sure he can make it to that destination.

Lennon's vocal performance is vigorous, even for him. He resurrects some of his barking and yelping sounds, not heard since The Beatles' "Hey Bulldog." There they were used for comic commentary and effect in relation to the song's topic, but here it is Lennon's sheer dynamism that propels him to make the noises. As the song fades, Lennon howls and then shouts in a startled manner, "every time I look in the mirror, I don't see anybody there! Whoo!" This remark was a key part of the lyrics for his unfinished song "Mirror, Mirror (On the Wall)."

Certainly it is pointless to argue with success, and this album produced three hits for Lennon. Had this track been a single, there might have been four. As it stands, the song justifiably takes its place as one of Lennon's better tracks, even in its not-quite-finished form.

Other recorded takes show a similar drive. In a version on the *John Lennon Anthology,* Lennon cues guitarist Earl Slick by shouting his name with a gusto not heard in other session recordings. At the end of this take, the playing breaks down into random noise, in a way similar to the connecting section between "I'm Losing You" and "I'm Moving On" from the earlier-issued *Double Fantasy* album. It sounds intentional and may have been an idea Lennon transferred to those other recordings. As the take finishes, Lennon notes, "my picks get half the size!" It is just that kind of performance.

What seems to be Ono's song in response to the anxiety of self-reflection is "Don't Be Scared," a song Lennon may have known in some form. The song suggests that fear of commitment to a relationship is really the fear of committing to life and that the joy is in the journey, not the destination. It is a sparse-sounding track, like several of Ono's efforts on this album. The approach may be her attempt not to overshadow Lennon's unpolished works, or to match the emotionally direct content of the lyrics with a direct unadorned sound.

A jaunty number called "Nobody Told Me" was the first single released from the album and is reputed to have been one of the titles Lennon was working on to give to Ringo Starr for his next album. A rolling bass line anchors the song that swings along merrily at a moderate rocking pace. A few instrumental flourishes here and there add a bit of spark to the piece, but the band functions at a point of being tight enough to allow themselves to be loose and the song's feeling of spontaneity has enough momentum for it all to gel.

The lyrics of the verses are more or less a series of inconsistencies from the start, with "everybody's talkin' but no one says a word" and such near-Zen observations as "everybody's flying, but never touch the sky." Each verse ends with an out-of-place statement that doesn't seem to follow from the preceding statements, such as the line repeated from "Move over Ms. L": "They're starvin' back in China, so finish what you got." Earlier, it was, "There's Nazis in the bathroom, just below the stair." The chorus doesn't try to make sense of these situations, but just accepts them with the comment that "nobody told me there'd be days like these" before adding "strange days indeed" and "most peculiar, mama!"

The mood is light and humorous with a slight undertone of possible unease that finally dissipates in the chorus. At first listen, the song seems slight and easily dismissible, a pleasurable effort with little substance. But repeated listening provides insight into some greater depth behind the innocuous perplexities of the words and the bouncy lilt of the music. The appeal of the song definitely grows, and that may partly account for its becoming a top-five hit in the United States.

Ono comments and builds on Lennon's observations by declaring that the only sane response to a world of peculiarities is to give up one's sanity in her short song "O'Sanity." Again, Ono uses humor to make her point: "psychotic builds a castle and neurotic lives in it."

At last, after a decade and a half of working reggae riffs into numerous compositions and recordings, Lennon composed "Borrowed Time," the closest he came to a full-out reggae effort. The song was released as a single and did not fare well in the United States; it failed to chart because reggae rhythms never caught on with the U.S. mass listening public as much as they had in England, where the song charted at number 32.[5]

The lyrics extol the idealistic virtues of growing older. The first section describes the hesitancy and unsure state of being younger, characterizing it as living in "deep despair" and the "illusion of freedom and power." The chorus reminds listeners that we are "living on borrowed time, without a thought for tomorrow." After the first verse, this emphasizes the callow lack of awareness of youth.

The second and third verses showcase that being older is better, because a little experience has brought understanding and clarity and "less complications." This time the chorus, verbally the same, says that it is possible to live in and for the moment without worry over the future. The song ends with a comic monologue from Lennon about leaving the angst of young love behind and trading it for physical infirmity. But having made the point, he cheerfully scat-sings a drum solo as the song moves toward its conclusion. Once again, Lennon's serious insights are kept from being either heavy handed or clichéd by his wry sense of humor.

In "Your Hands," Ono sings fully and powerfully in Japanese and concurrently gives a soft-spoken English translation of the words. Various aspects of the beloved's physical self are dreamt about (hands, skin, mouth, arms, eyes) between choruses that declare, "no matter how many times we meet," even over several life times, "it's not enough."

Presumably inspired by either May Pang or Ono, "(Forgive Me) My Little Flower Princess" has little going for it aside from a functional semi-shuffling rhythm. This is a very unfinished composition, and Lennon drops words and phrases in a song that appears to be about the power of forgiveness in romantic relationships. A couple of lines show a little promise, such as "take up the dance where we left off," for example, but the rest are banal and mundane. The song has no chorus or middle-eight section and offers only fragmentary and fractured lyrics. Taking this into consideration and in view of his store of other potential contenders, it is puzzling that Lennon even brought this one to the sessions. But, of course, it is not known what he ultimately had in mind.

If the male agenda set the topic of the dialogues previously, the female voice takes the lead at this point on the disc. In a conscious attempt to link sonically with Lennon's "Grow Old with Me," which existed only on a demonstration cassette, Ono provides a demo tape of her companion song "Let Me Count the Ways." Like Lennon's recording, the only accompaniment is piano.

In the album liner notes, Ono relates that the two songs were originally the inspiration and planned backbone for *Double Fantasy* but were put off so long that it was decided to make them the core of the follow-up album. The songs were inspired by the famous poems of Robert Browning and Elizabeth Barrett Browning. Ono's effort takes the first line of Elizabeth Barrett Browning's poem and the idea behind it, but then goes its own way in four stanzas that enumerate not only "the ways how I love you" but also how the loved one is missed, viewed, and has touched the speaker. Musically, the song has a simple intensity that underscores the verbal pleading for the chance to convince the loved one how much he is cared for.

"Grow Old with Me" is Lennon's companion song and shows greater closeness to its inspirational source and model, as if Lennon might have started off contemplating merely setting the poem to music at one point. In any event, it manages to be pure and exact in form and content—a guileless expression of idealized, heartfelt love.

Sadly, Lennon never created a professional recording of the song, and all that exists is the cassette version. On this, Lennon plays piano and is accompanied by a rhythm box that keeps time very well but spoils the mood of the song. Furthermore, Lennon sings in a high voice, possibly falsetto, and even taking into account the low sound quality of the source material, his voice sounds thin to the point of distraction. Some accounts claim that this was one of the four songs Ono gave the three surviving Beatles to work with and would have been the third release after "Free as a Bird" and "Real Love" for the Beatles' *Anthology* sets.[6] However, they opted to do nothing with the track after a quick try at creating some new backing for it.

In the album's liner notes, Ono relates that she and Lennon had planned on a big, lush orchestral arrangement and production for the song, hoping it would become a new standard for weddings and anniversaries. In fact, in the *John Lennon Anthology* collection, an overdubbed version of "Grow Old with Me" is included and it marks an intriguing posthumous collaboration between Lennon and The Beatles' producer, George Martin. It is not clear when this was done, but the reasonable assumption is that it was done after the Threetles, as fans called the surviving Beatles, officially abandoned their work on it.

Martin's arrangement has to be careful not to swamp the frail-sounding, low-fidelity original that does not sound as though it has been given as much of the studio restoration wizardry treatment that the Threetles gave the two tracks they completed. Even so, Martin's recognizable sound, so associated with The Beatles, is readily evident. His baroque-inspired arrangement begins with flowing strings and later includes a solo flute that provides short countermelody embellishments. Simple supporting brass variations can at times be heard, especially near the end, and pulsing strings support the chorus.

As enjoyable as it is to hear this version, the rhythm box still intrudes—but, unless some other performance by Lennon of this song surfaces, this is the closest we will get to how he may have envisioned the song. A simple version with only piano and voice by Mary Chapin Carpenter, stylistically much like Lennon's demonstration recording, became an adult contemporary hit in 1996.

As on *Double Fantasy*, Ono gets the last word in a production that is harsher and fuller sounding than her other tracks on the album, more so in view of the demo recordings that precede it. "You're the One" sets a strident tone with Ono vocally providing a percussion line. The song tells of a romantic pair's link having the strength of nature and the universe's inevitability. At first, the refrain of "how do I tell you you're the one?" refers to the difficulty of talking about the depth of the connection between the two. Yet a middle stanza talks about the couple in the past tense, shifting the implications of the questions considerably.

Curiously, the 2001 remastered and reissued CD version of the album has bonus cuts that would have been more appropriate for inclusion on *Double Fantasy*. Lennon's lead vocal version of "Every Man Has a Woman Who Loves Him"—a song of Ono's from *Double Fantasy* on which she sang lead—is appended to the album after "You're the One" as if it were part of the continuing dialogue. This version of the song was originally released on an album and as a single in 1984 and is discussed in the next section.

Also included on the *Milk and Honey* album is a home demo version of Lennon performing "I'm Stepping Out," simply called "Stepping Out" in this form. A demo version by Ono of her *Double Fantasy* song "Moving On" is also included, plus approximately 22 minutes of Lennon's last interview, given only hours before his death. In it, Lennon (and, to a limited degree at the start, Ono) discuss how they composed some of the songs on *Double Fantasy*, how they met, the social role of an artist, and their hopes for the future. Strangely, it is taken not from a reedit of the original interviews, but from an edit prepared for a radio broadcast that occasionally cuts to some of the songs from the album. In the original broadcast, the songs were overlaid with the interviews to blend from the speaking to the music, and musical fragments still remain.

"Every Man Has a Woman"

The Lennon single "Every Man Has a Woman"—with the flip side being the solo recording debut of his son Sean performing a composition of Ono's titled "It's Alright"—was released in November 1984, along with an album of the same name comprising Ono compositions performed by various other artists. In the album's liner notes, Ono explains that Lennon had planned an album of other artists performing Ono's work as a surprise present for her, and that he had recorded the track without her knowing. The track does not sound like an entirely new recording, and, since Lennon was reportedly remixing this song for an Ono EP during the last weeks of his life, he may have remixed it for his contribution to the future project as well, but this is conjecture.

This song was one of Ono's more lackluster efforts on *Double Fantasy,* and here "Every Man Has a Woman" sounds like a remixed and reedited version of the same track. A brief instrumental passage has been omitted, and Lennon's supporting vocals from the original have been mixed to the front. Ono's lead vocals have been eliminated, while her voice is clearly heard in parts of the chorus. It also does not sound as though Lennon recorded an additional new vocal track.

Like the original, the song traipses along well enough in counterpoint to the melancholy tone and performance. Corresponding to the title, the verses expound upon the inevitability of romantic pairing while the chorus voices a fearful hesitancy in accepting the personal reality of such a generalization, stating "why do I run when I know you're the one?" The music may have been designed to straddle the two dimensions of hesitancy and inevitability, but, instead of providing the needed supporting tension, it becomes droning.

In both Ono's and Lennon's versions, the track is an innocuous misfire, and—regrettably, but not surprisingly—the single failed to chart. In the early 2000s, however, a series of remixes of songs throughout Ono's career became dance-track hits, and a lyrically revamped remix of this song—including references to homosexual partnering and romance—was one of them. Ono also included Lennon's original version as a bonus track on the 2001 CD reissue of *Milk and Honey.*

Ono's *Every Man Has a Woman* album also included a version of her "Now or Never," a song she had included on her *Approximately Infinite Universe* album. This version was recorded during those sessions, and Lennon is credited as co-producer with Ono. Rather than Yoko's lead vocals, as on the original, a children's choir is featured, sounding much like the chorus of "Happy Xmas (War Is Over)." The idea gives extra contrast and urgency to Ono's interrogative lyrics, as if a very aware child were chastising the adults for what they were permitting the world to become.

Lennon's Appearances on Other Ono Releases

After his slaying, recordings of Lennon appeared on multiple releases, legal and otherwise. As the technique of electronic sampling began and intensified, fragments of Lennon's voice and music, with and without The Beatles, were used. This is by no means a comprehensive accounting, but rather a short look at the more interesting examples used by Yoko Ono in the five years after Lennon's killing. Not surprisingly, Ono has used Lennon's voice on later occasions as well, and the more notable examples are mentioned in the appropriate sections of this work.

Ono's first posthumous use of Lennon's voice was on "It Happened," a song of hers from the mid-1970s, which was reused as the flip side of "Walking on Thin Ice." Ono used a fragment of dialogue recorded as she and Lennon strolled through Central Park being filmed for promotional footage to be used for songs from the *Double Fantasy* album. Sound from a few seconds of the footage later turned up as a bonus cut on the CD reissue of *Double Fantasy*. Lennon can be heard taking the part of a startled fan, saying, "John Lennon! I can't believe it!" He also jokes about the set up of the filming. He comments, "Well, here we are, just two average people" and emits a short laugh that seems to be looped to approximate the fake laughter engaged in by The Beatles in the bicycle scene in *Help!* though it plays much briefer. The spoken introduction to the song ends with Lennon directing the filming by suggesting that he and Ono "bleach out into the sunset."

Lennon's voice next appeared on "Never Say Goodbye" from Ono's *It's Alright (I See Rainbows)* album of 1982. In the middle of the song, Lennon can clearly be heard yelling "Yoko!" from what sounds like a moment from their "John and Yoko" piece that makes up half of the *Wedding Album*. He says her name in a myriad of ways on that original recording. In this instance, Ono selected a full-fledged scream, and, given the context of his killing and this particular song, it is as harrowing as it is ironic.

As discussed previously, it is not precisely clear to what degree Lennon had input into Ono's recordings that make up the *Milk and Honey* album. "Don't Be Scared" was reportedly recorded with Lennon's involvement and, on the *Onobox* set, Ono includes enough of the lead-in so that Lennon can be heard asking Ono, "Mother, you listening?" In what might have been an attempt to make Ono's cuts from the *Milk and Honey* album better match Lennon's cuts by seeming less polished and to have been recorded when Lennon's cuts were, Ono added Lennon's voice to the fadeout of her song "You're the One" recorded, according to the *Onobox* booklet, in 1983. He is heard shouting in a near monotone, "Good night Sean, see you in the morning."

POSTHUMOUS RELEASES, 1985–1988

Even though there were still numerous Lennon recordings in various stages of professionalism and completion, all future Lennon releases would consist of live performances, studio outtakes, and demo recordings. Some would be excellent in terms of quality and content, others would be lacking in both, and many would fall somewhere in between. Casual fans might only have interest in the cream of the crop, but serious fans welcomed anything they could get. Even the most esoteric piece had something to offer, and the sheer amount and consistent quality only enhanced Lennon's posthumous reputation as a creative force of integrity and perseverance. Eventually, the amount of material that emerged from his home recordings made Lennon's claim of creative dormancy from 1975 to 1980 true only if taken to mean he did not complete any material in a professional recording studio.

Live in New York City

The 1986 *Live in New York City* album was an edited version of The Plastic Ono Band with Elephant's Memory's One to One concerts held in 1972 to raise money for and awareness of the situation of mentally handicapped children in New York. The album is gleaned from portions of the afternoon show, which Lennon half-joking calls "the rehearsal." To create a single disc album in 1986, Ono cut her feature numbers out, whereas two of her numbers (more were performed) are available on the video release. The encore is also edited significantly. Why, in the ensuing decades, the best performances of the concerts have not been reedited to fit a full CD (or parts of two) is unfathomable. With the abbreviated Toronto appearance, these two performances were Lennon's only full-fledged post-Beatles concerts, and legal issues—whatever they may be—should have been surmounted. The true joy of the album is that, faults and all—and no one expects perfection at a live show—it is both fun and interesting to hear Lennon perform these songs live. The CD reissue sounds edgier than the vinyl and video releases, both of which have a slightly muddy sound in comparison.

The album begins with the chant of "Power to the People," which blends into a rousing version of "New York City" that shows off the band to good effect and once again puzzles the listener as to why the song was not a single release at the time. In a nod to the journalist Geraldo Rivera, whose investigations spurred the event, Lennon changes the lyric "waitin' for Jerry" to "waitin' for Geraldo." "It's So Hard" follows and is performed with a nice rolling lilt with Lennon's vocals having real emotional flourish.

The *John Lennon Anthology* collection featured three performances from the second show, with all three numbers demonstrating that the later show was tighter musically and that Lennon took more care with his vocals. "It's So Hard" is one of three on the collection and keeps a more solid rhythm while losing none of the lilt. Lennon adds a few howls of emphasis to his vocals.

A live version of the couple's 1972 single follows on the 1986 release, with "Woman Is the Nigger of the World" and, on the video release, Ono's "Sisters, O Sisters." On these, as throughout the album, Lennon's rhythm guitar work, where it is discernable, is top notch. Lennon switches between guitar and electric piano later in the concert.

"Woman Is the Nigger of the World" is also available from the evening show and is also a superior performance. In the first performance, Lennon had forgotten his lyrics "while telling her not to be so smart, we put her down for being so dumb." Instead he sings, "while putting her down for being dumb, we put her down for being dumb." This time he admits he is defeated by his memory and sings, "this is the one that I can never remember but you get the message anyway."

"Well Well Well" is taken at a brisker pace than it is on the *Plastic Ono Band* release, and, in the live setting, it is all the better for it. It is one of the stronger numbers on the album. A perhaps too-ragged version of "Instant Karma!" prompts Lennon to remark that "we'll get it right next time" before an equally ragged version of "Mother." Lennon is straining at the vocals and chokes off a couple of times before getting to the throat-wrenching finale. The starkness of the studio version is a little undercut by the band, and Lennon jokes that he hopes people "recognized it" as a result.

The Beatles' "Come Together" is next, and, again, Lennon's vocals seem strained and he misses a couple of notes. However, paired with the loose feel of Elephant's Memory, the song trades the oddly threatening sound of the original for a nice rollicking effort that seems to please the crowd and Lennon himself. This is the third number that is also available from the evening set and, like the other two, sounds more assured overall, especially in Lennon's vocals but also noticeably stronger in the drumming and in the guitar work. Lennon shouts, "stop the war!" near the end, instead of "over me!" and then adds a couple of shrieks for extra emphasis, not needing to worry about saving his voice anymore.

Ono's "Born in a Prison" (video only) then leads into "Imagine," with Lennon pushing his nascent feminist awareness to the point of altering the lyrics to call for both a brotherhood "and sisterhood" of man. This time, however, the catch-as-catch-can feel of the band detracts from the gentle mood of the song, and it lacks some of the impact that Lennon's simpler live acoustic versions have.

For the third time, a recorded live version of "Cold Turkey" is presented, and it is somewhere between the lilting version from *Live Peace in Toronto* and the wonderfully harsh tour de force on the bonus disc of *Some Time in New York City*. The concert ends with an earnest version of "Hound Dog" that somehow never really gels, despite some good work from the band and Lennon's raucous vocals. An abbreviated version of "Give Peace a Chance" is chanted, bookending the concert with the opening chant from "Power to the People."

Menlove Ave.

The second Lennon album released in 1986—*Menlove Ave.*—is taken from material recorded during the misnamed "lost weekend" of September 1973 to February 1975. The first half contains two new Lennon compositions and some songs not used for the *Rock 'N' Roll* album (one was on *Roots*). The rest is made up of rehearsals of some of the numbers from *Walls and Bridges*.

It is interesting to compare the rehearsals to the final versions in view of how the songs sounded when finished, using the comparison to ponder what Lennon might have done with the similar-sounding rehearsals that made up his input to the posthumously released *Milk and Honey.*

The album opens with its strongest track, "Here We Go Again," a song-writing collaboration with Phil Spector, who produced as well. If the song has a weakness, it is the characteristic Spector background. Swirling and majestic at its best, the Spector signature sometimes becomes busy and distracting, dwarfing Lennon's vocal efforts but not enough to spoil the number. Lennon's vocals build and veer from rough, almost spoken whispers to full-on screams to great effect. The lyrics deal with the dreary and desultory and must reflect Lennon's sense of ennui at the start of his "lost weekend." "Nobody gives a damn," he sings before recalling his early Beatles hit by proclaiming "nobody wants to hold your hand."

The song would not fit as part of the proposed *Oldies but Goldies* project, but it might have been a worthwhile addition to *Walls and Bridges,* most closely of a piece thematically with "Nobody Loves You (When You're Down and Out)" or "Scared." A remake or different mix might have been needed to make it sonically closer to the album, but otherwise it would have been worthy.

"Rock 'n' Roll People" is the simple straight-ahead rocker that was attempted by Lennon during the *Mind Games* sessions but then abandoned and given to Johnny Winter, who made the most of its simple strengths. Lyrically, the song is another of Lennon's non sequitur wordplay pieces ("my father was a mother, my mother was a son") with a refrain that extols the virtues of "sweet sweet rock and roll." Lennon's version here has some strong guitar work, and the performance is good enough but lacks that special spark the song needs to lift it past the perfunctory. Other takes heard on *The Lost Lennon Tapes* are more exuberant, but, once finding the groove, Lennon was apparently unwilling to relinquish it. The takes go on until Lennon and the band totally exhaust themselves and all but wreck the proceedings, at least for a viable release at the time. It sounds like they were having fun, though.

The song does sound similar to the rough and ready, good but not polished performances that make up Lennon's contributions to *Milk and Honey.* Because those were partially done to get the performers to cohere as a band (as opposed to a collection of musicians), perhaps this recording served much the same purpose and explains Lennon's long takes.

Ultimately rejected by Lennon from the *Rock 'N' Roll* album, but included on the *Roots* album, "Angel Baby" is one of the Spector-produced pieces from early in the project, before the project started breaking down. Slow without being ponderous, stacked without sounding murky, the song is one where Spector's production succeeds and Lennon's vocals are earnest if a little flighty, as if he cannot quite totally commit to them—perhaps his reason for rejecting the song. Lennon begins his performance with a short narrative, dedicating the song to "Rosie" (Rose Hamlin of Rosie and the Originals), who wrote and recorded the original hit version of the song in 1960. All in all, a nice track, and arguably Lennon was being too hard on himself.

The rockabilly classic "Since My Baby Left Me" has an intriguing arrangement of a call and response between Lennon and a female chorus echoing his energetic, if erratic, vocals. It does not quite work, however, largely because the party-like sing-along atmosphere is forced and unconvincing. Lennon's introductory preamble loses focus, causing the number to stumble at the outset, and it never recovers. At one point, he forgets to pause and wait for the "response" to his "call." In fact, the call-and-response structure diminishes what should have been a raw vibrancy to something sputtering and lackluster. Not awful by any means, but considering what Lennon might have done with this in (for example) 1964, or compared to his then-recent "Tight A$," it is a missed opportunity.

Phil Spector's 1958 classic "To Know Her Is To Love Her" is revamped for Lennon, who somehow manages to give a performance that, remarkably and successfully, seems simultaneously tongue in cheek *and* sincere. The recording careens toward the overblown but stops just short with a middle section grounded by rapid martial-sounding snare drums and Lennon's impassioned vocals. As do most of the Spector-produced numbers for the project, this song suffers a bit from the slow pace but is not as hampered by that as others. The Beatles recorded this song at the 1962 Decca audition; Lennon also sang lead then, and a fun comparison can be made between the two.

The rest of the album is made up of rehearsals of five of the songs that were included on *Walls and Bridges*. All are stripped down compared to their final versions, though with the basic arrangements intact. Minus the polish and production, the bleakness of the numbers is accented. All have varying degrees of interest, with "Scared" coming off best. In some ways, the track is even improved, the emotional impact sounding something like an outtake from *Plastic Ono Band,* as others have noted. The other four songs, although intriguing at times—such as when Lennon offers alternate lyrics for "Nobody Loves You (When You're Down and Out)"—remain little more than sporadically fascinating curios.

Imagine: John Lennon

A compilation of key Lennon tracks released to coincide with the biographical documentary and photo book of the same name from 1988, a double album entitled *Imagine: John Lennon* includes Beatles recordings and two interesting, previously unreleased tracks, a unique attribute among Lennon compilations. The collection makes sense as a soundtrack of the film, less so if intended as a true representative encapsulation of his career.

The first of the two previously unreleased tracks is a short performance of "Imagine" that in the film is merely to familiarize fellow musicians with the basics of the song. Lennon talks his way through part of it, and finishes it in a mock cowboy drawl that punctures the solemnity of the piece in a comical, though startling, way.

Like the film, the album opens with "Real Love," an unfinished song of Lennon's that was later completed by the remaining Beatles as part of the *Anthology 2* set. This is a clear-sounding composing tape, done with guitar, and does not appear to be the version that The Beatles reworked. Oddly, it sounds better than the source material they had, and, as a matter of fact, so do other takes of the song. Further comments can be found under the discussion for The Beatles' treatment of Lennon's original recording.

The Lost Lennon Tapes Radio Series

The Lost Lennon Tapes, a syndicated radio series, proved to be alternately enthralling and frustrating for Lennon fans and historians. A significant amount of unaired Lennon work worth hearing was showcased along with material that even a hardcore fan would consider to be of marginal interest. It is important to note that a fair portion of the musical treasures broadcast has never turned up anywhere else legally, and the show has become the source of numerous bootleg collections and Internet downloads. All of which begs the question of why the material still languishes in the legal vaults at such a late date.

In 1988, *The Lost Lennon Tapes* was syndicated over the Westwood One Radio Network and hosted by disc jockey, and friend of Ono and Lennon, Elliot Mintz. The series began its near four-year run with a three-hour special. The show combined Mintz's commentary and historical accounts with various interviews he and others had conducted with Lennon over the years. Sanctioned by Ono and the Lennon Estate, the drawing power of the series was its promise of rare and previously unreleased recordings of Lennon from his earliest, even pre-Beatle, days up to the time of his slaying. These would encompass anything of near broadcast quality, including studio outtakes, rehearsals, live performances, jam sessions, composing tapes, home demos, and even studio chatter. For the first half of the series' run, it delivered.

Not surprisingly, many of the recordings that first were heard on this series were later included in such collections as The Beatles' *Anthology, John Lennon Anthology* and as bonus cuts on CD collections and reissues of Lennon's albums. Strangely, however, many others have not been legally released decades after being broadcast and, as a result, have turned up as popular bootlegs on the Internet and elsewhere. In fact, research shows that at least a dozen, if not twice that, additional Lennon compositions not heard on *The Lost Lennon Tapes* or released elsewhere have never yet been made public. Many are assuredly home demos, largely from his mid- to late-1970s hiatus. Despite the amount of written coverage on Lennon and The Beatles, it would seem that a book-length focus on his unfinished and unreleased musical materials is in order. The remarkable fact is that it is quite possible that two or even three hours of releasable, marketable John Lennon music awaits mass release decades after his killing. Here is a brief sampling of some of the more notable tracks from *The Lost Lennon Tapes* that are not covered elsewhere in this work.[7]

For his own pleasure or to work the kinks out of a group of musicians, Lennon enjoyed returning to his musical roots, time and time again. For Lennon, rock and roll wore the crown, of course, but, as mentioned, he had absorbed the pop music of his early childhood and had been entranced by the skiffle craze as well.

One of the most enjoyable recordings featured on the radio series was Lennon's performance of a medley of British Music Hall songs, with a skiffle revival number thrown in. Lennon sets up a rolling piano riff and eagerly tears his way through an impromptu selection of numbers, beginning with a sea shanty. The medley is not planned through, and part of the fun is to listen to Lennon vamp until ready at the keyboard, thinking of what song he will slip in next. The Music Hall classic "I Do Like To Be Beside the Seaside" is a good connection to the opening shanty, and both this song and skiffle king Lonnie Donegan's remake of "My Old Man's a Dustman" get a nod before two of George Formby's biggest hits, "Chinese Laundry Blues" and "Leaning on a Lamppost," are squeezed in. Lennon moves back into the shanty and seems reluctant to let the traipsing romp end.

Another medley from the series has a decidedly absurdist bent, as Lennon adopts a faux French accent for a turn at a comic introduction and performance of "Beyond the Sea" and "Blue Moon." The bit ends with Lennon shifting into another cartoon accent, this time cockney, for a section of "Young Love." The fun of these recordings is not in the musical mastery on display, by any means, but in Lennon's playful cleverness as he presents them.

One episode broadcast Lennon charging through a none-too-shabby version of "Rock Island Line," Donegan's biggest hit and a skiffle standard. Lennon flubs some of the lyrics but does not seem to mind at all since what he wants to do is get to the chorus and relive the liberating explosion that skiffle had in common with rockabilly. The recording has Ono audibly getting a phone call in the background and having trouble hearing the caller, but such was Lennon's delight that his spirited performance continued regardless. A similar version of "John Henry" was also broadcast.

The bluesy side of rock's roots was also a point of self-amusement for Lennon. In a home recording of "I'm a Man," Lennon once again opts for a comic take, performing most of the piece in an exaggerated Mississippi Delta drawl, with solid guitar accompaniment. The lyrics slip into a surreal parody of the macho bluesman, as Lennon gleefully sings about erectile dysfunction and not being able to find his feet! Before picking up the pace for the finale, Lennon drops the drawl and uses posh British inflection. That seems a comment, perhaps unconscious, on the influence of African American music on

Lennon's home country and his own eventual artistic drives, if not the entire British Blues movement.

Fifties rock and roll, though, remained Lennon's favorite music, and it comes as no surprise that he should parade his way through that era's musical product. Buddy Holly was always a big favorite and influence, and a nice, short but complete acoustic performance of Holly's "Maybe Baby" was included in one broadcast of the show. Lennon sounds relaxed and assured, and on the vocal refrain he jokes around during the lyricless passage and encourages himself or any listeners to join him with a reassuring "come on!" before slipping into a quick Holly impersonation. On another tape played during the series' run, Lennon starts an exhilarating version of Holly's "Peggy Sue" that is cut short by a phone call, much to Lennon's emphatic exasperation and likely the listener's as well.

During studio recording sessions, Lennon liked to both unwind and loosen up his musicians with off-the-cuff renditions of rock and roll classics. A handful of such attempts exist from the combined *Plastic Ono Band* sessions, including a version the *Lost Lennon Tapes* provided of Carl Perkins's "Matchbox." The song was a regular of the live performance repertoire of The Beatles, with Ringo Starr singing lead. In this recording, Lennon treads his way through the vocals (possibly trying to save his voice) with a few alternate lyrics and provides a sputtering, then ringing guitar solo before cutting things off with a quickly dismissive "ok, ok."

Preparing for the One to One concerts with Elephant's Memory required rehearsals and they, too, were recorded. A few performances from these were included in the radio series with Chuck Berry's "Roll over Beethoven" being one of the better examples. A fractured instrumental introduction is played, far enough off that Lennon laughingly feels the need to tell the band what it was, and then asks eagerly, "do you remember it?" Not waiting for an answer, he begins singing and the band does remember it, giving a raucous but more than passable recital of the piece, with Lennon keeping his vocals on track and cueing the band's guitarist with a hearty "hit it, Tex!"

Jerry Lee Lewis's "Whole Lotta Shakin' Goin' On" also gets a going over with saxophonist Stan Bronstein carrying the instrumental break and Lennon responding with a throaty cry of "Stan, the blues man, all right!" These presentations are sometimes rough, but, after all, they are rehearsals or private performances, never meant for public consumption. Still, Lennon's joy and energy are tangible, a feeling not always captured on his *Rock 'N' Roll* album recordings.

The Lost Lennon Tapes spent much of its air time tracing the compositional development of Lennon's music, and it was clearly the show's highlight. Assorted versions of songs in a variety of stages of completion from his Beatles years on were heard. It was fascinating and insightful listening. All the more interesting, though, were recordings of songs Lennon either never completed composing, never took to a professional studio, or decided against releasing.

One of the more complete and assumed to be finished songs also had one of the longer gestations of any of Lennon's works. Begun in 1970 and reworked in 1976, "Sally and Billy" is an ironic third-person narrative about two of the "beautiful people" who seem to be living successful lives but are empty inside. Sally is a modern, artistically inclined socialite, and Billy is a band singer. The separate verses emphasize the song's theme of disconnection from the essentials of life's experiences. The narration has some fine passages, and the tone is woven from simultaneous stances of condescension, sympathy, and sardonic detachment. The sarcasm is obvious, as in such lines as the one saying that Sally is "independent and beautiful—oh how beautiful!" The same tone is taken regarding Billy, who spends all his time "playing games with his mind," essentially fooling himself; yet he is seen by others as being a "lucky guy," even though in reality his heart is "running dry" (one of the better images in the song).

Both characters dream of "what might have been, hoping that Jesus will intervene," an event the narrator seems to imply is unlikely to occur. The narrator then presents them as not understanding what life is all about, and therefore missing out on what is truly important because it is "too late now" for them. Both characters cry in frustration over the awareness that their lives are hollow, but have no idea what to do about it, other than keep up the false hope that some outside force will save them. The song ends with the narrator urging them not to cry, despite just having proclaimed they have wasted their lives with no hope of redemption.

It is a singular piece in Lennon's post-Beatles output, its melodic and tuneful music undercutting the dark, third-person narrative from a chastising, yet basically disinterested, narrator. If it were not so well developed and executed, it would seem as if Lennon were parodying such songs rather than seriously creating one.

Also finished, and in the third person, is "She's a Friend of Dorothy," a song Lennon tweaked occasionally from 1976 until 1980. When, in 1978 and after, Lennon and Ono considered creating a musical based on their lives, this was one of the songs he thought of using for it. The phrase "a friend of Dorothy" was coded slang for being homosexual; little in the song makes that explicit if listeners did not already know the meaning.

The song is structured as if the narrator is convincing someone that the subject is indeed gay by listing her supposed characteristics, with a chorus of simple self-evident proclamations such as "she shows it…the way that she, the way that she is." The song's verses are litanies of the title character's traits. Some are quite witty, such as an early couplet "art deco decadent, TV dinner elegant" and "French jeans and sly boots" in the second verse. The song ends with Lennon as narrator comically spelling out "Dorothy" as if in a grade school primer with the letter "t" being for *Tea and Sympathy,* a well-known play and film partially concerned with homosexuality. Mid-paced, slightly wistful, and even mournful at times, yet quite melodic, the song remains one of the more fascinating of Lennon's home demo works.

Similar in mood and tone is the song "Tennessee" from 1975–1976. Not dedicated to the state, but to author Tennessee Williams, Lennon puts Williams in the limited category of real people he wrote about directly by name. This list included such people as his mother Julia, Mia Farrow's sister Prudence, Yoko Ono, Angela Davis, and John Sinclair. The song began as a statement of praise and acknowledgment of Williams's impact with the prosaic line "Tennessee, oh Tennessee, oh what you mean to me," and then presented the names of Williams's plays but did little else.

Part of the song evolved into a piece called "Memories," the title word replacing "Tennessee," and the rest of the song omitting the references to the play titles, thereby creating an odd cousin to one of his Beatle masterpieces, "In My Life." Some of "Memories," coupled with another developing song called "I'm Crazy," morphed into the nexus of "Watching the Wheels" and "Tennessee," as such, was long forgotten.[8]

One fragmentary composing effort is called "Pill" and was begun and abandoned in 1972. The work was never developed very far, but the jaunty guitar line and Lennon's breezy lyrical approach seem set to counter the more grave statement of, "you need a special pill to keep you on the line." Lennon must have decided the promising sound was little more than just that, and there is no evidence that he continued his efforts on the work.

Starting off with a similar chord structure to parts of the also unfinished "Grow Old with Me" is a song from 1977 called "Mirror, Mirror (On the Wall)." The opus is a decidedly morose self-investigation both musically and lyrically. Lennon's vocal performance is of questioning resignation as he intones that he looks "in the mirror and nobody's there," a line he would more or less repeat with a startled delivery in "I Don't Wanna Face It" from the posthumous *Milk and Honey* album. He sings that he keeps on "staring and staring" and finally asks, "can it be?" and "is it me?" repeatedly, followed by the droning but impassioned piano for over a minute before the song ends. Even in its undeveloped form, or perhaps because of its undeveloped form, the fragment creates a viable feeling of unease and distress.

Another fragment from the radio show was one of the last songs Lennon was working on at the time of his murder, a composition called "Gone from This Place." A lively guitar riff with a hint of melancholy underscores the few lyrical lines that are mostly variations on, "well I won't be satisfied 'til I'm gone from this place." Lennon whistles the melody contentedly and later hums his way through it before abruptly stopping. In this early form, there is no way of telling whether the song would have enhanced the irony implied in the lyrics when contrasted with the music or whether it would have solidified its outlook to one perspective or the other, turned into something totally different—or perhaps abandoned entirely. Like similar works of Lennon, it becomes a snapshot of the artist in process—tantalizing, but forever on the verge.

The Lost Lennon Tapes presented these songs and many more examples of how Lennon's creative processes worked. Among them were the harrowing "You Saved My Soul," and another third-person effort called "Whatever Became Of...?" In addition, there were "Emotional Wreck," "I Watch Your Face," and "One of the Boys," to name a few. Despite the wealth of Lennon material that has been legally released since the series went off the air in 1992, there remains a treasure trove of Lennon's creative legacy from the series and other sources that could, and in most cases probably should, be made available to the public.[9]

Gone from This Place:
The Continuing Legacy

More than a decade had passed since Lennon's murder and *The Lost Lennon Tapes* radio series was starting its third year and entering a phase of markedly diminishing returns. The series had exposed a wealth of material previously unheard by the general public, but it looked like there was little left to be collected and released, and certainly nothing that could be turned into pop music hits on the contemporary charts. Clearly, the well of material from Lennon's dormant years was dry, and only the most zealous fan would be interested in yet another demo variation of some fragmentary, incomplete song that was barely more than a couplet set to a guitar riff or piano run.

It was expected that the industry of Lennon releases would be relegated to reissues and the repackaging of previously issued materials, with a collection of the best of *The Lost Lennon Tapes* being the last release of "new" Lennon material. Such, however, was not to be the case.

LENNON

The fourth overview of Lennon's post-Beatles output is the most extensive, encompassing four CDs and entitled, simply, *Lennon*. Of special interest is the inclusion of several live tracks, including a sampling of cuts from *Live Peace in Toronto*, the Fillmore show with Frank Zappa, the One to One concert, and the appearance with Elton John. The only album present in its entirety is *John Lennon/Plastic Ono Band*, and, while personal taste may mark some disagreements with the remaining selections, it succeeds in its goal as a fairly comprehensive summary. Some quibbles include that "Move over Ms. L" is absent, while "Every Man Has a Woman Who Loves Him" is present;

and, as with all of the other collections, none of his experimental work with Ono and none of his studio work in collaboration with others is included.

PLAYGROUND PSYCHOTICS

In the early 1990s and near the end of his life, Frank Zappa embarked on a project of remastering and remixing his entire recorded output for digital issue, in addition to continuing to compose and record new material. He also reached back into his archived recordings to digitize and put his stamp on a strong collection of live recordings from throughout his career.

Included in this effort was Zappa's 1971 Fillmore East appearance with Lennon and Ono, released by them in 1972 as part of the bonus disc making up their *Sometime in New York City* album. Zappa released a two-CD album consisting of a variety of live music recordings and audio-vérité conversational snippets called *Playground Psychotics* that included his mixes of the material Lennon and Ono had released 20 years earlier. Because the performance was apparently a free-flowing jam, after Lennon's excellent performance of the song "Well," Zappa broke the numbers up differently than the earlier release and gave some of the numbers different titles, sardonically naming one "A Small Eternity with Yoko Ono." Zappa's versions are cleaner and more balanced than Lennon's, and the breaks make more sense musically. As such, they are the preferred versions. Ono's CD reissue of the *Some Time in New York City* album omits the jam entirely, apparently acquiescing to Zappa's judgments.

ONOBOX

In 1992, a six-CD set retrospective of Ono's recorded work, with and without Lennon, was released under the title *Onobox*. This set includes several previously unreleased recordings, including an entire abandoned album from 1974 called *A Story*. Some of the previously unissued material has contributions from Lennon.

The *Onobox* set has two more uses of Lennon's voice beyond what has previously been discussed. The work opens with "No Bed for Beatle John," with the brief added beginning of Lennon saying "Yoko's box." Later in the collection, a similar voice introduction from Lennon has been added to "Walking on Thin Ice." Lennon states, "[I] think you just got your first number one, Yoko."

Ono also used Lennon's voice on her contribution, "Georgia Stone," to a 1994 album honoring John Cage titled *A Chance Operation*.

LENNON LEGEND

A fifth Lennon retrospective collection, *Lennon Legend,* was the first single CD collection to include material from *Milk and Honey,* and the first designed solely for CD. Perhaps partially cashing in on the renewed Beatlemania as a result of The Beatles' *Anthology,* this compendium presents 20 cuts, and, once again, "Woman Is the Nigger of the World" and "Cold Turkey" are excluded. "Love," "Stand by Me," and "Jealous Guy" are back, with four instead of six of Lennon's *Double Fantasy* numbers, as were on the previous collection. The slots are replaced with two tracks from *Milk and Honey.* "Move over Ms. L" is not in the collection either, but there is the intriguing addition of "Working Class Hero," significant in that it was growing as a common phrase and attribute in the expanding Lennon mythos.

LIVERPOOL SOUND COLLAGE

Paul McCartney presented an art exhibit and prepared a set of sound collages and looped tapes to accompany the event. The recordings were subsequently released as *Liverpool Sound Collage,* and Lennon can be recognizably heard on two of the pieces, "Plastic Beetle" and "Made Up." Both tracks use short snippets of conversational dialogue or interviews recorded during the Beatles era.

COVERED #1

Q magazine released two different CDs of then-contemporary groups doing versions of Lennon's songs late in 2005. The occasion was an issue commemorating the 25th anniversary of Lennon's killing, or, alternatively, celebrating what would have been his 65th birthday. On *Covered #1,* the group Elbow performs "Working Class Hero" and ingeniously incorporates an excerpt from one of Lennon's last interviews wherein he proclaims that the social role of an artist is to express "what we all feel, not to tell people how to feel ... not as a preacher, not as a leader," as the lyrics ironically intone "just follow me."

THE BEATLES ANTHOLOGY

As *The Lost Lennon Tapes* radio series ended in 1992, fans expected a CD release of the most significant recordings unearthed for the project. But instead, rumors began that a long-delayed documentary and archive project titled *The Long and Winding Road* was at last underway. This would be The Beatles telling their own story, and eventually became the *Anthology* project.

As the 1980s came to a close, two projects commenced that would have far-reaching repercussions for the continuing legacy of Lennon's work. One was the projected release of an album of never legally released Beatle tracks called *Sessions;* the other was the radio series *The Lost Lennon Tapes,* discussed in the previous chapter.

The recordings on *Sessions* were neither jams nor unfinished fragments, nor a rehash of the U.S. version of *Rarities,* but were completed numbers that, for a variety of reasons, never were issued. The album was pulled from legal release at the last minute and, of course, became a best-selling bootleg, presumably influencing the Beatles' *Anthology* project. A roaring performance of Lennon leading the band at full throttle through a stellar cover version of Little Willie John's "Leave My Kitten Alone" was even selected for release as a single. Other obscure Lennon tracks, known only to those who collected bootlegged recordings, were to have been included. Fortunately, everything that would have been on *Sessions* did end up eventually in the *Anthology* collections.

Although this book does not cover Lennon's work as a Beatle, the *Anthology* project and its resulting publicity sparked a Beatles revival in the mid-1990s, renewed interest in the solo recordings of all four, and had a major impact on the reissuing of Lennon's posthumous materials in particular, and on his posthumous career in general. It is in this light that the *Anthology* project will be examined.

The first salvo was the 1994 release of The Beatles' *Live at the BBC.* This CD collection features 56 live but in the studio tracks recorded for broadcast by the British Broadcasting Corporation (BBC). The tracks were recorded from late 1962 through 1965, and over half the songs did not have a counterpart in the Beatles' officially released body of work. Most are covers, and Lennon lives up to his reputation as a rave-up rocker on several excellent cuts. Brief exchanges of dialogue were included where Lennon's humor shines.

More newsworthy was the fact that The Threetles—as fans took to calling McCartney, Harrison, and Starr—would be making new music together for the documentary. It was then disclosed that Ono had given some of Lennon's uncompleted recordings to The Threetles to see if they could finish them, thereby creating new Beatles recordings, of a sort.[1] Titles varied, but most sources said they had four songs to complete. They met and worked infrequently over a 15-month period in 1994 and 1995, completing two tracks, making progress on a third, and deciding to forgo work on a fourth.[2] Because of their clearly unique nature in The Beatles' output and their origins as post-Beatle Lennon compositions, they are discussed here.

By the mid-1990s, the project had become the *Anthology* series, and the surviving Beatles released three two-disc sets of unreleased finished tracks, outtakes and performances that spanned the time from their early days to the band's breakup. The first two volumes of the series opened with tracks whose foundations were two of Lennon's 1970s home demo recordings. Paul McCartney, George Harrison, and Ringo Starr added vocals and instruments to Lennon's demos of "Free as a Bird" and "Real Love," which appear on *Anthology 1* and *Anthology 2,* respectively. Assisting in the production of both songs was Jeff Lynne, a founding member of Electric Light Orchestra, and a member, with George Harrison, of The Traveling Wilburys. Lynne had also previously helped produce Harrison's *Cloud Nine* album with its Beatles-themed parody number "When We Was Fab." It seems not to have dawned on anyone that the sound Lynne and Harrison had created for parody was now somehow perceived as the way the reconstituted Beatles were supposed to sound.

Lennon's demo of "Free as a Bird" consists of a vocal with his piano accompaniment. The melody was completely developed, but the lyrics were not. McCartney, Harrison, and Starr added vocals, guitars, piano, bass, and drums in 1994 and altered the arrangement. The world will never know the final form Lennon may have released the song in, if any, had he lived, and in that light it is difficult to evaluate the recording with the contributions of his band mates. The issued production has a slow, almost plodding rhythm, attempting to capture a dreamlike quality. The track purposely and methodically gives each of the remaining Beatles a chance in the spotlight. McCartney sings the first bridge. Harrison sings the second, abbreviated bridge and follows it with a slide guitar solo. Both McCartney and Harrison seem to restrain their vocals to match better with the quality of the recording of Lennon's vocal that sounds thin and compressed to the point of distraction. After the false ending, Starr's drums come to the fore before the song closes with a George Formby–like banjolele and a snippet of Lennon speaking Formby's tag line, "turned out nice again," played backward (though the single version seems to just be Lennon saying, "uh, John Lennon," and not backward at all).

The subject of the song is a freedom that has evaporated. It could be a freedom that was felt because of the narrator's involvement in a romantic relationship, or it could be a freedom that resulted from his being in a more expansive surrounding (social or physical) in harmony. Harrison's slide guitar and some of the backing vocal harmonies are the most distinctive and successful parts of the recording.

The song was one of the compositions Lennon had decided to use in the proposed musical play *The Ballad of John and Yoko* and dated from 1977–1978.[3] Lennon had not written much in the way of lyrics. For the bridge, his demo recording has no lyrics after "the life that we once knew"; he fills in the melody with vocal sounds but no words. The lyrics McCartney sings, "where did we lose the touch that seemed to mean so much?" could relate to his relationship with Lennon, might be commentary on the dissolution of The Beatles, or could be addressed to an imaginary lover. With all the publicity around the group's *Anthology,* a clever promotional video, and 25 years of waiting for a Beatles reunion, it is surprising that the song only made it to number six on *Billboard* magazine's Hot 100 chart.

Lennon had developed the lyrics to "Real Love" more thoroughly, and the song had a long history. Lennon had begun it as "Real Life" in 1977, another of his songs for the proposed musical. As he developed it, he turned a section of the song into "I'm Stepping Out." Yet another section became part of the genesis of "Watching the Wheels." What remained became "Real Love" by 1978.[4] In 1980, Lennon returned to the song, now calling it "Boys and Girls." Many demos and rehearsals exist with either piano or guitar accompaniment, and at least one source claims that Lennon worked on it with the band during the *Double Fantasy* sessions.[5]

He sings of how his relationship with his love has changed him. He is self-assured. All the baggage of his past means nothing in the face of his "real love." Lennon's demo consisted of two vocal tracks, his piano accompaniment, and a drum machine. Surprisingly, some demos seem to be of better sound quality than the one used by The Threetles. Lennon's vocals are akin to his delivery on the Beatles' "Across the Universe" a decade earlier but sound slightly artificial due to the restoration. McCartney, Harrison, and Starr add acoustic guitars, electric guitar, electric and standup bass, drums and percussion, and backing harmony vocals. Unlike they did on "Free as a Bird," Lennon's band mates do not each take a turn in the spotlight on "Real Love." And, because the song was more completed to start with and the focus is on one lead vocalist, "Real Love" is in some ways the stronger of the two tracks, with Harrison's short guitar break a standout passage. Despite this, "Free as a Bird" performed better on the *Billboard* singles chart than "Real Love," which topped out at number 11 on *Billboard*'s Hot 100.

Once the excitement over The Beatles' "reunion" and the release of the third part of the *Anthology* compendium had died down, the *John Lennon Anthology* box set collection was released two years later in 1998. Then, beginning in 2000, an ambitious, multiyear project of remixing, remastering, and reissuing all of Lennon's solo material, along with bonus cuts, was begun. Occasionally these bonus tracks were songs that had not been legally released before.

JOHN LENNON ANTHOLOGY

With the overwhelming success of the Beatles' *Anthology* and the publicity that existed confirming the existence of many other John Lennon recordings in various stages of completion, it was to be expected that a parallel collection of Lennon's post-Beatles material would finally surface. Hardcore fans who knew of the bounty included in *The Lost Lennon Tapes* broadcasts busily compiled what they were sure would be on the collection.

If a collection of Lennon rarities and collectibles had indeed come out under the heading of the radio show and was tied to it, it surely would have included more of the highlights of that offering. But just as *The Lost Lennon Tapes* radio broadcasts had clearly influenced the *Anthology* sets, the Beatles' *Anthology* in turn influenced this collection, steering it away from some of the more esoteric inclusions and toward studio rehearsals and works in progress. While fans of *The Lost Lennon Tapes* may have been disappointed at some omissions and are still awaiting another release, *John Lennon Anthology* has some of the intriguing material from the radio series and a nice range of other materials, as these key examples not previously discussed elsewhere demonstrate.

The first disc in the four-disc set includes "Well (Baby Please Don't Go)," taken from the *Imagine* sessions and recorded a month after Lennon's performance of the song at the Fillmore show with Frank Zappa and the Mothers of Invention. Lennon had performed this in his early Beatles days, though certainly not with the hard-edged guitar he provides here to match his gritty vocals. The trio of Lennon, Klaus Voorman on bass, and Jim Gordon on drums is quite good, if a little spare sounding, even with the addition of sax work by stalwart Bobby Keyes bringing them up to a quartet.

The song is not a rehearsal jam and might have been intended for release as the flip side of a single, though the habit had already been established that Ono took the B-sides. Perhaps it had been posited that Ono should have her own releases, though Lennon kept her on his B-sides until his release of the "Mind Games" single in 1973. Phil Spector was co-producing on this album, and it is unfortunate that the sparer sound had no impact on his thinking two years later when Lennon and he began their project of recording similar rock and roll standards.

"Long Lost John" is a traditional folk song and does sound like a quick jam designed to clear the musical palette, though it may be a number Lennon learned in his skiffle craze days. The enjoyable recording comes from the *Plastic Ono Band* sessions. A tired-sounding Lennon seems to gain impetus and strength as he performs, until he hits a verse where he extemporizes lyrics that declare, "I got in about a half-past three, you don't look out you're gonna spew on me" before breaking himself up and stopping the band (which includes Ringo Starr and Voorman). Ono, who produced the CD collection, lets the track continue and we hear Lennon saying, "I'm defunct! That's one of the problems." Indeed it is.

Ono includes several fragments of dialogue and musical pieces throughout the set. This track is both. The band finishes its performance at the 1972 *Jerry Lewis MDA Labor Day Telethon,* and the crowd cheers for them. Lewis makes a comment about Lennon that it seems Ono wants us to ponder for its deeper implications beyond the show. Lennon "came here to help" Lewis states, and "he meant to say something." Lewis then adds, "he did both those things. He has split. Let's thank him very much."

"Be My Baby," along with "Angel Baby," had been included on *Roots,* but Lennon rejected them from the track list for *Rock 'N' Roll.* Lennon's performance of "Be My Baby" must be a spoof of the original, and he may have rejected it (needlessly it would seem) out of embarrassment. As with the other Spector-produced tracks, the song builds at a lethargic pace—at least when compared to the original. It takes over a minute to build to the point where Lennon begins his pseudo-ecstatic moans and chirping noises and another five seconds before the song gets to his affected, feminine, and fey-sounding performance of the lyrics. Based on accounts of the sessions, the likelihood is that Lennon was functional, but inebriated, for this performance. He s-stretches out the *s*-sounds at one point and s-somnambulates into a s-series of groaning orgasmic commentary as the s-song limps along to its fadeout.

The cut might have been rescued by new vocals, as Lennon succeeded in doing with some of the other Spector tracks; as it is, at least Lennon had the commitment to maintain the spoof all the way to the end. It is more odd than awful, and after a few drinks, listeners may be as amused as Lennon must have been.

Bob Dylan's 1979 album *Slow Train Coming* documented Dylan's conversion to Christianity and produced the hit "Gotta Serve Somebody." Lennon had acknowledged Dylan's influence on his songwriting many times and must have been listening, because Dylan's conversion was apparently so upsetting that he composed an answer song to Dylan's track titled "Serve Yourself." Multiple takes exist of the song taken at different speeds and performed on either piano or guitar. On this one, strumming angrily on an acoustic guitar, Lennon in a solo home recording from 1980, replies to Dylan, "ain't nobody gonna do for you." A person may variously put their trust in "devils" or "laws" or "Christ" or "Marx" or even "Marx and Spencer's" or "Woolworth's," but, in Lennon's purview, "you're gonna have to serve yourself." While on other home recordings of the late 1970s, Lennon either mocked Dylan by rhythmically reading newspaper stories in a Dylanesque drawl to a chugging guitar accompaniment or parodying Dylan's "Knocking on Heaven's Door" in another recording available in the CD set, this is decidedly different.

At his most sardonic and bitingly funny, Lennon spits out a series of condemning lyrics while referencing such wide-ranging and familiar pop music sources as "As Time Goes By" and "Down by the Riverside." Furthermore, he takes on the persona of a stereotypical parental authority figure and spouts a mesh of empty clichés from "put you back in the Stone Age" to "you should have been in the bloody war" to "get in there and wash your ears," mirroring the empty rhetoric of the religious authorities he challenges.

Interestingly, Lennon lists the religions' key figures (Jesus, Buddha, Mohammed, Krishna) and not the religions or beliefs. Lennon, 10 years after recording "Working Class Hero" with lyrics decrying a system in which people are being "doped with religion," is still railing against what he sees as palliatives and against people unwilling or unable to take responsibility for their situation and actions while clinging to a father figure.

Lennon can he heard justifiably chortling at the end of his fiery performance as Ono starts to comment. There's no evidence that Lennon planned to formally record the composition. What the song might have become had Lennon taken it into the studio is unclear, but in this raw form it remains one of Lennon's most powerful and intriguing works, much closer in spirit to the works of *Plastic Ono Band* than of *Double Fantasy*.

No studio recording of the song "Life Begins at 40" was done. The song is somewhat of a country and western parody, with fairly polished lyrics and an ironic sense of humor, with lines such as "I've been dead for 39" in response to the title's statement. As mentioned in chapter 5, some sources indicate that Lennon was composing this song for Ringo Starr to use on what would become his 1981 album *Stop and Smell the Roses,* and Starr did have a predilection for country and western in the past, even back to his Beatle days. The version on the CD set is fine but seems to be only about half of a song, needing another verse or two. Lennon's performance includes an amusing spoken introduction as if he were performing it at a country and western club lounge somewhere.

"The Rishi Kesh Song" is a 1980 home demo that starts out sounding like a combined parody of George Harrison and Lennon himself and then seems to turn into a harrowing fragment about feeling suicidal. The first part has a dry take on mysticism by asserting the claims that "the magics in the mantra will give you all the answers" and "everything that's not here's not there." The clanging guitar alters rhythm and tone as Lennon says, "but still" and then sings, "feel so suicidal" (a reference to the Beatles' White Album track "Yer Blues") before repeating "somethin' is wrong" several times for over a minute until the piece fades and ends. A significant number of the Beatles' White Album tracks were composed in Rishikesh, the location in India of the Maharishi Mahesh Yogi's ashram that the Beatles and their wives visited in 1968, and an earlier version of this song is reputedly one of them.

Lennon introduces the piece as "the happy Rishi Kesh song" with what is apparently sarcastic irony. The juxtaposition of what at first seems to be a parody to the grim desperation of the second section is so shocking that it takes a while to realize that they are part of the same work. The vapid sloganeering and nonsensical answers of the first part are no solace at all for a truly tortured soul. Whether this was all Lennon ever intended the song to be—it is so powerful it just might be—or if he had larger plans for the work is not known. But "The Rishi Kesh Song," "Serve Yourself," and few other songs he was working on at the time provide evidence that, despite the criticisms that his songs on *Double Fantasy* were too complacent, Lennon still had plenty of vitriol for injustice and righteous indignation for "hypocritics."

A home demo of Lennon singing and playing piano for a moderately paced song titled "Mr. Hyde's Gone (Don't Be Afraid)" sounds designed to placate a frightened child. Soon it is clear, however, that Lennon is singing to a woman ("girl, you've been good to me") about staying up to see the dawn and "drinking coffee from our favorite cup" as an apology for his boorish (the Hyde part of the Jekyll and Hyde combination) behavior. It sounds to be a composing tape that needs more work both lyrically and musically. Lennon employs lyrics similar to those he has used previously, sounding like he is feeling his way to what he might want to eventually use and bridging the gaps with intentional filler. At the end, he loses whatever grasp of lyrical structure he had and laughs at his own "bill and spoon in June, and croony woony woony" lyrics, asking finally "can you stand it?"

The song "Dear John" may be Lennon's last composing tape, comprising a double meaning on the famous relationship breakup notes called Dear John letters, and a missive to himself. Of course, it could also have become a companion piece to "Dear Yoko." The song is in an early stage of composition, with not quite two complete verses. The opening verse indicates that it might have also been related to the statements of self-support and assurance that make up "Hold On" from *John Lennon/ Plastic Ono Band* a decade previously. Here Lennon comforts himself as he approaches the start of middle age with "the race is over, you've won" and "don't be hard on yourself" in a soft, pleasantly relaxed voice. Riffing until he decides to try another verse, Lennon discovers that his chords are those of the famous, late-life romance ballad "September Song," which causes him to chuckle to himself, stop unexpectedly, and immediately begin again. It is a charming moment in what might have developed into a charming song of similar measure.

"The Great Wok" is one of a handful of "Dakota Mind Movies" Lennon prepared from 1977 to 1979, more of which were included in episodes of *The Lost Lennon Tapes.* They are usually ridiculous and silly but harmlessly amusing and creative. Most have out-of-place music playing in the background as Lennon, in the guise of some character (a French detective named Maurice Dupont was a favorite), unleashes a pun-filled stream of disconnected wordplay imagery and illogical narrative. The recordings varied in length and were clearly planned out and prepared, at least to some degree, with room to improvise on the irrational as the mood so struck him. If typed up and read, the content would not be out of place with any of Lennon's pieces from his first two books. Nor would the lyrics be atypical of the writings (roughly contemporary to the "mind movies" recordings) collected as the book *Skywriting by Word of Mouth,* which was published in 1986, almost six years after his slaying.

This particular recording was done for New Year's Eve 1979, and Lennon is in the guise of a guru called the Great Wok, who tells us that the truly "great wok must be done." His character is cut from the same cloth as the "Brahma from Burma" and he relates a holiday message. Included is his New Year's resolution to renounce everything but "complete luxury and self-indulgence," and he announces this sacrifice as his duty "not only as a human being, but as a person," based on the advice gleaned from that well-known "sage, George Formby" (the British Music Hall veteran). One way to look at it, the Great Wok relates, is "simply not to look at it at all."

"It's Real" is barely over a minute long and features Lennon pleasantly whistling a plaintive melody while strumming bouncy rhythmic chords on his acoustic guitar. If he had developed lyrics yet, he does not use them here, and the breezy tune does not seem to need them if he had.

WONSAPONATIME

Wonsaponatime is a single CD selection of cuts from *John Lennon Anthology,* largely favoring alternate studio takes and rehearsals and unexpectedly omitting some of the true rarities from the box set. If the larger collection is for serious fans, it might have made sense for *Wonsaponatime* to feature the rare selections such as the tracks discussed previously. Instead, it appears as though the idea was to make a collection of generally more easily recognized material; given the larger enterprise, the choice baffles.

WORKING CLASS HERO (COVERS COLLECTION)

Working Class Hero is an intriguing collection of covers and remakes of Lennon's post-Beatles career, sanctioned by his estate and used to raise funds for animal charities. Released in 1995, the lineup includes an eclectic selection of performances from such stalwarts as Cheap Trick and George Clinton as well as alternative groups Screaming Trees and Candlebox. Most versions of the songs do not stray too far from Lennon's performed or recorded conceptions of the songs, but each artist or group manages to put its characteristic imprint on its offering. Standouts include Clinton's near-delirious "Mind Games," The Flaming Lips' snarling "Nobody Told Me," Cheap Trick's "Cold Turkey," and "Well Well Well" by Super 8. "Grow Old with Me" by Mary Chapin Carpenter received some FM radio airplay, charting on the adult contemporary lists at number 17—and deservedly so for its quiet grace.

JOHN LENNON'S JUKEBOX

John Lennon's Jukebox, a unique two-CD set release, is reputedly made up of songs found on a jukebox once owned and stocked by Lennon, and a television documentary accompanied its release in 2004. This jukebox is not one of the fabled Dakota apartment jukeboxes, stocked with Bing Crosby and Elvis Presley, but a portable one owned by Lennon in the 1960s.[6]

One joy of the collection of 40 recordings is to hear many of the originals that either The Beatles or Lennon covered at some point in their respective recording careers. Even more interesting are certain musical riffs or snatches of lyrics that Lennon adapted to his own work. Some may be coincidence—such as "Steppin' Out" by Paul Revere and the Raiders, which perhaps inspired Lennon's "I'm Stepping Out"—but others have more significant and demonstrable connections.

"Some Other Guy" by The Big Three provides an example of a musical influence that Lennon would adapt in the future. This tune was a staple of The Beatles in their Hamburg and Cavern Club days and appears on the group's *Live at the BBC* collection. Lennon took the opening passage, three solid note-chords and transferred them almost verbatim for his own opening to "Instant Karma!" The songs could not be less alike after that, but the beginning is more than similar; it is the same.

A clear lyrical borrowing comes from Barrett Strong's "Oh I Apologize." The general approach of the song may have influenced such Lennon creations as "Jealous Guy," "Aisumasen (I'm Sorry)," and "(Forgive Me) My Little Flower Princess." But in the first verse, a more specific influence becomes apparent. Strong sings, "I don't expect you to take me back, after I've caused you so much pain" to a simple pounding rhythm similar to the passage from Lennon's "Isolation" in which he sings, "I don't expect you to understand, after you've caused so much pain." The line and Strong's performance of it is felt again in some of the demos of Lennon's "Real Love," where he sings, "I don't expect you to understand, the kingdom of heaven is in your hand" in a similar melodic rhythm. Interestingly, the version of "Real Love" completed by The Beatles for the *Anthology 2* collection does not contain the passage.

ACOUSTIC

In fall 2004, Ono sanctioned the release of *Acoustic,* which was Lennon performing acoustic versions of some of his songs. At the time of *Acoustic*'s release, there were still many unreleased home recordings of Lennon acoustically busking through various old rock and roll and rhythm and blues numbers (several had been broadcast on *The Lost Lennon Tapes*), and it reasonably might have been supposed that this collection would compile the best of them. The collection's running time of just under 45 minutes allows for another half hour of music on the CD. However, with three notable exceptions, the included tracks are all rehearsals or polished demos of Lennon accompanying himself on songs that he composed, so the idea behind the album is not just acoustic performances by Lennon, but acoustic guitar performances by Lennon of his own post-Beatles compositions—no acoustic piano and no non-Lennon compositions. Ono included charts of guitar chords and lyrics, explaining in her liner notes that she hoped to encourage future musicians to play from their hearts as Lennon always had.

Of special note is that many of the songs that are performed on piano in their finalized versions are here performed on guitar. Some of the recordings, especially "Woman Is the Nigger of the World, " It's Real," and "My Mummy's Dead," are so short or fragmentary as to be of limited interest and value. It is perplexing as to how they might be of use to guitar students.

Yet there are some real gems. For instance, "God" does not have the best sound quality, but Lennon's guitar work provides a rolling rhythm and the pace is faster than the studio version, making the mood oddly more upbeat and palatable. Lennon jokes around with the introduction, saying that angels must have sent him from above with a message about "our love."

It is akin to a 1950s teen romance parody, and Lennon almost breaks himself up, thereby softening the "God is a concept by which we measure our pain" line that follows. As noted previously, Lennon sings "I don't believe in Dylan" instead of "Zimmerman," which makes more thematic sense. After stating his belief in himself, he does not add the "Yoko and me" line as in the final version.

As for the rest, "Cold Turkey" features Lennon's intriguing shuddering as if in drug withdrawal and fractured vocals, and "What You Got" has a gutsy blues tinge that is a real joy because it is not as evident in the final version. "Watching the Wheels" shows its Dylansesque roots in a wonderful performance, and "Dear Yoko" sounds even more like the Buddy Holly songs that inspired it, at least musically. "Real Love" is not the same take as on the *Imagine: John Lennon* collection but is fairly close to that track and to the Beatles' completed version.

Three songs on the album are culled from live performances. "Imagine" comes from a concert at the Apollo Theater to support the families of those killed in the Attica State Prison riots and is one of the better versions extant for its gentle power in full effect. Also included are two numbers from the four-song set in Ann Arbor, Michigan, to support the release of John Sinclair from prison. "The Luck of the Irish" is a cut or two above passable, but after Lennon encourages the crowd to "start again" if attempts at social change do not work, "John Sinclair" is performed to great effect with lilting ease. While not the album fans may have been expecting, there is enough interesting material on *Acoustic* to make the collection worthwhile.

JOHN LENNON: THE MUSICAL

In 2004–2005, Ono collaborated on a production of a musical of Lennon's life and art, using his songs to tell the story of his life. Three songs never professionally recorded by Lennon during his life time were included in *John Lennon: The Musical*, and the availability of bootlegs of Lennon's demos of those songs increased as a result. One of the three songs was "Cookin' (In the Kitchen of Love)," his 1976 contribution to Ringo Starr's *Rotogravure* album, discussed in chapter 5. The other two were "India, India" and "I Don't Want To Lose You."

"India, India" seems to have been written for the autobiographical musical the couple planned off and on from the mid-1970s titled "The Ballad of John and Yoko." Lennon reportedly worked on it sporadically, though in earnest, in 1977 and 1978; the couple mentioned it as a future project in interviews publicizing *Double Fantasy;* and Ono discusses it in her introduction in Lennon's posthumously collected prose work *Skywriting by Word of Mouth*.

The song exists in a complete and overdubbed demo, sounding fairly polished as a result. As the title indicates, the song comments on Lennon's emotional state of mind during The Beatles' well-known trip to India in 1968.

It is an upbeat but wistful tune played on acoustic guitar. Lennon sings of India, asking it to take him to its heart and reveal its ancient mysteries. Immediately, however, he admits he has the answers he needs deep in his mind. The verse changes this awareness to his need to "follow my heart" which is "going home." Further verses carry this idea forward, saying he left his heart in England "with the girl I left behind." The song is a little obvious in the lyrics but very tuneful and somehow pleasant in its musical approximation of low-key anxiousness.

"I Don't Want To Lose You" is, according to rumor, one of the four songs Ono gave to The Threetles for them to consider overdubbing. They reportedly worked on it but then abandoned it. Since George Harrison's death in 2001, there have been recurring rumors that McCartney and Starr would complete it, and that if Harrison's input were judged sufficient, it would be considered a Beatles product.

The strikingly melancholic song, played on piano, opens with Lennon's emotionally drained voice intoning, "I know it's true, it's all because of you." The lyrics continue the thought that the singer is at the mercy of love and would be destroyed without it. The lyrics of the chorus do not seem completely finished, but the song has a rich melody with changes in tone and texture that mark it as potentially one of Lennon's more sophisticated harmonic efforts. If the surviving Beatles did indeed work on this track, it is unfortunate that they abandoned their attempt to complete it.

WORKING CLASS HERO: THE DEFINITIVE LENNON

Working Class Hero is yet another retrospective collection including Lennon's post-Beatles career output—the sixth to be exact, discounting the *John Lennon Anthology* and *Wonsaponatime* because of their singular nature. This issue is a two-CD set and was released in 2005 to celebrate what would have been Lennon's 65th birthday or to commemorate the quarter century mark of his slaying.

The "definitive" part of the subtitle is certainly debatable because the bulk of the collection consists of Lennon's pop hits and love ballads. As expected, none of the collaborative work with Ono or others in which Lennon was not the primary focus is included, nor is any of his avant-garde work from the three experimental albums.

As on *Lennon,* personal preference determines what might be included once the canon has been covered, yet there are some questionable choices. Among the more idiosyncratic inclusions are the only live cut being "Come Together" from *Live in New York City* and the version of "I'm Losing You" backed by members of Cheap Trick from the *John Lennon Anthology* instead of the official *Double Fantasy* release. Thankfully, all of the singles (with the understandable exception of "Every Man Has a Woman Who Loves Him") are here, but not the rare "Move over Ms. L" B-side. Only "New York City" and "Woman Is the Nigger of the World" make it from *Sometime in New York City,* but one of Lennon's demos of "Real Love" did make the cut. Fortunately, significant but less commercially oriented tracks, such as "God" and "Give Me Some Truth," help the collection to come closer to living up to its full title.

THE U.S. VS. JOHN LENNON

Fall 2006 saw another Lennon compilation CD, this one the soundtrack album for a documentary that had limited theatrical release. *The U.S. vs. John Lennon* focused on Lennon's immigration troubles, and the collection of songs makes sense in the context of the film but not as a coherent album collection on their own. A few of the numbers have Lennon's or Ono's voice layered on from interviews, inadvertently creating alternate versions of the songs when heard out of the film's context.

Two previously unreleased recordings are included. The first is a live version of "Attica State" from the 1971 Ann Arbor appearance in support of John Sinclair. Lennon introduces the song and set with a joke about his musical beginnings, "Ok, we're playing acoustic tonight, eh, you might call us The Quarry Men!" and then nervously adding "I haven't done this for years!" The performance is spirited but rough and more than a little erratic, teetering on the edge of losing time, though Lennon aggressively pushes it through with his forceful vocals. While ultimately a welcome release due to the paucity of Lennon's post-Beatles live appearances, the recording is of marginal interest to most. The other "new" release is a mix of "How Do You Sleep?" with Lennon's vocals removed. The change puts Harrison's stellar slide guitar work into sharper relief, but the ultimate result leaves large sections of the song sounding aimlessly repetitive. While McCartney fans may welcome this version, it creates a fear that similar karaoke-styled material might be created and issued in the future.

"CAMBRIDGE 1969"

Remixes of Ono's work had proven popular as electronica and dance-chart efforts. In 2007 the album *Yes, I'm a Witch* was released. Ono's vocals from previous recordings (both released and alternate unreleased takes) were taken by various artists and remixed into new versions of her songs. Lennon's contributions to those recordings were apparently not kept, with one obvious exception.

The Flaming Lips had done a version of "Nobody Told Me" for the charity album of Lennon covers *Working Class Hero* in 1995. Here, the band tackles the live recording of Ono's "Cambridge 1969," and a bit of Lennon's feedback guitar work is retained, possibly due to the technical aspects of the original live recording.

Both Ono's vocals and Lennon's guitar sounds waver in and out of prominence and are eventually subsumed to the sonic mesh the group provides. The raw vibrancy of the original and the interplay between Ono and Lennon are buried in a musical collage that surprisingly sounds much like the instrumental passages from George Harrison's Beatles track "It's All Too Much."

Afterword

Lennon's violent murder casts a backward shadow over his entire life, career, and creative output. Sometimes, it is hard to hear the fun or get through the retroactive irony that his work has been layered with by the event. Both he and his music deserve much better, of course. In addition, three or more decades of his potential creative output, artistic growth, and shared commentary is an unfathomable loss. In the years since his killing, there have been myriad portraits of Lennon produced by those who knew him, as well as numerous analyses of his life and work from various outsider perspectives. Many of those documents and studies have their strengths, yet what remains the most intriguing and ultimately significant effort are the self-portraits Lennon left in his songs. In holding the mirror up to himself and detailing what he saw for the public, Lennon went beyond himself, both inwardly and outwardly. That was the gift given to him as an artist, and that is the gift he gave to the public.

If Lennon had only produced what his output was as a Beatle, he would still be considered one of the major figures in all of popular music. In fact, if all Lennon had ever done were to produce popular music, he would still be considered a major figure of significance. But Lennon did much more than just create music, and he did much more than solely create music as a Beatle. As horribly curtailed as his life was, and even with almost half a decade of his career not professionally active, he still created a body of work that promises to be of continuing interest and importance.

Tributes to Lennon have commonly referred to him as the "spokesperson of his generation," and, while that is certainly meant as high praise, it is far too limiting. Lennon was able to transform the intensely personal into the deeply universal (as well as the reverse), often with humor and pointed insight. His songs spoke to, for, and about, the human condition. They continue to resonate with significance and meaning for new audiences in each succeeding generation.

At their core, Lennon's songs are simultaneously humanistic and transcendent. As such, they, and he, will undoubtedly continue to be relevant as long as humans are concerned with themselves, each other, and their place in the world.

EPILOGUE

I was working a third-shift job at a convenience store and going to graduate school. I had eagerly set an alarm so I could wake up and hear the debut broadcast of the new John Lennon single "(Just Like) Starting Over." A few days later, it was on a jukebox at a local Pizza Hut and I heard it again, and got to play Yoko's flip side "Kiss Kiss Kiss." Patrons were not amused, but I relished their annoyance. John and Yoko were back, and shaking up the complacent once again. I played both sides of the single every chance I had.

The album *Double Fantasy* came out a few weeks later and a friend and I rushed out to buy it. I liked it more than he did. He thought Lennon's work wasn't tough enough. We joked that if something bad happened to Yoko, the anguish might spur John to write gutsier songs.

I'd had a minor car accident, and my car radio didn't work. Usually I listened to the radio as I got ready for work, but on December 8, 1980, I overslept and was so rushed that I didn't have time to turn on the radio. When I got to my job, I was surprised to see my friend waiting for me. He said he was there since he knew how upset I'd be about the news. What news? Hadn't I heard on the radio that John Lennon had been shot? I thought it was a sort of practical joke, because he sometimes had a grim sense of humor and we sometimes imagined elaborate practical jokes we might play on friends. In view of our comments about Yoko, it seemed plausible to me that he might be pulling a joke on me. I even thought a coworker and customers in the convenience store were in on the gag until my exasperated coworker had me go out to his car and listen to the radio. I spun the dial, and station after station was playing Beatles and Lennon recordings.

I went back inside and asked my friend if the news had said how badly hurt Lennon was; and where was Yoko, was she hurt, too? He seemed startled. "I told you he's dead!" "No," I said, "you just said he'd been shot, you never said he was dead." "Well he is, he's dead" was his blunt reply, as my coworker nodded in assent. My friend later said it felt like he was saying Mickey Mouse had been killed. We all knew Lennon was a real person, but he was such an iconic figure that it was easy to lose sight of that fact—somewhat ironic in view of Lennon's uncanny ability to make his art so directly personal and simultaneously so popular. Or perhaps that's exactly why he seemed so real as to become unreal to us.

I called my girlfriend as soon as I thought she'd be home from her second-shift job. She picked up the phone, and, without saying hello, said, "Well, they finally got him." Another friend came to the store and stayed for five hours. In the morning I called my dad, a decorated Army Ranger Sharpshooter and had him explain just what was meant by the newspaper accounts that said Lennon's murderer had taken a "military crouch" to shoot at him.

A few days later I was going with my mom to some appointment, and The Beatles' Ed Sullivan performance of "This Boy" came on the car radio. I flashed back to when she had explained "Strawberry Fields Forever" to me in a similar car ride over 13 years earlier. As Lennon's vocals reached their peak, I burst out sobbing and told her it hurt too much to hear him scream with such anguish and emotion.

But it was my emotions I heard in his voice.

Just like I always had.

—Ben Urish

I was sitting at the kitchen table having breakfast with my mom before I went to work. The local New Brunswick station was on the radio. During the eight-o'clock news, the announcer spoke of the shooting at the Dakota the night before. John Lennon was dead. A Beatle was gone. My mother gasped. I had not heard the news the night before. *Monday Night Football* must have been turned off early in the house.

Stunned, I drove to work. I turned the radio dial to Dan Ingram, now the morning show host on WABC (the W-A-Beatle-C of 1964). WABC was the only Top-40 AM station left in New York. And I still did not have an FM radio in my 1972 Dodge Dart. Ingram was in a somber mood. He played a special set dedicated to John, including Neil Sedaka's "The Immigrant," a song about Lennon's problems with U.S. immigration in the 1970s. ABC was the right station to be listening to. No flashy jingles. Just a quiet, downplayed memorial.

That night my sister Joyce and I had tickets to see Bruce Springsteen at the Spectrum in Philadelphia. We would meet my sister Judy at the show. I was emotionally numb as I drove down the New Jersey Turnpike. We listened to the radio. An announcer read a police report in grisly detail explaining what had happened to John.

John had turned 40 only two months earlier. A friend at work had been driving along the Palisades and had seen Yoko's sky-written birthday greeting to John. I didn't pay close attention to John's doings in New York as an ex-Beatle, but I knew he was around.

When we arrived at the Spectrum, there were banners unfurled. Not for Bruce, though. They were tributes to John. Hand-printed proclamations on bed sheets. When Bruce came out, the first thing he did was talk. He said some things are hard to accept, but we have to live with them and go on from there. He said that "Twist and Shout," John's closing vocal on the

Beatles' first album 18 years earlier, was the first song he learned. And he said if it wasn't for John Lennon, we would all be someplace different that night. The band closed the show with "Twist and Shout" as its tribute. I read an account afterward that said Bruce broke into tears. From where I was sitting, I couldn't tell.

On the Sunday afternoon after John's murder, almost six days on, there was a memorial at Central Park, the park adjacent to the building where he and Yoko had made their home with their five-year-old Sean. Yoko asked for 10 minutes of silence in the afternoon. At least one of the New York television stations carried the memorial live.

My dad and I watched it. Throughout the past week, he kept telling me not to be upset about all this. Have to keep on going. For whatever reason, he was watching, too.

I remember the silence, the cameras panning across the crowd that had gathered at the band shell, the only sounds those of the chirping birds.

The guy who had brought with his Liverpool mates such a wonderful sound to our television screens less than two decades earlier was now being remembered with silence on TV.

All video, no audio.

Nothing but silence.

Silence.

—Ken Bielen

Discography

ALBUMS

Unfinished Music No. 1—Two Virgins. Yoko Ono, John Lennon vocals and speech, sound effects. "Two Virgins Section 1" (Yoko Ono, Lennon); "Together" (Yoko Ono, Lennon); "Two Virgins Section 2" (Yoko Ono, Lennon); "Two Virgins Section 3" (Yoko Ono, Lennon); "Two Virgins Section 4" (Yoko Ono, Lennon); "Two Virgins Section 5" (Yoko Ono, Lennon); "Two Virgins Section 6" (Yoko Ono, Lennon); "Hushabye Hushabye" (Yoko Ono, Lennon); "Two Virgins Section 7" (Yoko Ono, Lennon); "Two Virgins Section 8" (Yoko Ono, Lennon); "Two Virgins Section 9" (Yoko Ono, Lennon); "Two Virgins Section 10" (Yoko Ono, Lennon). 33 1/3 rpm phonodisc. Apple T-5001 (distributed by Tetragammaton Records), 1968. Reissued on compact disc in 1997 as Rykodisc 10411 with bonus track "Remember Love" (Yoko Ono).

Unfinished Music No. 2—Life with the Lions. Yoko Ono, John Lennon vocals and speech, sound effects. "Cambridge 1969" ("Song for John"; "Cambridge 1969"; "Let's Go on Flying"; "Snow Is Falling All the Time"; "Mummy's Only Looking for Her Hand in the Snow") (Yoko Ono, Lennon); "No Bed for Beatle John" (Yoko Ono); "Baby's Heartbeat" (Yoko Ono, Lennon); "Two Minutes Silence" (Yoko Ono, Lennon); "Radio Play" (Yoko Ono, Lennon). 33 1/3-rpm phonodisc. Zapple ST-3357, 1969. Reissued on compact disc in 1997 as Rykodisc 10412 with two bonus tracks: "Song for John" (Yoko Ono) and "Mulberry" (Yoko Ono).

Wedding Album. Yoko Ono, John Lennon vocals and speech, sound effects. "John and Yoko" (Yoko Ono, Lennon); "Amsterdam" (Yoko Ono,

Lennon). 33⅓-rpm phonodisc. Zapple SMAX-3361, 1969. Reissued on compact disc in 1997 as Rykodisc 10413 with three bonus tracks: "Who Has Seen the Wind?" (Yoko Ono), "Listen, the Snow Is Falling" (Yoko Ono), and "Don't Worry Kyoko (Mummy's Only Looking for Her Hand in the Snow)" (Yoko Ono, Lennon).

Plastic Ono Band—Live Peace in Toronto 1969. John Lennon vocals, guitar, piano; Yoko Ono vocals, Eric Clapton guitar, Klaus Voorman bass guitar, Alan White drums. "Blue Suede Shoes" (Carl Perkins); "Money (That's What I Want)" (Janie Bradford, Berry Gordy); "Dizzy Miss Lizzy" (Larry Williams); "Yer Blues" (Lennon, Paul McCartney); "Cold Turkey" (Lennon); "Give Peace a Chance" (Lennon, Paul McCartney); "Don't Worry Kyoko (Mummy's Only Looking for Her Hand in the Snow)" (Yoko Ono); "John John (Let's Hope for Peace)" (Yoko Ono). 33⅓-rpm phonodisc. Apple 076–90877, 1969. Reissued in 1995 on compact disc as Capitol 7904282.

John Lennon/Plastic Ono Band. John Lennon vocals, guitar, piano; various assisting instrumentalists and vocalists. "Mother" (Lennon); "Hold On" (Lennon); "I Found Out" (Lennon); "Working Class Hero" (Lennon); "Isolation" (Lennon); "Remember" (Lennon); "Love" (Lennon); "Well Well Well" (Lennon); "Look at Me" (Lennon); "God" (Lennon); "My Mummy's Dead" (Lennon). 33⅓-rpm phonodisc. Apple SW-3372, 1970. Reissued on compact disc in 2000 as Capitol CDP-724352874026. Includes the additional track "Do the Oz" (Lennon, Yoko Ono).

Imagine. John Lennon/Plastic Ono Band. John Lennon vocals, guitar, piano; various assisting instrumentalists and vocalists. "Imagine" (Lennon); "Crippled Inside" (Lennon); "Jealous Guy" (Lennon); "It's So Hard" (Lennon); "I Don't Wanna Be a Soldier" (Lennon); "Give Me Some Truth" (Lennon); "Oh My Love" (Lennon, Yoko Ono); "How Do You Sleep?" (Lennon); "How?" (Lennon); "Oh Yoko!" (Lennon). 33⅓-rpm phonodisc. Apple SW-3379, 1971. Reissued on compact disc as Capitol 724352485826.

Some Time in New York City. John Lennon Yoko Ono/Plastic Ono Band with Elephant's Memory and Invisible Strings. John Lennon vocals, guitar, piano; various assisting instrumentalists and vocalists. The last four tracks are recorded with Frank Zappa and the Mothers of Invention. "Woman Is Nigger of the World" (Lennon, Yoko Ono); "Sisters, O Sisters" (Yoko Ono); "Attica State" (Lennon, Yoko Ono); "Born in a Prison" (Yoko Ono); "New York City" (Lennon); "Sunday Bloody Sunday" (Lennon, Yoko Ono); "The Luck of the Irish" (Lennon, Yoko Ono); "John Sinclair" (Lennon); "Angela" (Lennon, Yoko Ono); "We're All Water" (Yoko Ono); "Cold Turkey" (Lennon); "Don't Worry Kyoko" (Yoko Ono); "Well (Baby Please Don't Go)" (Walter Ward); "Jamrag" (Lennon, Yoko Ono); "Scumbag" (Lennon, Yoko

Ono, Frank Zappa); "Au" (Lennon, Yoko Ono). 33⅓-rpm phonodisc. Apple SVBB-3392, 1972. A reissue on compact disc (Capitol CDP 094634097628) in 2005 replaces the last three live Zappa numbers with the "Happy Xmas (War Is Over)"/"Listen the Snow Is Falling" studio single.

Mind Games. John Lennon/Plastic U.F. Ono Band. John Lennon vocals, guitar, piano; various assisting instrumentalists and vocalists. "Mind Games" (Lennon); "Tight A$" (Lennon); "Aisumasen (I'm Sorry)" (Lennon); "One Day (At a Time)" (Lennon); "Bring on the Lucie (Freda Peeple)" (Lennon); "Nutopian International Anthem" (Lennon); "Intuition" (Lennon); "Out the Blue" (Lennon); "Only People" (Lennon); "I Know (I Know)" (Lennon) "You Are Here" (Lennon); "Meat City" (Lennon). 33⅓-rpm phonodisc. Apple SW-3414, 1973. Reissued on compact disc as Capitol 724354242526.

Walls and Bridges. John Lennon vocals, guitar, piano; with the Plastic Ono Nuclear Band, Little Big Horns, and the Philharmanic Orchestrange; various assisting instrumentalists and vocalists. "Going Down on Love" (Lennon); "Whatever Gets You through the Night" (Lennon); "Old Dirt Road" (Lennon, Harry Nilsson); "What You Got" (Lennon); "Bless You" (Lennon); "Scared" (Lennon); "#9 Dream" (Lennon); "Surprise Surprise (Sweet Bird of Paradox)" (Lennon); "Steel and Glass" (Lennon); "Beef Jerky" (Lennon); "Nobody Loves You (When You're Down and Out)" (Lennon); "Ya Ya" (Morgan Robinson, Lee Dorsey, Clarence Lewis). 33⅓-rpm phonodisc. Apple SW-3416, 1974. A 2004 reissue on compact disc (Capitol 094634097123) adds the live performance of "Whatever Gets You through the Night" with Elton John, an alternate take of "Nobody Loves You When You're Down and Out," and a brief in-house promotional interview for the album with Lennon.

Rock 'N' Roll. John Lennon vocals, guitar, piano; various assisting instrumentalists and vocalists. "Be-Bop-A-Lula" (Tex Davis, Gene Vincent); "Stand by Me" (Ben E. King, Jerry Leiber, Mike Stoller); Medley: "Ready Teddy" (Otis Blackwell, John Marascalco), "Rip It Up" (Otis Blackwell, John Marascalco); "You Can't Catch Me" (Chuck Berry); "Ain't That a Shame" (Antoine "Fats" Domino, Dave Bartholomew); "Do You Want To Dance" (Bobby Freeman); "Sweet Little Sixteen" (Chuck Berry); "Slippin' and Slidin'" (Richard Penniman, Edwin J. Bocage, Albert Collins, James Smith); "Peggy Sue" (Buddy Holly, Jerry Allison, Norman Petty); Medley: "Bring It on Home to Me" (Sam Cooke), "Send Me Some Lovin'" (John Marascalco, Lloyd Price); "Bony Moronie" (Larry Williams); "Ya Ya" (Morgan Robinson, Lee Dorsey, Clarence Lewis); "Just Because" (Lloyd Price). 33⅓-rpm phonodisc. Apple SK-3419, 1975. A 2004 reissue on compact disc (Capitol 724387432925) added "Angel Baby," "To Know Her Is To Love Her," "Since My Baby Left Me," and a reprise of "Just Because."

Shaved Fish. John Lennon vocals, guitar, piano; various assisting instrumentalists and vocalists. Medley: "Give Peace a Chance" (Lennon, Paul McCartney), "Cold Turkey" (Lennon); "Instant Karma!" (Lennon); "Power to the People" (Lennon); "Mother" (Lennon); "Woman Is the Nigger of the World" (Lennon, Yoko Ono); "Imagine" (Lennon); "Whatever Gets You through the Night" (Lennon); "Mind Games" (Lennon); "#9 Dream" (Lennon); Medley: "Happy Xmas (War Is Over)" (Yoko Ono, Lennon), "Give Peace a Chance" (reprise) (Lennon, Paul McCartney). 33⅓-rpm phonodisc. Capitol SW-3421, 1975. Reissued on compact disc as Capitol 077774664226. Consists of previously released material.

Double Fantasy: A Heart Play. John Lennon vocals, guitar, piano; Yoko Ono vocals; various assisting instrumentalists and vocalists. "(Just Like) Starting Over" (Lennon); "Kiss Kiss Kiss" (Yoko Ono); "Cleanup Time" (Lennon); "Give Me Something" (Yoko Ono); "I'm Losing You" (Lennon); "I'm Moving On" (Yoko Ono); "Beautiful Boy (Darling Boy)" (Lennon); "Watching the Wheels" (Lennon); "Yes, I'm Your Angel" (Yoko Ono); "Woman" (Lennon); "Beautiful Boys" (Yoko Ono); "Dear Yoko" (Lennon); "Every Man Has a Woman Who Loves Him" (Yoko Ono); "Hard Times Are Over" (Yoko Ono). 33⅓-rpm phonodisc. Geffen GHS-2001, 1980. A reissue on compact disc (Capitol 724352873920) added a Lennon home demo titled "Help Me To Help Myself," Ono's "Walking on Thin Ice," and the "Central Park Stroll" dialogue Ono had used as the introduction to her composition "It Happened," the original flip side of "Walking on Thin Ice."

The John Lennon Collection. John Lennon vocals, guitar, piano; various assisting instrumentalists and vocalists. "Give Peace a Chance" (Lennon, Paul McCartney); "Instant Karma!" (Lennon); "Power to the People" (Lennon); "Whatever Gets You through the Night" (Lennon); "#9 Dream" (Lennon); "Mind Games" (Lennon); "Love" (Lennon); "Happy Xmas (War Is Over)" (Yoko Ono, Lennon); "Imagine" (Lennon); "Jealous Guy" (Lennon); "Stand by Me" (Ben E. King, Jerry Leiber, Mike Stoller); "(Just Like) Starting Over" (Lennon); "Woman" (Lennon); "I'm Losing You" (Lennon); "Beautiful Boy (Darling Boy)" (Lennon); "Watching the Wheels" (Lennon); "Dear Yoko" (Lennon); "Move over Ms. L" (Lennon); "Cold Turkey" (Lennon). 33⅓-rpm phonodisc. Geffen GHSP-2023, 1982. Reissued on compact disc as Capitol C2–91516. Consists of previously released material.

Milk and Honey: A Heart Play. John Lennon vocals, guitar; piano; Yoko Ono vocals, piano; various assisting instrumentalists and vocalists. "I'm Stepping Out" (Lennon); "Sleepless Night" (Yoko Ono); "I Don't Wanna Face It" (Lennon); "Don't Be Scared" (Yoko Ono); "Nobody Told Me" (Lennon); "O'Sanity" (Yoko Ono); "Borrowed Time" (Lennon); "Your Hands" (Yoko Ono); "(Forgive Me) My Little Flower Princess" (Lennon);

"Let Me Count the Ways" (Yoko Ono); "Grow Old with Me" (Lennon); "You're the One" (Yoko Ono). 33⅓-rpm phonodisc Polydor 817–160–1; compact disc Polydor 817–160–2, 1984. A reissue on compact disc in 2001 (Capitol CDP 7243535959 20) added Lennon's lead vocal version of "Every Man Has A Woman Who Loves Him," demo versions of "Stepping Out" and "I'm Moving On," plus part of a 12-8-80 radio interview.

Live in New York City. John Lennon vocals, guitar, piano; various assisting instrumentalists and vocalists. "New York City" (Lennon); "It's So Hard" (Lennon); "Woman Is the Nigger of the World" (Lennon, Yoko Ono); "Well, Well, Well" (Lennon); "Instant Karma! (We All Shine On)" (Lennon); "Mother" (Lennon); "Come Together" (Lennon, Paul McCartney); "Imagine" (Lennon); "Cold Turkey" (Lennon); "Hound Dog" (Jerry Leiber, Mike Stoller); "Give Peace a Chance" (Lennon, Paul McCartney). 33⅓-rpm phonodisc. Parlophone PCS 7301, 1986. Recorded in 1972. Reissued on compact disc as Capitol 077774619622. These performances are also included on Sony videocassette RO-172 with the following additional songs: "Power to the People" (Lennon); "Sisters, O Sisters" (Yoko Ono); and "Born in a Prison" (Yoko Ono).

Menlove Ave. John Lennon vocals, guitar, piano; various assisting instrumentalists and vocalists. "Here We Go Again" (Lennon, Phil Spector); "Rock and Roll People" (Lennon); "Angel Baby" (Rose Hamlin); "Since My Baby Left Me" (Arthur Crudup); "To Know Her Is To Love Her" (Phil Spector); "Steel and Glass" (Lennon); "Scared" (Lennon); "Old Dirt Road" (Lennon, Harry Nilsson); "Nobody Loves You" (Lennon); "Bless You" (Lennon). 33⅓-rpm phonodisc. Parlophone PCS 7308, 1986. Reissued on compact disc as Capitol 077774657624. Outtakes and alternate versions from the *Walls and Bridges* and *Rock 'N' Roll* recording sessions.

Imagine: John Lennon. John Lennon vocals, guitar, piano; various assisting instrumentalists and vocalists. "Real Love" (Lennon); "Twist and Shout" (P. Medley, B. Russell); "Help!" (Lennon, Paul McCartney); "In My Life" (Lennon, Paul McCartney); "Strawberry Fields Forever" (Lennon, Paul McCartney); "A Day in the Life" (Lennon, Paul McCartney); "Revolution" (Lennon, Paul McCartney); "Ballad of John and Yoko" (Lennon, Paul McCartney); "Julia" (Lennon, Paul McCartney); "Don't Let Me Down" (Lennon, Paul McCartney); "Give Peace a Chance" (Lennon, Paul McCartney); "How?" (Lennon); "Imagine" (rehearsal) (Lennon); "God" (Lennon); "Mother" (live) (Lennon); "Stand by Me" (Ben E. King, Jerry Leiber, Mike Stoller); "Jealous Guy" (Lennon); "Woman" (Lennon); "Beautiful Boy (Darling Boy)" (Lennon); "(Just Like) Starting Over" (Lennon); "Imagine" (Lennon). Compact disc. Capitol 077779080328, 1988. Soundtrack to documentary about Lennon. Primarily consists of previously released material.

Lennon. John Lennon vocals, guitar, piano; various assisting instrumentalists and vocalists. "Give Peace a Chance" (Lennon, Paul McCartney);

"Blue Suede Shoes" (Carl Perkins); "Money" (Janie Bradford, Berry Gordy); "Dizzy Miss Lizzy" (Larry Williams); "Yer Blues" (Lennon, Paul McCartney); "Cold Turkey" (Lennon); "Instant Karma!" (Lennon); "Hold On" (Lennon); "I Found Out" (Lennon); "Working Class Hero" (Lennon); "Isolation" (Lennon); "Remember" (Lennon); "Love" (Lennon); "Well Well Well" (Lennon); "Look at Me" (Lennon); "God" (Lennon); "My Mummy's Dead" (Lennon); "Power to the People" (Lennon); "Well (Baby Please Don't Go)" (Walter Ward); "Imagine" (Lennon); "Crippled Inside" (Lennon); "Jealous Guy" (Lennon); "It's So Hard" (Lennon); "Give Me Some Truth" (Lennon); "Oh My Love" (Lennon, Yoko Ono); "How Do You Sleep?" (Lennon); "How?" (Lennon); "Oh Yoko!" (Lennon); "Happy Xmas (War Is Over)" (Yoko Ono, Lennon); "Woman Is the Nigger of the World" (Lennon, Yoko Ono); "New York City" (Lennon); "John Sinclair" (Lennon); "Come Together" (Lennon, Paul McCartney); "Hound Dog" (Jerry Leiber, Mike Stoller); "Mind Games" (Lennon); "Aisumasen (I'm Sorry)" (Lennon); "One Day (At a Time)" (Lennon); "Intuition" (Lennon); "Out the Blue" (Lennon); "Whatever Gets You through the Night" (Lennon); "Going Down on Love" (Lennon); "Old Dirt Road" (Lennon, Harry Nilsson); "Bless You" (Lennon); "Scared" (Lennon); "#9 Dream" (Lennon); "Surprise Surprise (Sweet Bird of Paradox)" (Lennon); "Steel and Glass" (Lennon); "Nobody Loves You (When You're Down and Out)" (Lennon); "Stand by Me" (Ben E. King, Jerry Leiber, Mike Stoller); "Ain't That a Shame" (Antoine "Fats" Domino, Dave Bartholomew); "Do You Want To Dance" (Bobby Freeman); "Sweet Little Sixteen" (Chuck Berry); "Slippin' and Slidin'" (Richard Penniman, Edwin J. Bocage, Albert Collins, James Smith); "Angel Baby" (Rose Hamlin); "Just Because" (Lloyd Price); "Whatever Gets You through the Night" (live version) (Lennon); "Lucy in the Sky with Diamonds" (Lennon, Paul McCartney); "I Saw Her Standing There" (Lennon, Paul McCartney); "(Just Like) Starting Over" (Lennon); "Cleanup Time" (Lennon); "I'm Losing You" (Lennon); "Beautiful Boy (Darling Boy)" (Lennon); "Watching the Wheels" (Lennon); "Woman" (Lennon); "Dear Yoko" (Lennon); "I'm Stepping Out" (Lennon); "I Don't Wanna Face It" (Lennon); "Nobody Told Me" (Lennon); "Borrowed Time" (Lennon); "(Forgive Me) My Little Flower Princess" (Lennon); Every Man Has a Woman Who Loves Him" (Yoko Ono); "Grow Old with Me" (Lennon). Four compact discs. Capitol C2–95220, 1990. Contains previously released material.

Lennon Legend. John Lennon vocals, guitar, piano; various assisting instrumentalists and vocalists. "Imagine" (Lennon); "Instant Karma!" (Lennon); "Mother" (single edit) (Lennon); "Jealous Guy" (Lennon); "Power to the People" (Lennon); "Cold Turkey" (Lennon); "Love" (Lennon); "Mind Games" (Lennon); "Whatever Gets You through the Night" (Lennon); "#9 Dream" (Lennon); "Stand by Me" (Ben E.

King, Jerry Leiber, Mike Stoller); "(Just Like) Starting Over" (Lennon); "Woman" (Lennon); "Beautiful Boy (Darling Boy)" (Lennon); "Watching the Wheels" (Lennon); "Nobody Told Me" (Lennon); "Borrowed Time" (Lennon); "Working Class Hero" (Lennon); "Happy Xmas (War Is Over)" (Yoko Ono, Lennon); "Give Peace a Chance" (Lennon, Paul McCartney). Compact disc. Capitol 724382195429, 1997. Consists of previously released material.

John Lennon Anthology. John Lennon vocals, guitar, piano; various assisting instrumentalists and vocalists. "Working Class Hero" (Lennon); "God" (Lennon); "I Found Out" (Lennon); "Hold On" (Lennon); "Isolation" (Lennon); "Love" (Lennon); "Mother" (Lennon); "Remember" (Lennon); "Imagine" (Lennon); "Fortunately" (Lennon); "Baby Please Don't Go" (Walter Ward); "Oh My Love" (Lennon, Yoko Ono); "Jealous Guy" (Lennon); "Maggie Mae" (traditional); "How Do You Sleep?" (Lennon); "God Save Oz" (Lennon, Yoko Ono); "Do the Oz" (Lennon, Yoko Ono); "I Don't Want To Be a Soldier" (Lennon); "Give Peace a Chance" (Lennon, Paul McCartney); "Look at Me" (Lennon); "Long Lost John" (Lennon); "New York City" (Lennon); "Attica State" (live) (Lennon, Yoko Ono); "Imagine" (live) (Lennon); "Bring on the Lucie (Freda Peeple)" (Lennon); "Woman Is the Nigger of the World" (Lennon, Yoko Ono); "Geraldo Rivera—One to One Concert"; "Woman Is the Nigger of the World" (live) (Lennon, Yoko Ono); "It's So Hard" (live) (Lennon); "Come Together" (live) (Lennon, Paul McCartney); "Happy Xmas (War Is Over)" (Yoko Ono, Lennon); "Luck of the Irish" (live) (Lennon, Yoko Ono); "John Sinclair" (live) (Lennon); "The David Frost Show"; "Mind Games" (I Promise) (Lennon); "Mind Games" (Make Love, Not War) (Lennon); "One Day (At a Time)" (Lennon); "I Know" (Lennon); "I'm the Greatest" (Lennon); "Goodnight Vienna" (Lennon); "Jerry Lewis Telethon"; "A Kiss Is Just a Kiss (As Time Goes By)" (Herman Hupfield); "Real Love" (Lennon); "You Are Here" (Lennon); "What You Got" (Lennon); "Nobody Loves You (When You're Down and Out)" (Lennon); "Whatever Gets You through the Night" (home) (Lennon); "Whatever Gets You through the Night" (studio) (Lennon); "Yesterday" (parody) (Lennon, Paul McCartney); "Be-Bop-A-Lula" (Tex Davis, Gene Vincent); Medley: "Rip It Up" (Otis Blackwell, John Marascalco); "Ready Teddy" (Otis Blackwell, John Marascalco); "Scared" (Lennon); "Steel and Glass" (Lennon); "Surprise Surprise (Sweet Bird of Paradox)" (Lennon); "Bless You" (Lennon); "Going Down on Love" (Lennon); "Move over Ms. L" (Lennon); "Ain't She Sweet" (Jack Yellen, Milton Ager);"Slippin' and Slidin'" (Richard Penniman, Edwin J. Bocage, Albert Collins, James Smith); "Peggy Sue" (Buddy Holly, Jerry Allison, Norman Petty); Medley: "Bring It on Home to Me" (Sam Cooke)/"Send Me Some Lovin'" (John Marascalco, Lloyd Price); "Phil and John 1" (Lennon, Phil Spector); "Phil and John 2" (Lennon, Phil Spector); "Phil and John 3" (Lennon, Phil Spector); "When in Doubt,

Fuck It" (Lennon); "Be My Baby" (Jeff Barry, Ellie Greenwich, Phil Spector); "Stranger's Room" (Lennon); "Old Dirt Road" (Lennon, Harry Nilsson); "I'm Losing You" (Lennon); "Sean's 'Little Help'"(Lennon, Paul McCartney); "Serve Yourself" (Lennon); "My Life" (Lennon); "Nobody Told Me" (Lennon); "Life Begins at 40" (Lennon); "I Don't Wanna Face It" (Lennon); "Woman" (Lennon); "Dear Yoko" (Lennon); "Watching the Wheels" (Lennon); "I'm Stepping Out" (Lennon); "Borrowed Time" (Lennon); "The Rishi Kesh Song" (Lennon); "Sean's 'Loud'" (Lennon); "Beautiful Boy (Darling Boy)" (Lennon); "Mr. Hyde's Gone (Don't Be Afraid)" (Lennon); "Only You" (Ande Rand, Buck Ram); "Grow Old with Me" (Lennon); "Dear John" (Lennon); "The Great Wok" (Lennon); "Mucho Mungo" (Lennon); "Satire 1" (Lennon); "Satire 2" (Lennon); "Satire 3" (Lennon); "Sean's 'In the Sky'" (Lennon, Paul McCartney); "It's Real" (Lennon). Four compact discs: Disc 1, "Ascot." Disc 2, "New York City." Disc 3, "The Lost Weekend." Disc 4, "Dakota." Capitol 30614, 1998. Contains previously unissued material.

Wonsaponatime. John Lennon vocals, guitar, piano; various assisting instrumentalists and vocalists. "I'm Losing You" (Lennon); "Working Class Hero" (Lennon); "God" (Lennon); "How Do You Sleep?" (Lennon); "Imagine" (take 1) (Lennon); "Baby Please Don't Go" (Walter Ward); "Oh My Love" (Lennon, Yoko Ono); "God Save Oz" (Lennon, Yoko Ono); "I Found Out" (Lennon); "Woman Is the Nigger of the World" (live) (Lennon, Yoko Ono); "A Kiss Is Just a Kiss (As Time Goes By)" (Herman Hupfield); "Be-Bop-A-Lula" (Tex Davis, Gene Vincent); Medley: "Rip It Up" (Otis Blackwell, John Marascalco), "Ready Teddy" (Otis Blackwell, John Marascalco); "What You Got" (Lennon); "Nobody Loves You (When You're Down and Out)" (Lennon); "I Don't Wanna Face It" (Lennon); "Real Love" (Lennon); "Only You" (Ande Rand, Buck Ram); "Grow Old with Me" (Lennon); "Sean's 'In the Sky'" (Lennon, Paul McCartney); "Serve Yourself" (Lennon). Compact disc. Capitol 97639–1, 1998. Selections from *John Lennon Anthology.* Title is taken from a phrase invented by Lennon and included in his book *Skywriting by Word of Mouth.*

Acoustic. John Lennon vocals, guitar, piano; various assisting instrumentalists and vocalists. "Working Class Hero" (Lennon); "Love" (Lennon); "Well Well Well" (Lennon); "Look at Me" (Lennon); "God" (Lennon); "My Mummy's Dead" (Lennon); "Cold Turkey" (Lennon); "The Luck of the Irish" (live) (Lennon, Yoko Ono); "John Sinclair" (live) (Lennon); "Woman Is the Nigger of the World" (Lennon, Yoko Ono); What You Got" (Lennon); "Watching the Wheels" (Lennon); "Dear Yoko" (Lennon); "Real Love" (Lennon); "Imagine" (live) (Lennon); "It's Real" (Lennon). Compact disc. Capitol 724387442825, 2004. Contains previously unissued versions of Lennon's songs.

Working Class Hero: The Definitive Lennon. John Lennon vocals, guitar, piano; various assisting instrumentalists and vocalists. "(Just Like)

Starting Over" (Lennon); "Imagine" (Lennon); "Watching the Wheels" (Lennon); "Jealous Guy" (Lennon); "Instant Karma! (We All Shine On)" (Lennon); "Stand by Me" (Ben E. King, Jerry Leiber, Mike Stoller); "Working Class Hero" (Lennon); "Power to the People" (Lennon); "Oh My Love" (Lennon, Yoko Ono); "Oh Yoko!" (Lennon); "Nobody Loves You (When You're Down and Out)" (Lennon); "Nobody Told Me" (Lennon); "Bless You" (Lennon); "Come Together" (live) (Lennon, Paul McCartney); "New York City" (Lennon); "I'm Stepping Out" (Lennon); "You Are Here" (Lennon); "Borrowed Time" (Lennon); "Happy Xmas (War Is Over)" (Yoko Ono, Lennon); "Woman" (Lennon); "Mind Games" (Lennon); "Out the Blue" (Lennon); "Whatever Gets You through the Night" (Lennon); "Love" (Lennon); "Mother" (Lennon); "Beautiful Boy (Darling Boy)" (Lennon); "Woman Is the Nigger of the World" (Lennon, Yoko Ono); "God" (Lennon); "Scared" (Lennon); "#9 Dream" (Lennon); "I'm Losing You" (*Anthology* version) (Lennon); "Isolation" (Lennon); "Cold Turkey" (Lennon); "Intuition" (Lennon); "Gimme Some Truth" (Lennon); "Give Peace a Chance" (Lennon, Paul McCartney); "Real Love" (*Anthology* version) (Lennon); "Grow Old with Me" (*Anthology* version) (Lennon). Two compact discs. Capitol 094634039123, 2005. Consists of previously released material.

The U.S. vs. John Lennon (Soundtrack). John Lennon vocals, guitar, piano; various assisting instrumentalists and vocalists. "Power to the People" (Lennon); "Nobody Told Me" (Lennon); Working Class Hero" (Lennon); "I Found Out" (Lennon); "Bed Peace" (Lennon, Yoko Ono); "Ballad of John and Yoko" (Lennon, Paul McCartney); "Give Peace a Chance" (Lennon, Paul McCartney); "Love" (Lennon); "Attica State" (live) (Lennon, Yoko Ono); "Happy Xmas (War Is Over)" (Yoko Ono, Lennon); "I Don't Wanna Be a Soldier Mama I Don't Wanna Die" (Lennon); "Imagine" (Lennon); "How Do You Sleep?" (instrumental score) (Lennon); "New York City" (Lennon); "John Sinclair" (live) (Lennon); "Scared" (Lennon); "God" (Lennon); "Here We Go Again" (Lennon, Phil Spector); "Gimme Some Truth" (Lennon); "Oh My Love" (Lennon, Yoko Ono); "Instant Karma! (We All Shine On)" (Lennon). Compact disc. Capitol 094637491225, 2006. Consists of previously released material except for "Attica State" (live) and "How Do You Sleep?" (instrumental).

SINGLES

"Give Peace a Chance" (Lennon, Paul McCartney); "Remember Love" (Yoko Ono). 45-rpm phonodisc. Apple 1809, 1969.
"Cold Turkey" (Lennon); "Don't Worry Kyoko (Mummy's Only Looking for a Hand in the Snow" (Yoko Ono). 45-rpm phonodisc. Apple 1813, 1969.
"Instant Karma! (We All Shine On)" (Lennon); "Who Has Seen the Wind?" (Yoko Ono). 45-rpm phonodisc. Apple 1818, 1970.

"Mother" (Lennon); "Why" (Yoko Ono). 45-rpm phonodisc. Apple 1827, 1970.

"Power to the People" (Lennon); "Touch Me" (Yoko Ono). 45-rpm phonodisc. Apple 1830, 1971. Issued with "Open Your Box" (Yoko Ono) as the B-side in the United Kingdom. "Open Your Box" was later titled "Hirake."

"Imagine" (Lennon); "It's So Hard" (Lennon). 45-rpm phonodisc. Apple 1840, 1971.

"Happy Xmas (War Is Over)" (Yoko Ono, Lennon); "Listen, the Snow Is Falling" (Yoko Ono). 45-rpm phonodisc. Apple 1842, 1971.

"Woman Is the Nigger of the World" (Lennon, Yoko Ono); "Sisters, O Sisters" (Yoko Ono). 45-rpm phonodisc. Apple 1848, 1972.

"Mind Games" (Lennon); "Meat City" (Lennon). 45-rpm phonodisc. Apple 1868, 1973.

"Whatever Gets You through the Night" (Lennon); "Beef Jerky" (Lennon). 45-rpm phonodisc. Apple 1874, 1974.

"#9 Dream" (Lennon); "What You Got" (Lennon). 45-rpm phonodisc. Apple 1878, 1974.

"Stand by Me" (Ben E. King, Jerry Leiber, Mike Stoller); "Move over Ms. L" (Lennon). 45-rpm phonodisc. Apple 1881, 1975.

"Imagine" (Lennon); "Working Class Hero" (Lennon). 45-rpm phonodisc. Apple R-6009, 1975. Issued in United Kingdom only.

"(Just Like) Starting Over" (Lennon); "Kiss Kiss Kiss" (Yoko Ono). 45-rpm phonodisc. Geffen K 79186, 1980.

"Woman" (Lennon); "Beautiful Boys" (Yoko Ono). 45-rpm phonodisc. Geffen K 79185, 1981.

"Watching the Wheels" (Lennon); "Yes, I'm Your Angel" (Yoko Ono). 45-rpm phonodisc. Geffen K 79207, 1981.

"Love" (Lennon); "Give Me Some Truth" (Lennon). 45-rpm phonodisc. Parlophone R 6059, 1982.

"Nobody Told Me" (Lennon); "O'Sanity" (Yoko Ono). 45-rpm phonodisc. Polydor POSP 700, 1984.

"Borrowed Time" (Lennon); "Your Hands" (Yoko Ono). 45-rpm phonodisc. Polydor POSP 701, 1984. Released in the United Kingdom with additional B-side track, "Never Say Goodbye" (Yoko Ono).

"Give Peace a Chance" (Lennon, Paul McCartney); "Cold Turkey" (Lennon). 45-rpm phonodisc. EMI G 45 2, 1984.

"I'm Stepping Out" (Lennon); "Sleepless Nights" (Yoko Ono). 45-rpm phonodisc. Polydor POSP 702, 1984. Released in the United Kingdom with additional B-side track, "Loneliness" (Yoko Ono).

"Every Man Has a Woman Who Loves Him" (Yoko Ono); "It's Alright" (Yoko Ono). 45-rpm phonodisc. Polydor POSP 172, 1984.

"Jealous Guy" (Lennon); "Going Down on Love" (Lennon). 45-rpm phonodisc. Parlophone R 6117, 1985. U.K. release only.

"Jealous Guy" (Lennon); "Give Peace a Chance" (Lennon, Paul McCartney). 45-rpm phonodisc. Capitol B 442230, 1988. U.S. release only.

"Imagine" (Lennon); "Jealous Guy" (Lennon). 45-rpm phonodisc. Parlophone R 6199, 1988. U.K. release only.

"Love" (Lennon); "Stand by Me" (Ben E. King, Jerry Leiber, Mike Stoller). Compact disc single. EMI International 2555, 1999.

Notes

INTRODUCTION

1. The *Billboard* best-seller chart information cited throughout this volume is from Joel Whitburn, *Top Pop Albums, 1955–1996* (Menomonee Falls, WI: Record Research, 1996); and Joel Whitburn, *Top Pop Singles, 1955–1996* (Menomonee Falls, WI: Record Research, 1997).

2. John Lennon, *Testimony: The Life and Times of John Lennon in His Own Words,* Thunder Bolt Compact Disc CDTB 095.

CHAPTER 1

1. There are a vast number of reliable sources for information on Lennon's life. One of the best is Ray Coleman, *Lennon* (New York: McGraw-Hill, 1984).

2. The full account of Lennon's relationship with his father can be found in Pauline Lennon, *Daddy Come Home* (New York: HarperCollins, 1990).

3. This side of Lennon's life is best told in Julia Baird with Geoffrey Giuliano, *John Lennon, My Brother*, foreword by Paul McCartney (New York: Henry Holt, 1988).

4. For articles that approach this undeveloped area of Lennon criticism, see Alun Nash, "John Lennon and the Influence of Lewis Carroll," *Jabberwocky: The Journal of the Lewis Carroll Society* 7 (1978): 36–39; Michael E. Roos, "The Walrus and the Deacon: John Lennon's Debt to Lewis Carroll," *Journal of Popular Culture* 18 (Summer 1984): 19–29; and Iain Ellis, "From Mop-Top to Walrus: Some Funny Sides of The Beatles," *Popmatters.com*.

5. Numerous comments from Lennon himself support this, as can be seen throughout John Lennon and Yoko Ono, *All We Are Saying: The Last Major Interview with John Lennon and Yoko Ono* (New York: St. Martin's Press, 2000).

6. Also much covered in Beatles lore, the insider account of this phase of Lennon's life and career is told in Pete Shotton and Nicholas Schaffner, *John Lennon: In My Life* (New York: Stein and Day, 1983).

7. Paul McCartney has said numerous times that this oft-repeated story is not entirely accurate.

8. Lennon and Ono, *All We Are Saying,* 173.

9. Chris Ingham, *The Rough Guide to the Beatles,* 2nd Edition (New York: Penguin, 2006), 306.

10. Ingham, 306.

11. Another much-documented story of Beatles lore.

12. Thanks to Beatle expert Jim Cummer for clarifying this and other Beatle rumors mentioned herein.

CHAPTER 2

1. January 9, 1975, for those keeping track.

2. This odd little recording is credited to "Musketeer Gripweed and the 3rd Troop," Gripweed being the name of Lennon's character in the film. Lennon used a variety of joking pseudonyms throughout his career, most famously Dr. Winston O'Boogie.

3. In addition to Clapton, the band included Mitch Mitchell on drums and Keith Richards on bass.

4. Bill Harry, *The John Lennon Encyclopedia* (London: Virgin, 2000), 775.

5. In particular, Cage's composition *4′33″*.

6. For the whole story, see *John and Yoko Give Peace a Song,* produced and directed by Alan Lysaght and Paul McGrath. DVD, 1 hr. 40 min. (Canadian Broadcasting Corporation, 2005).

7. John Robertson, *The Art and Music of John Lennon* (Secaucus, NJ: Carol, 1991), 119.

8. Robertson, *Art and Music,* 114.

9. John Robertson, *Lennon: 1940–1980* (London: Omnibus Press, 1995), 74.

10. The credit given on the original release of the *Live Peace in Toronto* album is for Lennon and McCartney; on subsequent releases, Lennon receives sole credit.

11. Chris Ingham, *The Rough Guide to the Beatles,* 2nd Edition (New York: Penguin, 2006), 304–309.

12. Lennon introduces the song that way in *John Lennon Live in New York City,* produced by Gerald Meola; directed by Steve Gebhardt (1972) and Carol Dysinger (1985). 55 min. (Capitol, 1985).

13. Robertson, *Art and Music,* 119.

CHAPTER 3

1. The article that started it all was Maureen Cleave, "How Does a Beatle Live? John Lennon Lives Like This," *London Evening Standard* March 4, 1966; but see also Leonard Gross, "John Lennon: Beatle on His Own," *Look* 30 (December 13, 1966): 58–60 ff.

2. *John Lennon: The Rolling Stone Interview.* Podcast, December 3, 2005 through January 17, 2006, I-tunes; and Jann Wenner, *Lennon Remembers: New Edition* (New York: Verso, 2000), 94–95.

3. Bill Harry, *The John Lennon Encyclopedia* (London: Virgin, 2000), 564.

4. *John Lennon,* podcast; and Wenner, 21.

5. Terry Burrows, *John Lennon: A Story in Photographs* (London: Brown Partworks, 2000), 135.

6. Jerry Hopkins, *Yoko Ono* (New York: Macmillan, 1986), 227.

7. The comment is included in several documentaries, including *John and Yoko's Year of Peace,* produced by Alan Lysaght, directed by Paul McGrath. Videocassette, 52 min. (Canadian Broadcasting Corporation, 2000); and *The U.S. vs. John Lennon,* directed by David Leaf and John Scheinfeld. 1 hr. 45 min. (Lionsgate, 2006).

8. Interestingly, two of *Ram*'s musicians, Hugh McCracken and David Spinozza, would later record with Lennon and Ono.

9. Johnny Rogan, *The Complete Guide to the Music of John Lennon* (London: Omnibus Press, 1997), 57.

10. John Robertson. *Lennon: 1940–1980* (London: Omnibus Press, 1995), 87.

11. Rogan, 153.

12. Robertson, *Lennon,* 87.

13. Lennon reads the statement of support from Congressman Dellums on *The Dick Cavett Show: John Lennon and Yoko Ono.* DVD, 4 hr. (Shout Factory, 2005).

14. The comment occurs in Ono's interview in the March 1969 issue of *Nova.*

15. Robertson, *Lennon,* 87; and John Robertson, *The Art and Music of John Lennon* (Secaucus, NJ: Carol, 1991), 146.

CHAPTER 4

1. For the details, see Jon Wiener, *Gimme Some Truth: The John Lennon FBI Files* (Los Angeles: University of California, 2001); and *The U.S. vs. John Lennon,* directed by David Leaf and John Scheinfeld. Film, 1 hr. 45 min. (Lionsgate, 2006).

2. The insider account for this time of Lennon's life is May Pang and Henry Edwards, *Loving John: The Untold Story* (New York: Warner, 1983).

3. Once again, common knowledge among Beatlemaniacs.

4. John Robertson, *The Art and Music of John Lennon* (Secaucus, NJ: Carol, 1991), 130.

5. Lennon tells the story most completely in *The Mike Douglas Show with John Lennon and Yoko Ono.* DVD, 6 hr. 40 min. (Rhino, 1998).

6. Ringo Starr used several of the same musicians for his *Goodnight Vienna* album sessions as well.

7. Johnny Rogan, *The Complete Guide to the Music of John Lennon* (London: Omnibus Press, 1997), 31.

8. Rogan, 31.

9. The promotional film is included in *Lennon Legend: The Very Best of John Lennon.* DVD, 1 hr. 40 min. (2003).

10. The story is well documented by Lennon's biographers, and Lennon commented on it several times, as early as the 1970 *Rolling Stone* interview and again in the 1975 *Rolling Stone* interview. See Jann Wenner, *Lennon Remembers: New Edition* (New York: Verso, 2000), 89–90; and Pete Hamill, "Long Night's Journey into Day: A Conversation with John Lennon," *Rolling Stone* June 5, 1975.

Chapter 5

1. Such a statement was a staple comment of the last *Double Fantasy* publicity interviews. See, for example, John Lennon, *The Lennon Tapes: John Lennon and Yoko Ono in Conversation with Andy Peebles, 6 December 1980* (London: British Broadcasting Corporation, 2001), 57–61; multiple sections of John Lennon and Yoko Ono, *All We Are Saying: The Last Major Interview with John Lennon and Yoko Ono* (New York: St. Martin's Press, 2000); and recordings made from those and other September through December 1980 interviews.

2. John Robertson, *Lennon: 1940–1980* (London: Omnibus Press, 1995), 105; and John Robertson. *The Art and Music of John Lennon* (Secaucus, NJ: Carol, 1991), 181.

3. Lennon, *Lennon Tapes,* 70.

4. Bill Harry. *The John Lennon Encyclopedia* (London: Virgin, 2000), 546; Robertson, *Art and Music,* 191.

5. This comes from the unsubstantiated memory of one of the authors.

6. Robertson, *Lennon,* 110.

7. Lennon, *Lennon Tapes,* 89.

8. Robertson, *Lennon,* 106.

9. Robertson, *Lennon,* 121.

10. Lennon, *Lennon Tapes,* 89.

11. Robertson, *Art and Music,* 192.

Chapter 6

1. John Robertson, *Lennon: 1940–1980* (London: Omnibus Press, 1995), 120.

2. Johnny Rogan, *The Complete Guide to the Music of John Lennon* (London: Omnibus Press, 1997), 154–155.

3. Robertson, *Lennon,* 109.

4. John Robertson, *The Art and Music of John Lennon* (Secaucus, NJ: Carol, 1991), 192–193.

5. Rogan, 154.

6. Bill Harry, *The John Lennon Encyclopedia* (London: Virgin, 2000), 297.

7. The information related in the upcoming section was obtained by listening to off-air recordings one of the authors made of the series during its original broadcast.

8. As explained and illustrated in various episodes of *The Lost Lennon Tapes.*

9. A step in this direction occurred when the series began being podcast in March of 2007.

Chapter 7

1. John Robertson, *Lennon: 1940–1980* (London: Omnibus Press, 1995), 127.

2. Chris Ingham, *The Rough Guide to the Beatles,* 2nd Edition (New York: Penguin, 2006), 74.

3. Bill Harry, *The John Lennon Encyclopedia* (London: Virgin, 2000), 54–55, 258.

4. Harry, 758.

5. Robertson, *Lennon,* 110.

6. Jerry Hopkins, *Yoko Ono* (New York: Macmillan, 1986), 211, 226.

Annotated Bibliography

Ali, Tariq and Robin Blackburn. "The Lost Lennon Interview." *BeatlesNumber9.com* (n.d.). Accessed February 23, 2007, at http://beatlesnumber9.com/lostlennon. html. The 1971 interview originally appeared in the activist British journal *The Red Mole* and was republished in *CounterPunch*. Lennon is both thoughtful and wary of the lessons the history of radicalism have taught as he considers a range of ideas from rigid Maoism to workers' uprisings.

Allison, Sue. "Strawberry Fields: John Lennon's Song Becomes a Landmark—Forever." *Life* (November 1985): 61–64. An article about the unveiling of the Strawberry Fields area of New York's Central Park dedicated to Lennon.

Alverson, Charles. "Plastic: Wailing with Mrs. Lennon." *Rolling Stone* 51 (February 7, 1970): 13. Review of a UNICEF benefit concert in London in late 1969 that featured Lennon singing "Cold Turkey" with backing by George Harrison, Eric Clapton, Billy Preston, and Delaney and Bonnie.

Arden, Patrick. "Some Time Remains in New York." *Metro* (New York) (December 8, 2005): 2. Summary of Lennon's life in New York City written for the 25th anniversary of his death.

Arnest, Mark. "Ready To Leave Beatles Behind: Lennon's 1st Wife 'in Happy Space' in Her Life." *Gazette* (Colorado Springs, Colorado) (March 17, 2006). Accessed March 17, 2006, at http://www.gazette.com/onset?id=9815&template=article. html. Author converses with Cynthia Lennon, who was in the United States to promote her book *John*.

Austin, Anthony. "Soviet Newspapers Comment on Lennon—Death Attributed to 'Pathological Violence' in U.S. Praise Is Lavished on the Beatles." *New York Times* (December 14, 1980): 42. The reaction to Lennon's death in the Soviet Union of the Cold War era.

Badman, Keith. *The Beatles after the Breakup, 1970–2000*. London: Omnibus, 1999.

Bailey, Rosemary. "Lennon Biographer Defends Controversial Tome." *Ann Arbor News* (September 17, 1988): B1–B2. An article about Goldman's justification for his Lennon book.

Baird, Julia with Geoffrey Giuliano. *John Lennon, My Brother.* Foreword by Paul McCartney. New York: Henry Holt, 1988. Insightful perspective on Lennon by one of his three younger half sisters, including life in the household of Lennon's mother Julia in the 1950s.

Bangs, Lester. "Thinking the Unthinkable about John Lennon." *Los Angeles Times* (December 11, 1980): VI-3. Less than 72 hours after Lennon's slaying, the author, in an unsentimental piece, suggests that the mourning for Lennon is really a mourning for the Beatles' "moment" and its fans. Bangs is absolutely right except that he is totally wrong.

Barnes, Anthony. "The US vs. John Lennon." *The Independent* (July 17, 2006). Accessed July 17, 2006, at http://news.independent.co.uk/world/americas/article1180239.ece. Short article about the documentary focusing on Lennon's immigration troubles that was released in September 2006.

Barrow, Tony. *P.S. We Love You.* London: Mirror Books, 1982.

Bartimole, John. "John Lennon (October 9, 1940–December 8, 1980)." *Song Hits* (March 1981): 22. An appreciation of Lennon written to acknowledge his death.

Bashe, Philip. "An Expression of Sorrow." *Circus* (January 31, 1981): 36. A tribute to and appreciation of Lennon published by the popular music periodical in response to his passing.

Batterson, David. "Lennon as Lenin." *Creem* (November 1972): 32.

Bauder, David. "Many Still Grapple with Lennon's Death." *Ledger* (Lakeland, Florida) (December 4, 2005). Accessed March 3, 2007, at http://www.theledger.com/apps/pbcs.dll/article?AID=/20051204/NEWS/512040315/1021. Reflections on Lennon's passing by Associated Press music writer. Includes comments from Dolly Parton, Neil Diamond, and Patrick Stump of Fall Out Boy.

Beckley, Timothy Green, ed. *Lennon, Up Close and Personal.* New York: Sunshine, 1980. Quickly written, short biography (full of inaccuracies) prepared within days of Lennon's murder.

Beifus, John. "Memphis Leaders Gave Beatles Icy Reception." *Commercial Appeal* (Memphis, Tennessee) (August 20, 2006). Accessed August 20, 2006, at http://www.tennessean.com/apps/pbcs.dll/article?AID=/20060820/NEWS01/608200359/1006/NEWS. On the occasion of the 40th anniversary of the last Beatles concert in Memphis, the author describes the concert in detail. Lennon was the center of attention due to his "Jesus" remark. The article includes the little-known fact that The Beatles wanted to record the *Revolver* album in Memphis, but Brian Epstein was wary of security and housing options.

Black, Elvira. "John Lennon: New Yorker." *Blogcritics.org* (February 1, 2006). Accessed February 4, 2006, at http://blogcritics.org/archives/2006/02/01/085237.php. Thoughtful op-ed piece that relates encounters with Lennon in New York City. Author is uneasy with the devotion of those who continue to make pilgrimages to Strawberry Fields. Previously posted in *Shithouse Rat* on December 8, 2005.

Blake, John. *All You Needed Was Love: The Beatles after the Beatles.* New York: Perigee, 1981. Fairly detailed account of the individual Beatles during their first decade as solo stars, ending with the immediate aftermath of Lennon's murder. The book doesn't sugar coat any of the foursome's less than savory actions.

Blake, John. "John and Yoko." *Us* (December 8, 1981): 70.

Blangger, Tim. "Imagine Lennon in the Valley." *Morning Call* (Allentown, Pennsylvania) (December 5, 2005): E-1. Musings on whether it was Lennon or a look-alike who frequented parks in Allentown's Lehigh Valley in the late 1970s.

Brasor, Philip. "Yoko Just Can't Keep Her Hands off Her John." *Japan Times* (November 27, 2005). Accessed March 4, 2007, at https://search.japantimes.co.jp/member/member.html?file=fd20051127pb.html. Discussion of Yoko's stewardship of the Lennon legacy and how it is viewed in Japan.

Bream, Jon. "Imagine, After 25 Years...Music Stars Share the Moment They Learned of Lennon's Slaying." *Minneapolis Star-Tribune* (December 8, 2005). Accessed March 4, 2007, at http://www.jsonline.com/story/index.aspx?id=375927&format=print. Memories of the night of Lennon's passing by musical celebrities.

Bresler, Fenton S. *Who Killed John Lennon?* New York: St. Martin's Press, 1989. British barrister unfolds conspiracy plot involving CIA, YMCA, and mind control to assassinate Lennon. The author provides a well-researched and detailed account of the days surrounding Lennon's murder. More sensible than might be expected, but still rife with speculation while making much of random coincidences with thinly supported assertions.

Breslin, Jimmy. "Pray for John, then Point the Finger at D.C." *Daily News* (New York) (December 14, 1980): 3 ff. The author, incorporating personal anecdotes, presents one of the many appeals for gun control that were published in the days after Lennon's murder.

Bronson, Fred. *The Billboard Book of Number One Hits.* New York: Billboard, 1985. The author devotes a full page each to "Whatever Gets You through the Night" and "(Just Like) Starting Over" in his exposition of *Billboard* number-one hits from 1955 to 1985.

Brookhiser, R. "John Lennon: R.I.P." *National Review* (December 31, 1980): 1555. An appreciation of Lennon written on the occasion of his passing.

Brownmiller, Susan. "John and Yoko." *Rolling Stone* 335 (January 22, 1981): 25. The author analyzes the relationship between Lennon and his wife and muses over why he needed her.

Buckley, William F., Jr. "Grief for Lennon." *News Tribune* (Woodbridge, New Jersey) (December 1980). An op-ed piece that analyzes the reaction to Lennon's murder.

Buckley, William F., Jr. "John Lennon's Almanac." *National Review* (April 6, 1971): 391.

Burchill, Julie. "John Lennon? What a Phoney!" *Guardian* (Manchester, England) (December 9, 2000). Accessed March 4, 2007, at http://www.guardian.co.uk/print/0,,4102526-103390,00.html. On the occasion of the 20th anniversary of Lennon's death, the author attempts to dismantle the Lennon legend in a spiteful antihagiographic attack.

Burr, Ty. "A Lennon Love Fest, and an Evocative Tour of the '60s." *Boston Globe* (September 29, 2006). Accessed March 4, 2007, at http://www.boston.com/news/globe/living/articles/2006/09/29/a_lennon_love_fest_and_an_evocative_tour_of_the_60s/. An intelligently written, mostly favorable review of *The U.S. vs. John Lennon* documentary.

Burrows, Terry. *John Lennon: A Story in Photographs.* London: Brown Partworks, 2000. Part of "Icons of Rock" series. The story is half black-and-white photographs (many rarely seen) and half text (consisting of one-page essays covering the range of Lennon's life) in a coffee table book format.

Butler, Robert W. "Historic Documentary or an Anti-War Primer?" *Miami Herald* (October 20, 2006). Accessed October 20, 2006, at http://www.miami.com/ mld/miamiherald/entertainment/movies/15794774.htm. A favorable review by the *Kansas City Star* correspondent of the *U.S. vs. John Lennon* documentary.

Byron, S. "John and Yoko Becoming Unmoored." *Village Voice* (January 18, 1973): 75.

Cameron, Gail. "The Cool Brain behind the Bonfire." *Life* (August 26, 1964): 58–66.

Carlozo, Louis R. "Musician Contributed More than Attitude." *Blade* (Toledo, Ohio) (December 7, 2005): D1. An appreciation of Lennon written on the occasion of the 25th anniversary of his murder.

Carpozi, George. *John Lennon: Death of a Dream.* New York: Manor, 1980. A newsstand paperback quickly published on the occasion of Lennon's killing.

Carroll, Jon and Jon Caulfield. "John Goes One Way, Toronto the Other." *Rolling Stone* 55 (April 2, 1970): 10. A summary of the controversy surrounding the Toronto Peace Festival that was announced by Lennon and Ono and planned for the summer of 1970.

Carroll, Maurice. "Reagan, Visiting New York, Talks with the Cardinal and Top Blacks." *New York Times* (December 10, 1980): 8. The article includes the soon-to-be president's comments on the murder of Lennon.

Cassidy, Martin. "On the 25th Anniversary of John Lennon's Death, Residents Reflect on His Life and Music." *Greenwich Time* (Greenwich, Connecticut) (December 8, 2005): A-1. Interviews with those who had contact with the Lennons, and with other Greenwich, Connecticut, residents whose lives were touched by Lennon.

Castleman, Harry and Walter J. Podrazik. *All Together Now: The First Complete Beatles Discography 1961–1975.* Ann Arbor, MI: Pierian, 1976. The book includes all of Lennon's releases through 1975.

Castleman, Harry and Walter J. Podrazik. *The End of the Beatles?* Ann Arbor, MI: Pierian, 1985.

Catlin, Roger. "John Lennon." In *Rock: The Essential Album Guide,* ed. Gary Graff. Detroit, MI: Visible Ink, 1996: 405–406. A consumer guide to Lennon's releases.

Cepican, Bob and Ali Waleed. *Yesterday ... Came Suddenly.* New York: Arbor House, 1984.

Chapple, Mike. "Row over TV Psychic's Bid To Contact Lennon Spirit." *Daily Post.co.uk* (Liverpool, England) (April 17, 2006). Accessed April 17, 2006, at http://icliverpool.icnetwork.co.uk/0800beatles/0050news/tm_objectid=16 960186&method=full&siteid=50061&headline=row-over-tv-psychic-s-bid-to-contact-lennon-spirit-name_page.html#story_continue. The author speaks with medium Joe Power, who was in Liverpool to visit places frequented by Lennon in his life.

Charters, David. "Lennon—The Last Big Interview." *Daily Post.co.uk* (Liverpool, England) (December 8, 2005). Accessed March 4, 2007, at http://icliverpool. icnetwork.co.uk/0800beatles/0050news/tm_objectid=16459670%26method =full%26siteid=50061%26headline=lennon%2d%2d%2dthe%2dlast%2dbig%2din terview-name_page.html. The remembrances of Andy Peebles, the BBC disc jockey who conducted the last substantial interview of Lennon.

Christgau, Robert. "John Lennon, 1940–1980." *Village Voice* (December 10, 1980): 1–2. The weekly's chief music critic's obituary, tribute to, and appreciation of Lennon.

Christgau, Robert. *Rock Albums of the '70s*. New York: Da Capo, 1981. The critic wrote capsule reviews of *Plastic Ono Band* (A); *Imagine* (A); *Some Time in New York City* (C); *Mind Games* (C+); *Walls and Bridges* (B−); *Rock 'N' Roll* (B−); and *Shaved Fish* (B+).

Christopher, Michael. "UFOs and Chocolate Cake." *Popmatters.com* (December 8, 2005). Accessed February 4, 2006, at www.popmatters.com/music/features/051208-lennon-christopher.shtml. Using extensive quotes from May Pang, who lived with Lennon in the mid-1970s, the author unfolds Pang's part in the Lennon saga, a contribution that has largely been erased.

Clancy, Michael. "John: All Those Years Ago." *am New York* (December 8, 2005): 3. The memories of people in New York City at the 25th anniversary of Lennon's death.

Clancy, Michael. "NYC Remembers." *am New York* (December 9–11, 2005): 3. Local coverage of the gathering in Central Park to commemorate the 25th anniversary of Lennon's death.

Clayton, Marie and Gareth Thomas. *John Lennon: Unseen Archives*. Bath, England: Parragon, 2002. A coffee table biography in photos and text using British newspaper photos from the Beatle years through the solo years.

Cleave, Maureen. "How Does a Beatle Live? John Lennon Lives Like This." *London Evening Standard* (March 4, 1966). Accessed March 4, 2007, at http://www.geocities.com/nastymcquickly/articles/standard.html. This article quotes Lennon extensively on a variety of topics and includes the notorious paragraph about his thinking that The Beatles were more popular than Jesus and that Christianity would fade away.

Cocks, Jay. "The Last Day in the Life." *Time* (December 22, 1980): 18–24. In a tribute cover story, the author gives a broad overview of Lennon's life and career and presents the details of his murder.

Cohan, Jillian. "Local Fans of Lennon Imagine." *Wichita Eagle* (December 8, 2005): 1-A. Wichita residents discuss Lennon's musical legacy.

Coker, Matt. "Strange Days Indeed: The Gipper, Tricky Dick, *American Hardcore*, *The U.S. vs. John Lennon* and Déjà vu All over Again." *www.ocweekly.com* (September 21, 2006). Accessed March 4, 2007, at http://www.ocweekly.com/film/film/strange-days-indeed/25872/. Excellent, culture studies–based article that compares the documentary *The U.S. vs. John Lennon* with the hardcore punk documentary *American Hardcore*, and how both films are connected to Orange County, California.

Coleman, Ray. *Lennon*. New York: McGraw-Hill, 1984. An expansive biography by the former editor of *Melody Maker*.

Coles, Robert. "On the Death of John Lennon." *Mademoiselle* (June 1981): 124.

Collins, Paul. "John Lennon: The Dream Is Over." *icLiverpool.co.uk* (February 6, 2006). Accessed February 6, 2006, at http://icliverpool.icnetwork.co.uk/0800beatles/0050news/. A thoughtful essay that notes the contradictions in Lennon's life, the wide range of his music creations, and provides an argument for "In My Life" as the best Beatles' song.

"A Comedy of Letters." *Times Literary Supplement* (March 26, 1964): 35. A review of Lennon's book *In His Own Write*.

Compton, Todd. "McCartney or Lennon: Beatle Myths and the Composing of the Lennon-McCartney Songs." *Journal of Popular Culture* 22 (Fall 1988):

99–131. The author discusses the myth that Lennon wrote the hard rockers and McCartney wrote the soft ballads.

Connelly, Christopher. "A Survival LP for Yoko Ono: With a Little Help from Some Friends." *Rolling Stone* 434 (November 8, 1984): 53 ff. The author speaks with Yoko Ono about the release of the Lennons' *Milk and Honey: Every Man Has a Woman,* a collection of Ono songs recorded by various artists, and the burden of wearing the mantle of "Mrs. Lennon."

Connolly, Ray. *John Lennon, 1940–1980.* London: Fontana, 1981. A newsstand biography published on the occasion of Lennon's death.

Constantine, Alex. *The Covert War against Rock: What You Don't Know about the Deaths of Jim Morrison, Tupac Shakur, Michael Hutchence, Brian Jones, Jimi Hendrix, Phil Ochs, Bob Marley, Peter Tosh, John Lennon, the Notorious B.I.G.* Venice, CA: Feral House, 2000.

Coppage, N. "The Ex-Beatles: Surmounting the Aftermath." *Stereo Review* (March 1974): 88.

Corbin, Carole Lynn. *John Lennon.* Chicago: Franklin Watts, 1982.

Corbyn, Zoe. "Where Were You the Day Lennon Died?" *Guardian* (Manchester, England) (December 8, 2005). Accessed March 4, 2007, at http://arts.guardian.co.uk/features/story/0,,1661857,00.html. Prominent art scene Londoners remember the impact of hearing of Lennon's assassination.

Cott, Jonathan. "A Conversation." *Rolling Stone* 335 (January 22, 1981): 37–39. For what was to be a *Rolling Stone* cover story about Lennon's return to music, the author and the artist had a long talk on December 5, 1980.

Cott, Jonathan. "The Eggman Wears White." *Rolling Stone* (September 14, 1968): 1.

Cott, Jonathan. "John Lennon Talks." *Vogue* (March 1969): 170–171 ff. The author conducts a long interview that covers Lennon's Beatles' compositions, Bob Dylan, India, and the *Two Virgins* album cover. The interview took place at the time of the recording of the White Album.

Cott, Jonathan and Christine Doudna, eds. *The Ballad of John and Yoko.* Garden City, NY: Doubleday/Rolling Stone Press, 1982.

Crossland, David. "The Stars in St. Pauli: Hamburg's Heady Days of Rock & Roll." *Spiegel* (February 15, 2006). Accessed February 15, 2006, at http://www.spiegel.de/international/0,1518,400870,00.html. The author speaks with Horst Fascher, who founded the Star Club in Hamburg and has published his autobiography, *Let the Good Times Roll.*

"Los Cubanos Recuerdan a John Lennon." *BBCMundo.com* (December 20, 2005). Accessed February 4, 2006, at http://news.bbc.co.uk/go/pr/fr/-/hi/spanish/learn_english/newsid_4522000/4522820.stm. Short note about a tribute concert held in John Lennon Park in Havana to commemorate the 25th anniversary of his passing.

Curiel, Jonathan. "Art and Politics Frightened the FBI: Lennon Most Notable Example of Government Monitoring Celebrities." *San Francisco Chronicle* (September 24, 2006). Accessed September 24, 2006, at http://sfgate.com/cgi-bin/article.cgi?file=/c/a/2006/09/24/INGQ3LAA3E1.DTL. Using the documentary *The U.S. vs. John Lennon* as a launchpad, the author highlights other examples of artists who have been persecuted by the U.S. government, including Pete Seeger, Charlie Chaplin, and Pablo Picasso.

Dalton, David. "Rock and Roll Circus." *Rolling Stone* 54 (March 19, 1970): 36–39.
A firsthand account of the Rolling Stones' BBC-TV special from December 1968
that had not yet aired at the time of the article. Lennon and friends performed
"Yer Blues."

Danton, Eric R. "Lennon Recalled as Bono Powers U2." *Hartford Courant*
(December 8, 2005). Accessed March 4, 2007, at http://www.u2achtung.
com/01/articles/article.php?id=138. Concert review of U2 show notes the
lead singer's nods to Lennon on the anniversary of his death.

Davies, Hunter. "For the Record." *Guardian* (Manchester, England) (December
8, 2005). Accessed March 4, 2007, at http://arts.guardian.co.uk/features/
story/0,11710,1662006,00.html. The author, who wrote the only authorized
biography of The Beatles, sets the facts straight about Lennon's opinion of the
book.

"Davies Relates to Lennon after Shooting." *Contactmusic.com* (January 31, 2006).
Accessed March 4, 2007, at http://www.contactmusic.com/new/xmlfeed.
nsf/mndwebpages/davies%20relates%20to%20lennon%20after%20shooting_
31_01_2006. Ray Davies of the Kinks speaks of his shooting experience in New
Orleans and comments on the pain Lennon would have gone through.

Davies, Rod. "All He Was Saying Is Give Peace a Chance." *Texas Observer* (December
26, 1980): 2. An appreciation of Lennon written on the occasion of his
murder.

Davis, T. N. "Of Many Things: Beatle John Lennon's Statement." *America* 115
(August 20, 1966): 164. The author, editor-in-chief of the Jesuit periodical,
basically agrees with Lennon's assertion that popular music artists were more
popular with youth than the Christian religion.

DeCurtis, Anthony. *Rocking My Life Away: Writing about Music and Other Matters.*
Durham, NC: Duke University Press, 1998. The author is a contributing editor
at *Rolling Stone* magazine. The collection of essays includes "Plastic Ono Band/
John Lennon" written in 1987 for *Rolling Stone* as part of a feature on the
100 best albums of the past 20 years and another titled "John Lennon: The
Man," also written for *Rolling Stone* on the occasion of the 10th anniversary of
Lennon's death.

DeGuisti, Tony. "End of an Odyssey." *Oklahoma Observer* (January 10, 1981): 6.
Thoughts on the passing of Lennon and the end of an era.

DeLuca, Dan. "When John Lennon Rattled Richard Nixon." *Philadelphia Inquirer*
(September 29, 2006). Accessed September 29, 2006, at http://www.philly.
com/mld/inquirer/entertainment/weekend/15633161.htm. The author
asserts that, despite the failings of the creators of the documentary *The U.S. vs.
John Lennon,* Lennon himself makes the film a success.

DeLuca, Dan. "Yoko Ono Brings Some of Lennon's Art Here." *Philadelphia
Inquirer* (June 2, 2006). Accessed June 2, 2006, at http://www.philly.com/
mld/inquirer/entertainment/weekend/14719301.htm. For the exhibit "In
My Life: The Artwork of John Lennon," presented in suburban Philadelphia,
the author conducts a telephone interview with Yoko Ono about her role in
sharing Lennon's legacy.

Denberg, Jody. "When Hearts Are Trumps: 'Milk and Honey,' John Lennon and
Yoko Ono." *Record* 3 (May 1984): 54–56. A review of the posthumously
released album.

DeWitt, David and Tara Mulholland. "Web-Only Guide: Lennon Lore and More." *International Herald Tribune* (February 9, 2006). Accessed February 9, 2006, at http://www.iht.com/articles/2006/02/08/features/lennonweb.php. A brief, annotated listing of Web sites and books about Lennon and his music.

The Dick Cavett Show: John Lennon and Yoko Ono. 4 hr. Shout Factory. 2005. DVD. This collection contains all three appearances the couple made on Cavett's talk show in their completion. The original interview was edited to fit into two different shows, so it is presented unedited as well as on the DVD. Cavett provides his memories in newly filmed introductions. During the third show, Lennon performs "Woman Is the Nigger of the World."

"Discography." *Rolling Stone* 335 (January 22, 1981): 68. A listing of all authorized studio recordings (singles, albums, EPs) that Lennon performed on from June 1961 to November 1980.

"The Doctor Who Pronounced John Lennon Dead Remembers That Night." Associated Press online news wire service (December 2005). Accessed March 4, 2007, at http://www.kfor.com/global/story.asp?s=4199249&ClientType= Printable. A short article recalling what happened to medical records and linens.

Donald, D. K. "Anatomy of a Bed-In." *Montrealer* (July–August 1969): 28. Local coverage of the Lennons' peace efforts in Canada.

Doncaster, Patrick. *Tribute to John Lennon.* London: Mirror Books, 1980. A biography of Lennon quickly published on the occasion of his death.

Doney, Malcolm. *Lennon and McCartney.* London: Omnibus, 1982.

Du Noyer, Paul. *John Lennon: Whatever Gets You through the Night.* New York: Thunder's Mouth Press, 1999.

Dupont, David. "Why Lennon Mattered." *Sentinel-Tribune* (Bowling Green, Ohio) (December 8, 2005). The author contemplates Lennon's contribution to the world of music today.

Durchholz, Daniel. "World Keeps Spinning, But It's Poorer for John Lennon's Death." *Post-Dispatch* (St. Louis, Missouri) (December 7, 2005). Accessed March 5, 2007, at http://english.cri.cn/ce_critoday/archieves/2005/12/07/ news/World%20Keeps%20Spinning.htm. An appreciation of Lennon and what he might have brought to the world if he lived.

Edgers, Geoff. "Imagine Lennon as Himself, Not an Icon." *Boston Globe* (December 7, 2005). Accessed February 4, 2006, at http://www.boston.com/ae/music/ articles/2005/12/07/imagine_lennon_as_himself_not_an_icon/. Imagine if Lennon had lived: what would he have said about the U.S. response to Hurricane Katrina? What producers would he have worked with?

Elliott, Anthony. *The Mourning of John Lennon.* Berkeley: University of California Press, 1999.

Ellis, Francis L. "A Meditation on John Lennon." *San Francisco* (January 1981): 7. Thoughts of Lennon written on the occasion of his passing.

Ellis, Iain. "From Mop-Top to Walrus: Some Funny Sides of The Beatles." *Popmatters. com.* Accessed March 4, 2007, at http://www.popmatters.com/pm/columns/ article/6706/from-the-mop-top-to-the-walrus-some-funny-sides-of-the- beatles/. The author posits that The Beatles' (especially Lennon's)sometimes surreal humor is a form of rebellion.

Eltman, Frank. "Fans Mark Anniversary of Lennon's Murder." Associated Press online news wire service (December 8, 2005). Accessed March 4, 2007, at

http://www.happynews.com/news/1282005/fans-mark-lennon-anniverary-
.htm. Verbal snapshots of the activities of those gathered to remember the
anniversary of Lennon's death.

Eremo, J. "In Memory of John Lennon." *Guitar Player* (October 1981): 14. An
appreciation of Lennon.

Ervolino, Bill. "Icon's Murder Is Just as Senseless 25 Years Later." *Blade* (Toledo,
Ohio) (December 7, 2005): D1. A profile of Lennon written on the anniversary
of his death.

Evans, M. Stanton. "Lennon and the Gun Controllers." *Human Events* 41 (January
10, 1981): 7. An article about the renewed call for gun control in the wake of
Lennon's murder.

Evans, Paul. "John Lennon (with Yoko Ono)." In *The Rolling Stone Album Guide,*
eds. Anthony DeCurtis and James Henke with Holly George-Warren. New
York: Random House, 1992: 419–420. A short review of Lennon's solo output
released through 1990.

Evans, Peter. "The Breakup of the Beatles and the Buildup of Their Wives."
Cosmopolitan (February 1972): 122.

Fallon, Beth. "Wounded Memories of the Millions." *Daily News* (New York)
(December 10, 1980): 24. An almost stream-of-consciousness op-ed piece
written in reaction to the murder of Lennon. The shooting rekindled memories
of the dark side of the 1960s for the author.

Farrell, William E. "About New York: Mourners Come and Go to Sad Tones of
Beatles' Music." *New York Times* (December 10, 1980): B6. An observant
snapshot of those gathered around the Dakota in the hours after Lennon's
slaying.

Fawcett, Anthony. *John Lennon: One Day at a Time: A Personal Biography of the Seven-
ties.* New York: Grove Press, 1976. Revised 1980, 1981. The author was a personal assistant to the Lennons in the late 1960s and 1970. He provides a unique
point of view (as a Lennon staffer) of the twilight years of The Beatles. He also
explores (with varying success) what makes the creative Lennon tick, in episodes
dealing with the birth of the song "Instant Karma!" and Lennon's decision and
indecision about whether to play the Toronto Rock and Roll Revival in 1969.

Ferguson, Andrew. "Slimy Portrait of an Ex-Beatle." *Wall Street Journal* (October
21, 1988): A13. A negative review of the Goldman biography.

Ferris, Timothy. "Lennons' Concert: NY Benefit Nets a Quarter Million." *Rolling
Stone* 118 (September 28, 1972): 6. A review of the August 30, 1972, benefit
concert at Madison Square Garden that featured the Lennons.

Fink, Mitchell. *The Last Days of Dead Celebrities.* New York: Miramax, 2006.
Accessed July 11, 2006, at http://www.abcnews.go.com/GMA/Books/
story?id=2165256&page=1. One chapter is about Lennon. The narrative covers
the Lennons' time in New York City. The comments from photographer Bob
Gruen and Yoko Ono spokesperson Elliot Mintz are the most useful parts.

Finlayson, Ann. "Volumes of Virulence." *MacLean's* 101 (October 17, 1988): 42. The
author discusses Albert Goldman's paranoia over the reaction to his biography
of Lennon.

Finn, Timothy. "Collecting Lennon for Christmas." *Kansas City Star* (December
8, 2005). Accessed March 5, 2007, at http://ccadp.proboards40.com/index.
cgi?board=victims&action=display&thread=1134041342&page=3. An article

about Lennon-related CDs, books, DVDs, and memorabilia available for the holiday season.

Finn, Timothy. "Dream, Was It Just a Dream?" *Kansas City Star* (December 8, 2005). Accessed March 5, 2007, at http://ccadp.proboards40.com/index.cgi?board= victims&action=display&thread=1134041342&page=3. A short, thoughtful essay about the meaning of Lennon written for the anniversary of his death.

"The 500 Greatest Songs of All Time: 'Imagine'." *Rolling Stone* 963 (December 9, 2004): 68. Lennon's "Imagine" is ranked number three among *Rolling Stone* magazine's top 500 songs of all time.

Flake, Carol. "Message from the Eggman." *Village Voice* (September 3, 1979): 66. A reaction to the open letter the Lennons published in newspapers in New York, London, and Tokyo.

Flippo, Chet. "For the Record." *Rolling Stone* 335 (January 22, 1981): 18 ff. The author recounts the Lennon shooting announcements to the press by the emergency room director at midnight and by the chief of detectives at 2:00 A.M.

Flippo, Chet. "Imagine: John Lennon Legal." *Rolling Stone* 221 (September 9, 1976): 14. A report about the court decision allowing Lennon permanent residency.

Flippo, Chet. "Lennon in Court Again: $42 Million of Old Gold." *Rolling Stone* 210 (April 8, 1976): 12 ff. A summary report about Morris Levy's lawsuit against Lennon over the *Rock 'N' Roll* album.

Flippo, Chet. "Lennon's Lawsuit: Memo from Thurmond." *Rolling Stone* 192 (July 31, 1975): 16. A report on Lennon's lawsuit against former Attorney General John Mitchell for interfering with the artist's attempt to stay in the United States.

Flippo, Chet. "The Private Years." *Rolling Stone* 380 (October 14, 1982): 38–40 ff. An excerpt from *The Ballad of John and Yoko* by the editors of *Rolling Stone*. The emphasis is on a Tokyo trip taken by the couple and Elliot Mintz.

Flippo, Chet. "Radio: Tribal Drum." *Rolling Stone* 335 (January 22, 1981): 19. Using the example of disc jockey Vin Scelsa, who was on the air at WNEW-FM in New York City at the time of Lennon's death, the author explains how radio stations across the country became centers of community as listeners learned of the shooting.

Fogo, Fred. *"I Read the News Today": The Social Drama of John Lennon's Death.* Lanham, MD: Rowman & Littlefield, 1994. Sociologist teases out the meaning of the journalism regarding Lennon's death and its relationship to the passing of the sixties generation.

Fong-Torres, Ben. "Christ, They Know It Ain't Easy." *Rolling Stone* (July 26, 1969): 8. A summary of the controversy over the release of "The Ballad of John and Yoko" due to the use of the word *Christ* in the lyric.

Fong-Torres, Ben. "Lennon's Song: The Man Can't F**k Our Music." *Rolling Stone* 76 (February 18, 1971): 1 ff. The author writes of how most FM stations around the country are not airing "Working Class Hero" due to Lennon singing the word *fucking* twice in the lyrics.

Fong-Torres, Ben. "Ringo Starr Was in the Crowd; John and Yoko Stayed in Bed." *Rolling Stone* (July 29, 1976): 9. The article includes a brief note about the Lennons not showing up at the Paul McCartney and Wings concert at Madison Square Garden in New York City.

Forrest, John. "Yellow Matter Custard and the Brilliance of Lennon." *Nanaimo News Bulletin* (British Columbia) (June 1, 2006). Accessed June 1, 2006, at

http://www.nanaimobulletin.com/portals-code/list.cgi?paper=51&cat=47&
id=660252&more=). While learning to play "I Am the Walrus" on accordion,
the author discusses the qualities of the song.

Foss, Karen A. "John Lennon and the Advisory Function of Eulogies." *Central States Speech Journal* 34 (1983): 187–194. The author analyzed the exhortative and encouraging tone of eulogies given in the wake of Lennon's death.

Frankel, Glenn. "And She Loved Him: Cynthia Lennon Pens a Memoir of Her Beatle." *Washington Post* (October 3, 2005). Accessed March 4, 2007, at http://www.washingtonpost.com/wp-dyn/content/article/2005/10/02/AR2005100201301_pf.html. The author has a candid conversation with Lennon's first wife as she returns to Liverpool for a book signing.

Fremont-Smith, Eliot. "A Death in the Family." *Village Voice* (December 17, 1980): 61. An appreciation of Lennon written on the occasion of his passing.

Fricke, David. "Live! Twenty Concerts that Changed Rock & Roll: John Lennon and the Plastic Ono Band, Varsity Stadium, Toronto, September 13th, 1969." *Rolling Stone* 501 (June 4, 1987): 67 ff. The Plastic Ono Band performance at the rock and roll revival concert is included among *Rolling Stone* magazine's greatest live shows.

Fricke, David. "Yoko Ono." *Rolling Stone* 512 (December 10, 1987): 53–54. An interview with Yoko Ono about the Lennons' involvement in the peace movement.

Fricke, David and Jeffrey Ressner. "Imaginary Lennon: The True Story behind Albert Goldman's Character Assassination of John Lennon." *Rolling Stone* 537 (October 20, 1988): 42–44 ff. An extensive defense of Lennon against the accusations presented in the Goldman biography.

Frost, David. "John's Gospel." *The Spectator* 7207 (August 12, 1966): 198–199. The author finds Lennon's remarks about the popularity of The Beatles versus Christianity to be refreshing and challenging.

Garbarini, Vic and Brian Cullman with Barbara Graustark. *Strawberry Fields Forever: John Lennon Remembered*. New York: Bantam, 1980. A quickly prepared biography of Lennon with input from *Newsweek* reporter Graustark, who interviewed Lennon in the months before his death.

Garbarini, Vic and Barbara Graustark. "John Lennon." *Musician, Player and Listener* (March 1981): 56. An appreciation of Lennon written on the occasion of his murder.

Garry, Len. *John, Paul & Me before the Beatles: The True Story of the Very Early Days*. London: Collector's Guide, 1997.

Gates, David et al. "Lennon: The Battle over His Memory." *Newsweek* (October 17, 1988): 64–73. The author discusses the controversy over the Goldman biography and the mythmaking in the film biography *Imagine*.

Geffen, David. "A Reminiscence." *Rolling Stone* 335 (January 22, 1981): 59 ff. The owner of the Lennons' record label writes of convincing the couple to sign with his fledgling company in 1980 and of comforting Yoko Ono at Roosevelt Hospital on the night of her husband's murder.

Geringer, Ken. *Nobody Told Me: From Basement Band to Jack and the John Lennon Sessions*. New York: Hipway, 2002.

Germain, David. "Tracing Lennon's Path to Peace: Film Shows Evolution from Flippant Rocker to Passionate Activist." *Charlotte Observer* (October 29, 2006). Accessed October 29, 2006, at http://www.theeveningbulletin.com/site/news.

cfm?newsid=17191934&BRD=2737&PAG=461&dept_id=576361&rfi=6. A favorable review by the Associated Press correspondent of the *U.S. vs. John Lennon* documentary with quotes from Yoko Ono.

Gewen, Barry. "Stepping on a Beatle." *New Leader* 71 (December 12, 1988): 18–19. The author presents a negative review of the Goldman biography.

Giles, Jeff. "Lennon Lives." *Newsweek* (November 29, 2005). Accessed March 4, 2007, at http://www.msnbc.msn.com/id/10115403/site/newsweek/. A wrap-up of the struggles that have gone on over the past 25 years between Lennon's widow, his ex-wife, his sons, employees, biographers, and former band mates.

Gilmore, Mikal. "Lennon Lives Forever." *Rolling Stone* 989 (December 15, 2005): 56–58 ff. A well-written 6,600-word summary of the life and death of Lennon and the impact of each on contemporary culture.

Gimme Some Truth: The Making of John Lennon's "Imagine" Album. Produced and directed by Andrew Solt. 73 min. Andrew Solt Productions. 1999. DVD. Intriguing documentary shows Lennon at work on the *Imagine* album. Lennon's humor, anger, frustrations, joys, and talents are all apparent, and are fascinating viewing. Highlights include his interactions with George Harrison and Phil Spector.

Gitlin, Todd. "John Lennon Speaking." *Commonweal* 96 (September 22, 1972): 500–503. The author discusses the Jann Wenner interview with Lennon from a culture studies point of view. The author is critical of Wenner's interviewing skills but states that Lennon's candidness made the interview an excellent piece.

Gitlin, Todd. "John Lennon's Legacy." *The Center Magazine* (May–June 1981): 2–4.

Giuliano, Geoffrey. *Lennon in America.* New York: Cooper Square Press, 2000.

Giuliano, Geoffrey. *Two of Us: John Lennon & Paul McCartney Behind the Myth.* New York: Penguin, 1999.

Giuliano, Geoffrey and Vrnda Devi. *The Lost Beatles Interviews.* New York: Cooper Square, 2002. The book includes interviews with Lennon, Yoko Ono, and Lennon's family members and associates. The author plays fast and loose with the facts in the interviews he conducts.

Giuliano, Geoffrey and Brenda Giuliano. *The Lost Lennon Interviews.* Holbrook, MA: Adams Media, 1996. A bit overladen with repetitive interviews from the bed-ins, but more than worthwhile for the rest, including some telling interviews with Lennon's family members.

Glassman, Bruce S. *John Lennon and Paul McCartney: Their Magic and Their Music.* Farmington Hills, MI: Gale Group, 1995.

Gogerly, Liz. *John Lennon: Voice of a Generation.* Chicago: Raintree, 2002.

Goldman, Albert H. "John and Yoko's Troubled Road." *People Weekly* (August 22, 1988): 70–78 ff. The second half of excerpts from Goldman's biography of Lennon.

Goldman, Albert H. *The Lives of John Lennon.* New York: William Morrow, 1988. The wide-ranging, ambitious biography by the late author who was sometimes too spiteful for his own good. Controversial upon publication, some of the author's revelations have since been substantiated.

Goldman, Albert H. "John Lennon: In the Hard Day's Light." *People Weekly* (August 15, 1988): 68–69 ff. The first half of excerpts from Goldman's biography of Lennon.

Goldman, Julia. "The Two Women Who Broke Up the Beatles." *McCall's* 98 (July 1971): 72–73 ff. The author presents a biographical piece about Yoko Ono and Linda Eastman with a focus on the affairs and marriages.

Goldmine, Editors of. *The Beatles Digest.* Iona, WI: Krause, 2000. The compilation of articles includes Gillian G. Gaar's "Love Calls: The Inside Story of John Lennon and Yoko Ono Week on *The Mike Douglas Show*"; William Ruhlmann's "John Brower, Promoter of Toronto Lennon Concert, Says Goldman's Book Got It All Wrong"; Dave Thompson's "Just a Pair of *Pussy Cats:* The Lennon/Nilsson Collaboration"; Gillian G. Gaar's "It Was 20 Years Ago Today ... The (Ex-) Beatles in 1974"; and Rick Whitesell's "John Lennon (1940–1980)."

Gonick, Jean. "A Rubber Soul Was Saved by St. Lennon." *San Francisco Chronicle* (December 24, 2005). Accessed February 4, 2006, at http://sfgate.com/cgi-bin/article.cgi?file=/c/a/2005/12/24/DDG4SGC9S61.DTL. An amusing reminiscence (related to the holiday season) written by a Catholic, female Beatlemaniac.

Goodman, Ellen. "Lennon Made a Life Late and Died Early." *Los Angeles Times* (December 12, 1980): II–11. An appreciation of Lennon written in response to his murder.

Goodwin, Karin. "Lennon Movie Leaves Little to the Imagination." *Sunday Times* (Scotland) (August 13, 2006). Accessed March 5, 2007, at http://ono.proboards15.com/index.cgi?board=LENNON&action=display&thread=1156867361. Mixed review of *The Killing of John Lennon* documentary with quotes from director Andrew Piddington.

Goodykoontz, Bill. "Give Grief a Chance: Coverage Gave Us Time To Reflect." *Arizona Republic* (December 4, 2005). Accessed March 4, 2007, at http://www.azcentral.com/arizonarepublic/ae/articles/1204lennon1204goody.html. A discussion of how the Internet and cable television would have changed the reaction to Lennon's murder.

Gordon, Andrew M. "Lennon's Leaping Whimsey." *Jazz and Pop* (March 1969): 45.

Gorov, Lynda. "They Say They Filmed an Evolution." *Boston Globe* (September 24, 2006). Accessed September 24, 2006, at http://www.boston.com/news/globe/living/articles/2006/09/24/they_say_they_filmed_an_evolution/. The author interviews David Leaf and John Scheinfeld, the creators of the documentary *The U.S. vs. John Lennon,* about the process and the barriers to making the film. They had tried for more than 10 years to get interest, but it was not until after 9/11 that people who could help became interested.

Grant, Peter. "Day the Music Died." *Liverpool Echo* (December 8, 2005). Accessed March 4, 2007, at http://icliverpool.icnetwork.co.uk/0800beatles/0050news/tm_method=full%26objectid=16462976%26siteid=50061-name_page.html. A remembrance of Liverpool's memorial concert for Lennon shortly after he died.

Grant, Peter. "The Night John Died." *Liverpool Echo* (December 8, 2005). Accessed March 4, 2007, at http://icliverpool.icnetwork.co.uk/0800beatles/0050news/tm_method=full%26objectid=16462973%26siteid=50061-name_page.html. The author's discussion at the Cavern Club with Lennon's ex-wife Cynthia and Lennon's ex-lover May Pang.

Graustark, Barbara. "An Ex-Beatle 'Starting Over.'" *Newsweek* (December 22, 1980): 45–46. The author focuses on Lennon's post-Beatles career, drawing on a September 1980 interview and an interview with Yoko Ono after Lennon's death.

Graustark, Barbara. "The Real John Lennon." *Newsweek* (September 29, 1980): 76. An interview spotlighting Lennon's comeback as *Double Fantasy* was weeks from release.

Green, Joey. *Marx and Lennon: The Parallel Sayings.* New York: Hyperion, 2005. Humorous collection of similarly themed or structured quotes from Lennon and Groucho Marx, with Ono and Marx's son Arthur in on the joke. Somewhat flawed by matching acknowledged McCartney lyrics with Groucho witticisms known to have been penned by movie scenarists.

Green, John. *Dakota Days.* New York: St. Martin's Press, 1983. Tales of numerology and tarot cards in the Lennon household in the 1970s. Written by Yoko Ono's card reader.

Greenfield, Meg. "Thinking about John Lennon." *Newsweek* (December 29, 1980): 68. An op-ed piece written in reaction to the slaying of Lennon.

Gross, Leonard. "John Lennon: Beatle on His Own." *Look* 30 (December 13, 1966): 58–60 ff. The author presents a candid, early solo spotlight on Lennon. Includes rarely seen photos and Lennon's remarks on religion, similar to those that brought him a lot of negative publicity earlier in the year.

Grove, Martin A. "'Lennon' Docu Could Score Oscar Nom." (August 30, 2006). Accessed August 30, 2006, at http://www.hollywoodreporter.com/thr/columns/grove_display.jsp?vnu_content_id=1003054830. Good, long interview with David Leaf and John Scheinfeld, who wrote, directed, and produced the documentary *The U.S. vs. John Lennon.*

Gruen, Bob. *John Lennon: The New York Years.* New York: Stewart, Tabori and Chang, 2005. The author photographed the Lennons through most of the 1970s. The book combines his reminiscences with his photographic work.

Gruen, Bob. *Listen to These Pictures: Photographs of John Lennon.* New York: William Morrow, 1985.

"Gunfire Kills John Lennon." *Philadelphia Inquirer* (December 9, 1980): 1A. A report on Lennon's murder.

Haberman, Clyde. "Silent Tribute to Lennon's Memory Is Observed throughout the World." *New York Times* (December 15, 1980): 1. Coverage of the memorials to Lennon in New York's Central Park and in Liverpool, England.

Hamill, Pete. "Long Night's Journey into Day: A Conversation with John Lennon." *Rolling Stone* (June 5, 1975). Accessed December 12, 2006, at http://www.geocities.com/~beatleboy1/dbjl6575.html. Lennon discusses his immigration status, his legal and personal relations with the other Beatles, his life with Ono, and his plans for the future.

Hamill, Pete. "The Death and Life of John Lennon." *New York* (December 22, 1980): 38–50. A long essay, somewhat personal, written in reaction to Lennon's death. The author provides details of his encounters with Lennon and reports on the murder.

Hampton, Wayne. *Guerrilla Minstrels: John Lennon, Joe Hill, Woody Guthrie and Bob Dylan.* Knoxville: University of Tennessee Press, 1986. The author relates the idea and culture of the protest singer to hero worship. Lennon's murder was the impetus behind the work, which first saw light in the author's doctoral dissertation in political science.

Harrington, Richard. "Meeting the Beatle, Again." *Washington Post* (October 7, 1988): B1 ff. An article about the flurry of interest in Lennon caused by the release of the Goldman biography and the *Imagine* documentary.

Harrington, Richard. "Missing Peace: John Lennon's Legal Battles with the U.S." *Washington Post* (September 29, 2006). Accessed September 29, 2006, at http://www.washingtonpost.com/wp-dyn/content/article/2006/09/29/AR2006092900225.html. The author provides a historical framework for the documentary *The U.S. vs. John Lennon*, including a conversation with co-creator David Leaf.

Harris, Bill. "Fifth Beatle Liked Lennon Best." *Toronto Sun* (December 8, 2005). Accessed March 4, 2007, at http://jam.canoe.ca/Music/Artists/L/Lennon_John/2005/12/08/pf-1343427.html. The author focuses on drummer Pete Best's thoughts of Lennon during the solo years and the Lennon legacy.

Harry, Bill. *The Book of Lennon.* London: Aurum, 1984.

Harry, Bill. *The John Lennon Encyclopedia.* London: Virgin, 2000. Mind-bogglingly detailed compendium of Lennon-related information, over 1,000 pages in length.

Harting, Al. "'Turn Me Loose, Mate' Lennon Told Dallas Boy." *Dallas Morning News* (December 14, 1980): 6C. Local reminiscences published on the occasion of the passing of Lennon.

Heatley, Michael. *The Immortal John Lennon, 1940–1980.* Stamford, CT: Longmeadow Press, 1992.

Hendrix, Kathleen. "Beatlemania Reached around the World—Even to the Jungle of Borneo." *Los Angeles Times* (December 12, 1980): II-11. An appreciation of Lennon and The Beatles written on the occasion of his slaying.

Henke, James. *Lennon: His Life and Work.* Cleveland, OH: Rock and Roll Hall of Fame, 2000. The exhibit catalog for the retrospective hosted by the Rock and Roll Hall of Fame to commemorate the 60th anniversary of Lennon's birth.

Henke, James. *Lennon Legend: An Illustrated Life of John Lennon.* San Francisco: Chronicle Books, 2003. The scrapbook format publication (including pockets of reproductions of Lennon souvenirs) is a companion to the special exhibit about Lennon at the Rock and Roll Hall of Fame, where the author is curator. The exhibit commemorated the 60th anniversary of Lennon's birth. Includes a CD of interview segments with Lennon from *The Mike Douglas Show;* the WNEW-FM, New York, radio appearance with Dennis Elsas; the *Playboy* interviews; and a live performance of "Imagine."

Henry III, William. "Authentic Voice of the 60's." *Daily News* (New York) (December 10, 1980): 28. A well-written introduction to a 12-page retrospective put together by the newspaper the day after Lennon's death.

Hicks, Tony. "Out of This World: Séance Attempts To Contact Lennon." *Seattle Times* (April 16, 2006). Accessed March 4, 2007, at http://seattletimes.nwsource.com/html/artsentertainment/2002930687_lennon16.html. A tongue-in-cheek opinion piece about the scheduled séance with Lennon.

Higson, Rosalie. "Play Imagines Lennon's Final Thoughts." *The Australian* (February 13, 2006). Accessed February 13, 2006, at http://www.theaustralian.news.com.au/story/0,20867,18126872-16947,00.html. The author speaks with

Valentine Pelka, who acts as Lennon in the play *And in the End,* which opened in Sydney in March 2006.

Hilburn, Robert. "The Flip Side of 'Lennon' Bio." *Los Angeles Times* (September 3, 1988): IV-1. The music critic's thoughts on the *Imagine* documentary.

Hilburn, Robert. "A Heartless Portrait of Lennon." *Miami Herald* (September 6, 1988): 7C. The *Los Angeles Times*' music critic's negative review of the Goldman biography.

Hilburn, Robert. "John Lennon: No Secret Interior, Just Integrity." *Los Angeles Times* (December 14, 1980): 1. An appreciation by the newspaper's chief music critic written on the occasion of Lennon's slaying.

Hilburn, Robert. "Making Up: McCartney Says in Song What He Wishes He Had Told Lennon." *Philadelphia Inquirer* (April 25, 1982): 7A.

Hinckley, David. "Night that Stopped City Cold." *Daily News* (New York) (December 4, 2005): 38. The reporter talks with Vin Scelsa, who was on the air on New York's flagship FM rock station the night Lennon died.

Hinson, Hal. " 'Imagine': The Artist as Nowhere Man." *Washington Post* (October 7, 1988): B1. A review of the *Imagine* documentary.

Hinson, Mark. "Join Hands and Meet a Beatle." *Tallahassee.com* (April 2, 2006). Accessed April 2, 2006, at http://www.tallahassee.com/apps/pbcs. dll/article?AID=/20060402/COLUMNIST08/604020317/1005/ ENT&template=printart. After the announcement of an upcoming séance, the author provides a mock transcript of Lennon's angry words from the beyond.

Holden, Stephen. "Lennon's Music: A Range of Genius." *Rolling Stone* 335 (January 22, 1981): 64–67 ff. The critic walks through Lennon's recorded output from the days of The Beatles to *Double Fantasy.*

Hopkins, Jerry. "Genitalia Slips Quietly under the Counter." *Rolling Stone* (March 1, 1969): 6. An article about the controversial *Two Virgins* album cover.

Hopkins, Jerry. *Yoko Ono.* New York: Macmillan. 1986. Not surprisingly, Lennon is extensively covered in this grudgingly appreciative but often harshly written biography of Ono.

How I Won the War. Directed by Richard Lester. 1 hr. 50 min. MGM. 2002. DVD. Lennon plays a supporting role in this absurdist antiwar film released in 1967.

Hume, Martha. "Growing with … Grieving for." *Daily News* (New York) (December 14, 1980): Leisure-1 ff. The author, wife of rock critic Chet Flippo, presents a personal essay in reaction to Lennon's death.

"Imagine." *Rolling Stone* 537 (October 20, 1988): 57–61 ff. Photo essay excerpted from Andrew Solt and Sam Egan's companion book to the *Imagine* film.

Imagine. Directed by John Lennon and Yoko Ono. 55 min. Joko Films. 1986. Videocassette. A film Lennon and Ono made to accompany the *Imagine* and *Fly* albums. The production consists of short films for each song that are linked by footage of the couple doing a variety of activities around their home and property. Some of the films are interesting, such as the one for "Imagine" wherein Ono opens the windows in an all-white room as Lennon plays the song on a white piano, and "Crippled Inside," which is visualized as Lennon sitting for a photograph portrait intercut with party footage.

Imagine: John Lennon. Produced by David L. Wolper and Andrew Solt. Directed by Andrew Solt. 1 hr. 46 min. Warner. 2005. DVD. A documentary film done with the cooperation of Lennon's estate. The feature covers his entire life from his parents' meeting until the immediate shock of his killing. Some remarkable moments are captured on film and audio. They present Lennon in every mood from thoughtful and passionate to vindictive and spiteful to an exhausted state. The deluxe edition DVD has footage not seen in movie theaters or in the original video release.

"'Imagine' Tops Favourite Song Survey." *News.Scotsman.com* (December 30, 2005). Accessed February 4, 2006, at http://news.scotsman.com/latest. cfm?id=2478072005. Article about U.K. survey conducted by Virgin Radio. Lennon's song "Imagine" was number one.

"In Praise of John Lennon: The Liverpool Lad as Musician, Husband, Father and Man." *People Weekly* (December 22, 1980): 26–36. The celebrity magazine's profile of Lennon on the occasion of his murder.

Infusino, Divina. "Yoko Ono Is Not Alone." *McCall's* 112 (January 1985): 60 ff. The author speaks with Yoko Ono about her first four years without her husband.

Ingham, Chris. *The Rough Guide to the Beatles,* 2nd Edition. New York: Penguin, 2006. This handy compendium covers a variety of Beatles topics, with a nice section on Lennon's post-Beatles career and other solo activities.

Interview with a Legend: John Lennon. 58 min. Karl Video Corporation. 1981. Videocassette. This rare video is an edited version of the December 9, 1980, broadcast of the *Tomorrow Show* with Tom Snyder on NBC. Snyder introduces Lennon's 1975 appearance on the show, which then plays in slightly edited form. Lennon amiably answers Snyder's questions about Beatlemania and fame before being joined by his lawyer to discuss his immigration troubles. The show then returns to the 1980 segment as Snyder discusses Lennon with *New York Post* columnist Lisa Robinson. Lastly, *Double Fantasy* co-producer Jack Douglas, still in shock only 24 hours after Lennon's murder, tells Snyder of Lennon's mood during his last day.

"Is It Worth a Fab $4M?" *Sydney Morning Herald* (February 1, 2006). Accessed March 4, 2007, at http://www.smh.com.au/news/music/are-beatles-lyrics-worth-4-million/2006/02/01/1138590540354.html. A short article about the auction of Lennon's handwritten lyrics to "A Day in the Life."

Isfeld, Gordon. "Cynthia Lennon: In Her Own Write." *CNN.com* (December 8, 2005). Accessed February 4, 2006, at http://www.cnn.com/2005/ SHOWBIZ/Music/09/28/cynthia.lennon.book/index.html. A review of *John,* the book by Lennon's first wife. Includes comments from Cynthia Lennon speaking about the book at a Foreign Press Association gathering in London.

"'It's a Hard Night,' Says Springsteen." *Philadelphia Inquirer* (December 10, 1980): A14. A review of a Springsteen concert held at the Spectrum in Philadelphia the night after Lennon's murder.

Ivins, Molly. "Lennon and Gun Laws." *Texas Observer* (February 27, 1981): 24.

Jackson, John Wyse. *We All Want To Change the World: The Life of John Lennon.* New York: Haus, 2005. Breezy canonical biography of Lennon, heavy on well-chosen photo illustrations with a good index and thorough citations.

Januszczak, Waldemar. "Albert and Lennon." *Guardian Weekly* (September 25, 1988): 27. An article about the controversy that swirled around the Goldman biography.

Jenkin, Eve. "Psychics Get in Touch with John Lennon." *undercover.com.au* (March 14, 2006). Accessed March 4, 2007, at http://www.undercover.com.au/

news/2006/mar06/20060314_johnlennon.html. Report about an upcoming pay-per-view séance during which psychics will attempt to communicate with Lennon and gather music from him.

Jennings, Nicholas. "The Storm over John Lennon." *MacLean's* 101 (October 17, 1988): 40–43. The author discusses the controversial Goldman biography as well as Lennon's half-sister Julia Baird's biography.

John and Yoko Give Peace a Song. Produced and directed by Alan Lysaght and Paul McGrath. 1 hr. 40 min. Canadian Broadcasting Corporation. 2005. DVD. The story of Lennon's peace anthem and first non-Beatles song release is thoroughly documented by the same team that covered the entire 1969 year in an earlier film. The song's instant absorption into the counterculture is remarkably portrayed. The DVD contains additional interviews not seen in the original 50-minute broadcast.

John and Yoko's Year of Peace. Produced by Alan Lysaght. Directed by Paul McGrath. 52 min. Canadian Broadcasting Corporation. 2000. Videocassette. Lennon and Ono's campaign for peace is put in a sociohistorical context, focusing on global events taking place in 1969. The same team later did a CBC television special about the composition of "Give Peace a Chance."

"John Lennon." In *The New Dakota Dictionary of Skiffle,* eds. Fred Stanley and Keith George. Liverpool, England: Merseytime Press, 1999. An encyclopedia entry about Lennon's skiffle years and its influence on his career, making much of his irreverent humor.

"John Lennon." In *The Penguin Encyclopedia of Popular Music,* ed. Donald Clarke. New York: Viking Penguin, 1989: 696–697. Includes an informative entry about Lennon.

"John Lennon and Yoko Ono." In *The Rolling Stone Encyclopedia of Rock & Roll,* eds. Holly George-Warren and Patricia Romanowski. New York: Fireside, 2005: 557–560. A long, informative entry about Lennon and Yoko Ono.

"John Lennon: Dominant Role in a Pop Music Revolution." *The Times* (London) (December 10, 1980): 17F. An obituary and profile of Lennon.

John Lennon Live in New York City. Produced by Gerald Meola. Directed by Steve Gebhardt (1972) and Carol Dysinger (1985). 55 min. Capitol. 1985. The afternoon show of the One to One concerts is presented, including a few songs performed by Ono that were not available on the simultaneously released album.

John Lennon: The Rolling Stone Interview. Podcast, December 3, 2005–January 17, 2006. I-tunes.

The John Lennon Video Collection. Produced by Martin R. Smith. 1 hr. 17 min. Picture Music International. 1992. Videocassette. A handful of television appearances and promotional films for his songs made by Lennon are included with several newly made films to provide videos for the bulk of Lennon's hits and few of his other recordings. Most welcome are Lennon's experimental film for "Cold Turkey" and his television performances of "Instant Karma! (We All Shine On)," "Imagine," and "Slippin' and Slidin'."

"John Lennon's Death." *Columbus Citizen-Journal* (December 11, 1980). Thoughts on the passing of Lennon.

"John Lennon's Death Memorialized by Atlanta Global Peace Project." *Emediawire. com* (December 8, 2005). Accessed February 4, 2006, at http://www. emediawire.com/releases/2005/12/emw319433.htm   accessed   2/4/06.

A peace organization, Friends of Gandhi-King-Carter, uses the occasion of the anniversary of Lennon's death to promote upcoming events related to their peace project.

"John Lennon's Dream Is Over." *Philadelphia Evening Bulletin* (December 10, 1980): B6. An obituary and profile of Lennon.

"John Lennon's Girl." *XLibris.com* (February 1, 2006). Accessed February 4, 2006, at http://www.primezone.com/newsroom/news.html?d=93270. A review of a book by Janet Celia Waters, who alleges that as a teenager she had a long-running affair with Lennon in Pensacola, Florida.

Kakutani, Michiko. "A Revisionist View of the Odd Life of Beatle John." *New York Times* (August 31, 1988): III-21. A report on the controversial Goldman biography.

Kane, Larry. *Lennon Revealed.* Philadelphia: Running Press, 2005. Former Philadelphia disc jockey during the Beatlemania years reminisces about his relationship with Lennon and includes quotes from many Lennon friends and acquaintances, including his lover May Pang. Includes a DVD with a 1968 interview with Lennon and Paul McCartney and a brief clip of Lennon broadcasting the weather on WPVI-TV, Philadelphia, in 1975.

Kanzler, George. "From World Leaders to Beatles Fans, Millions Mourn Gifted Songwriter." *Star-Ledger* (Newark, New Jersey) (December 10, 1980): 1 ff. Popular music critic covers the reactions to Lennon's death, including those of New Jerseyans Don Kirshner (rock producer) and "Cousin" Bruce Morrow (disc jockey on New York's W-A-Beatle-C in 1964).

Katz, Gregory. "Inside the Dakota." *Rolling Stone* 335 (January 22, 1981): 17 ff. The author relates the experience of Jay Hastings, one of the doormen stationed at the Dakota on the night of Lennon's death.

Kaufman, Murray (the K). "John Was Honest and Brave." *Daily News* (New York) (December 10, 1980): 4. The legendary New York disc jockey who was in the middle of the Beatlemania fray reminisces about Lennon the day after his murder.

Kaye, Laurie, Ron Hummel, and Dave Sholin. "Lennon's Last Interview." *Daily News* (New York) (December 10, 1980): 31. Insightful and poignant excerpts from an RKO Radio Network interview conducted eight hours before Lennon's murder.

Keene, Kerry. "It Was 40 Years Ago Today ... Remembering the Beatles' Final Concert from Candlestick Park." *Contra Costa Times* (California) (August 29, 2006). Accessed August 29, 2006, at http://www.contracostatimes.com/mld/cctimes/news/local/states/california/15387345.htm. A remembrance of the final Beatles performance. Protestors picketed outside because of Lennon's remark about The Beatles being more popular than Jesus.

Keough, Peter. "The Gospel According to Lennon and Marx." *The Phoenix* (September 27, 2006). Accessed September 27, 2006, at http://www.thephoenix.com/article_ektid23774.aspx. The author puts the creators of the documentary *The U.S. vs. John Lennon* on the defensive regarding their politics and their point of view.

Kesey, Ken. "Burned by the Big Eye: On the Passing of John Lennon." *Rolling Stone* 338 (March 5, 1981): 22–25 ff. The author remembers his encounter in London with Lennon at Christmas 1968. He discusses the vulnerability of celebrities before obsessive, dangerous fans.

King, Douglas. "John Lennon: The New York Years." *LibraryJournal.com* (December 13, 2005). Accessed February 4, 2006, at http://www.libraryjournal.com/article/CA6290411.html. A favorable review of the 2005 photo biography by music photographer Bob Gruen.

Kirchherr, Astrid and Klaus Voorman. *Hamburg Days.* Guildford, England: Genesis, 1999.

"Klein: It's Lennon's Peace Festival." *Rolling Stone* 54 (March 19, 1970): 8. A short article about the controversy over the planned Toronto Peace Festival and Lennon's demand for complete control.

Kopkind, Andrew. "I Wanna Hold Your Head: John Lennon after the Fall." *Ramparts* (April 1971): 18.

Kopkind, Andrew. "Lennon without Tears." *SoHo News* (December 17, 1980). A tribute to Lennon written at the time of his murder.

Kordosh, J. "John Lennon, 1940–1980: Nothing To Do To Save His Life." *Creem* (March 1981): 2. A profile and appreciation of Lennon written in response to his killing.

Kornheiser, Tony. "The Beatle We Wanted To Be." *Washington Post* (December 9, 1980): B1. An appreciation of Lennon written at the time of his murder.

Kornhiser, Toni and Tom Zito. "Lennon: Always Up Front." *Washington Post* (December 10, 1980). An obituary and profile of Lennon written at the time of his passing.

Kozinn, Allan. "An Embattled Albert Goldman Defends His Book on Lennon." *New York Times* (September 12, 1988): 17–18. The author speaks with the author of the controversial *The Lives of John Lennon.*

Kozinn, Allan. "Lennon? A Film Joins the Fray." *New York Times* (October 2, 1988): 13 ff. An article about the upcoming release of the *Imagine* documentary.

Kozinn, Allan. "A New Lennon Mystery Tour." *New York Times* (March 20, 1988): 25.

Kramer, Marcia. "George and Paul May Follow Ringo Here." *Daily News* (New York) (December 10, 1980): 4. A local report on the reactions of the remaining Beatles after Lennon's murder.

Kramer, Marcia. "Millions To Mourn for Lennon Today." *Daily News* (New York) (December 14, 1980): 3 ff. A local report on the observances scheduled in honor of Lennon at the time of his passing.

Kroll, Jack. "Strawberry Fields Forever." *Newsweek* (December 22, 1980): 41–44. As part of a tribute issue, the author looks at Lennon's contributions to The Beatles and his attempts to demythologize the pop-star image.

Lapidos, Mark and Carol Lapidos. *A Loving Tribute to John Lennon.* Westwood, NJ: Lapidos Productions, 1981. A newsstand publication prepared for quick release at the time of Lennon's murder.

Lawrence, Ken. *John Lennon in His Own Words.* Kansas City, MO: Andrews McMeel, 2005. A nice collection of aphoristic quotes and pungent commentaries, with citations (though often secondhand)

Lefcowitz, Eric. *Tomorrow Never Knows: The Beatles' Last Concert.* San Francisco: Terra Firma, 1987. This book documents The Beatles' last stage performance held at Candlestick Park in San Francisco on August 29, 1966. It was the end of the beginning and the beginning of the end. The backdrop for the U.S. leg of the 1966 concert tour was Lennon's controversial remarks regarding the popularity of The Beatles versus Jesus. The volume includes many black-and-white photos by rock photographer Jim Marshall.

Lefsetz, Bob. "A Remembrance: In My Life." *The Lefsetz Letter* (December 9, 2005). Accessed February 4, 2006, at http://www.whatgoeson.com/story.20051209. html. An insightful 1,200-word op-ed piece about the importance of Lennon to the youth of the 1960s.

Leigh, Vanora. *John Lennon*. Chicago: Franklin Watts, 1986.

"Lennon Asks for Peace: TV Séance." *Sydney Morning Herald* (April 25, 2006). Accessed April 25, 2006, at http://www.smh.com.au/news/people/lennon-asks-for-peace-tv-seance/2006/04/25/1145861319686.html#. In a pay-per-view séance, mediums claimed that Lennon told them, "Peace, the message is peace."

"The Lennon Connection." *Boston Globe* (December 10, 1980): 18. An appreciation of Lennon written at the time of his slaying.

Lennon, Cynthia. *John*. Foreword by Julian Lennon. New York: Crown, 2005. The author pens another autobiography of life with Lennon with much more frankness and detail, though with some factual lapses as in her previous work.

Lennon, Cynthia. *A Twist of Lennon*. New York: Avon, 1978, 1980. Lennon's first wife's (the former Cynthia Powell and later Cynthia Twist) autobiography (salted with Liverpool [Northern] slang) provides a look at Beatlemania from the point of view of a spouse. Occasionally, the author mixes up the chronology—for example, having The Beatles' first visit to the United States take place in the summer of 1964 after the premiere of *A Hard Day's Night*. The final chapter is simply titled "Yoko Ono." Pen-and-ink illustrations by the author, who met Lennon in art college.

"Lennon Has a Legacy." *Nation* (December 20, 1980): 657. Thoughts on the passing of Lennon.

Lennon, John. *Ai: Japan through John Lennon's Eyes, a Personal Sketchbook*. Foreword by Yoko Ono. San Francisco: Cadence Books, 1992. A collection of often amusing sketches Lennon made for word associations to help him understand Japanese language and culture.

Lennon, John. *Bag One: A Suite of Lithographs*. New York: Lee Nordness Galleries, 1970.

Lennon, John. "Have We All Forgotten What Vibes Are?" *Rolling Stone* 56 (April 16, 1970): 1 ff. Lennon's side of the story regarding the controversy over the proposed Toronto Peace Festival.

Lennon, John. *In His Own Write/A Spaniard in the Works*. New York: Signet, 1964, 1965. Verse and pen-and-ink drawings by the author. *In His Own Write* was published in hardcover in 1964. *A Spaniard in the Works* was published in hardcover in 1965. The Signet edition combines the two works in one paperback.

Lennon, John. *John Lennon: In His Own Words*. New York: Quick Fox, 1981. Compiled by Barry Miles. Designed by Pearce Marchbank. Compilation of excerpts from Lennon's interviews and other communications. Organized chronologically.

Lennon, John. *The Last Lennon Tapes*. New York: Dell, 1983.

Lennon, John. *The Lennon Tapes: John Lennon and Yoko Ono in Conversation with Andy Peebles, 6 December 1980*. London: British Broadcasting Corporation, 2001. Full transcript of three-hour interview by BBC journalist of Lennon and Yoko Ono conducted two evenings before Lennon was shot and killed. Intelligent questions cover full range of Lennon's solo career, with special emphasis on Lennon's approach to songwriting and his growing embrace of feminism. Lennon's interest in and knowledge of then-contemporary Great Britain affairs and his plans to return after almost a decade's absence are especially poignant.

Lennon, John. *Real Love: The Drawings for Sean.* Introduction by Yoko Ono. New York: Random House, 1999. Picture book for children. Graphics are adapted by Al Naclerio from drawings created by the author for his young son.

Lennon, John. *Skywriting by Word of Mouth, and Other Short Works, Including the Ballad of John and Yoko.* Afterword by Yoko Ono. New York: Harper & Row, 1986. Drafted in 1975 and 1976 (most of the sketches come from 1978) but abandoned and unfinished at the time of his death, this primarily consists of short prose pieces with occasional verses plus pen-and-ink drawings by the author, similar to his 1960s volumes.

Lennon, John. *Testimony: The Life and Times of John Lennon in His Own Words.* Thunder Bolt Compact Disc CDTB 095. A CD of the last interview Lennon gave, hours before being killed, conducted by Bob Miles.

Lennon, John and Yoko Ono. *All We Are Saying: The Last Major Interview with John Lennon and Yoko Ono.* New York: St. Martin's Press, 2000. Interviews conducted by David Sheff. Edited by G. Barry Golson. Complete transcript of magazine interview that hit the newsstands two days prior to Lennon's death. Lennon and Ono were ready to talk after years away from the media, and Sheff offered the right prompts in an extensive, in-depth review of Lennon's career. Originally published in 1981 as *The Playboy Interviews with John Lennon and Yoko Ono.*

Lennon, John, Adrienne Kennedy, and Victor Spinetti. *The Lennon Play: In His Own Write.* New York: Simon & Schuster, 1969. Lennon's early writings turned into a play in the style of theater of the absurd.

Lennon Legend: The Very Best of John Lennon. 1 hr. 40 min. 2003. DVD. More or less the DVD version of *The John Lennon Video Collection* yet substantially different, hence the change of title. It is also designed to parallel the CD collection of the same name. Additional numbers have been added, some of the films have been re-edited, and the linking voice commentaries are absent as well. A different television performance of "Instant Karma! (We All Shine On)" replaces the version in the video release. An inexcusable misjudgment: Lennon's exciting and highly energized performance of "Slippin' and Slidin'" for *The Old Grey Whistle Test* has the studio version dubbed over it except for the end.

"Lennon of Beatles Sorry for Making Remark on Jesus." *New York Times* (August 12, 1966): 38. An article covering the press conference in which Lennon said his remarks about the popularity of The Beatles versus Jesus were misunderstood.

Lennon, Pauline. *Daddy Come Home.* New York: HarperCollins, 1990. Reputedly based on a lengthy autobiographical manuscript of Lennon's father and finished by the elder Lennon's widow, this book tells Alfred Lennon's side of the story. He claims he did not abandon John, but rather was thwarted by a conspiracy of the Stanley family to keep him away.

Lennon, Yoko Ono. "In Gratitude." *New York Times* (January 18, 1981): E24. An open letter from Lennon's widow in response to all that happened in the weeks after the shooting of Lennon.

"Lennon's Cheque Sells for £2,000." *News.BBC.Co.UK* (December 14, 2005). Accessed February 4, 2006, at http://news.bbc.co.uk/go/pr/fr/-/2/hi/uk_news/england/hereford/worcs/4529206.stm. A short article noting the auction of a check Lennon had written to the Inland Service. The check was owned by a former madam named Lindi St. Clair, who was known as Miss Whiplash.

"Lennon's Exercise Book for Sale." *U.TV* (December 12, 2005). Accessed February 4, 2006, at http://www.u.tv/newsroom/indepth.asp?id=9644&pt=e. The article notes the auction of a 1952 school book of Lennon that contains eight of his original drawings.

Leonard, John. "Lennon Energized High Art with Pop." *New York Times* (December 14, 1980): II-1. The classical music critic looks at the contributions of Lennon and his fellow Beatles, with a peppering of puns, to high culture.

Leopold, Todd. "Review: Beatles Myth, Beatles Facts." *CNN.com* (December 7, 2005). Accessed February 4, 2006, at http://www.cnn.com/2005/SHOWBIZ/books/12/07/review.beatles/index.html. Mostly favorable reviews of Bob Spitz's *The Beatles* and Tony Bramwell's *Magical Mystery Tours: My Life with the Beatles*.

"Letter from Lennon to Critic of Beatles Sells for Evans for ,12,000." *Belfast Telegraph* (May 25, 2006). Accessed May 25, 2006, at http://www.belfasttelegraph.co.uk/lifestyle/music/story.jsp?story=692562. The article details the contents of a letter written in defense of The Beatles by Lennon in 1971 in response to an article by Craig McGregor of the *New York Times,* who accused the band of exploiting black American music.

"A Library of Lennon." *Post-Dispatch* (St. Louis, Missouri) (December 7, 2005). A summary of recent books focusing on Lennon written on the occasion of the 25th anniversary of his death.

Life, Editors of. *Life: Remembering John Lennon: 25 Years Later.* New York: Life Books, 2005. A magazine-format hardcover with many color photos and reminiscences by some who knew Lennon, including Astrid Kirchherr.

"Liverpool, NYC Remember Lennon." *CNN.com* (December 8, 2005). Accessed March 4, 2007, at http://www.cnn.com/2005/SHOWBIZ/Music/12/08/lennon.tributes/index.html. Comments from Liverpudlians and New Yorkers as tributes are held for Lennon to commemorate the anniversary of his death.

"Liverpool Sings Praises of Its Lost Son." *Liverpool Echo* (December 9, 2005). Accessed February 4, 2006, at http://icliverpool.icnetwork.co.uk/0800beatles/0050news/tm_objectid=16467493&method=full&siteid=50061&headline=liverpool-sings-praises-of-its-lost-son-name_page.html. A cursory survey of activities that took place in Lennon's birthplace to commemorate the 25th anniversary of his murder.

Livingston, Victor. "Lennons' Fortune Estimated at $150M." *Daily News* (New York) (December 10, 1980): 23. The author reports on the investments made by the Lennons during their time in New York.

Lloyd, Eric. "Reading for Pleasure: A Slice of Lennon." *Wall Street Journal* (June 3, 1964): 18. A review of Lennon's first published literary effort *In His Own Write*.

Loder, Kurt. "The Last Session." *Rolling Stone* 335 (January 22, 1981): 67. The author relates producer Jack Douglas's thoughts about the recording session with the Lennons at the Hit Factory on the evening of December 8, 1980.

"The Long and Winding Road." *Louisville Courier-Journal* (December 14, 1980): 12-page supplement. A tribute to Lennon and The Beatles published on the occasion of Lennon's death.

Maass, Alan. "The Pop Star the FBI Declared a 'Threat': John Lennon's Revolution." *Socialist Worker Online* (October 6, 2006). Accessed October 6, 2006, at http://www.socialistworker.org/2006-2/604/604_13_Lennon.shtml. A well-written, politicized, favorable review of *The U.S. vs. John Lennon* documentary.

"Macca on Lennon." *UK.News.Launch.Yahoo.com* (December 9, 2005). Accessed February 4, 2006, at http://uk.news.launch.yahoo.com/dyna/article.html?a=/051209/340/fywbb.html&e=l_news_dm. A report based on Paul McCartney's conversation with Steve Wright of BBC Radio 2.

Majendie, Paul. "Lennon Top Icon for U.S. Rock Photographer." Reuters online news wire service (October 28, 2005). Accessed March 4, 2007, at http://www.signonsandiego.com/news/features/20051028-0607-arts-lennon-photographer.html. Ethan Russell, the rock photographer, remembers his time with The Beatles and the Lennons.

Makela, Janne. *John Lennon Imagined: Cultural History of a Rock Star.* New York: P. Lang, 2004.

Marcus, Greil. "Life and Life Only." *Rolling Stone* 335 (January 22, 1981): 26–27. The author attempts to figure out why Lennon was the target of an assassin, and why it happened at this point in U.S. cultural history.

Marsh, Dave. "Another Open Letter to John." *Rolling Stone* 298 (August 23, 1979): 28. The author admires Lennon for remaining silent while his musical peers embarrass themselves. In light of Lennon's three Beatle band mates performing together at Eric Clapton's recent wedding, Marsh pleads with Lennon to not allow a Beatles reunion.

Marsh, Dave. "Ghoulish Beatlemania." *Rolling Stone* 335 (January 22, 1981): 28–29. The author looks at the role of the U.S. assassination culture in the death of Lennon.

Marsh, Dave. "The Year in Review." *Rolling Stone* (December 25, 1980): 1–6. A sweeping review of the popular music world in 1980, including the return of the Lennons.

Martin, Bernice. "Not Marx but Lennon." *Encounter* 56 (June 1981): 49–51. The author provides an intelligent analysis of the disenchantment with conventional politics and how Lennon's attempt to bring the personal to politics was a refreshing and necessary change.

Martin, Nancie S. *John Lennon, Julian Lennon.* New York: Avon, 1986. A short, newsstand biography of Lennon with emphasis on his relationship with his first son.

Maslin, Janet. "'Imagine: John Lennon': Portrait of a Generation." *New York Times* (October 7, 1988): III–7. A review of the *Imagine* documentary.

Mayer, Allan J. "Death of a Beatle." *Newsweek* (December 22, 1980): 31–36. A report on the last hours and the shooting of John Lennon.

McCabe, Peter and Robert D. Schonfeld. *John Lennon: For the Record.* New York: Bantam, 1984. A 1971 interview with Lennon and Ono as the background for a book about The Beatles. The couple covers a wide range of topics, emphasizing The Beatles' dissolution, with Lennon still in a mood similar to that of his *Rolling Stone* interview the previous year.

McCarry, Charles. "John Rennon's Excrusive Gloupie." *Esquire* (December 1970): 204–205 ff. The author conducted an extensive interview with Lennon and Ono while they were in Los Angeles for primal scream therapy with Arthur Janov. The article provides extensive background on Yoko Ono's growing up in Japan and about the creation of her manuscript *Grapefruit*.

McCracken, Melinda. "Rock and Roll Revival Surprise: John and Yoko." *Rolling Stone* 44 (October 18, 1969): 1 ff. A review of Toronto's September 13, 1969, Rock and Roll Revival concert featuring the Lennons.

McGuigan, Cathleen. "Yoko Ono: A Widow Guards Her Husband's Legacy." *Newsweek* (October 17, 1988): 66–67. A feature article about Lennon's widow's defense against the Goldman biography assault and her role in the production of the *Imagine* documentary.

McKeen, William. *The Beatles: A Bio-Bibliography*. New York: Greenwood, 1989. The work includes an extensive bibliography of the band, including the solo years.

McKenna, Kristine. "Lennon and the Legend." *American Film* 14 (October 1988): 32–37. The author speaks with David Wolper, Andrew Solt, and Yoko Ono about the making of the documentary *Imagine: John Lennon*.

McShane, Larry. "John Lennon's Death Lingers for Witnesses." Associated Press online news wire service (December 4, 2005). Accessed March 4, 2007, at http://www.foxnews.com/story/0,2933,177744,00.html. The reporter focuses on four actors in the tragedy of Lennon's passing: the emergency room doctor who attended to him; the two police officers who were first on the scene of the shooting; and a television producer whose injuries were being attended to when Lennon was brought to Roosevelt Hospital.

Meagher, L. D. "Review: Lennon 'Revealed' and Remembered." *CNN.com* (December 8, 2005). Accessed March 4, 2007, at http://edition.cnn.com/2005/SHOWBIZ/books/12/07/review.lennon/. Reviews of Larry Kane's *Lennon Revealed* and Yoko Ono's *Memories of John Lennon*. The Kane book is given a positive review, but the author is disappointed that Ono does not share much of her memories. He also finds some of the memories are too much in the image of what Ono wants to portray of her late husband.

The Mike Douglas Show with John Lennon and Yoko Ono. 6 hr. 40 min. Rhino. 1998. DVD. All five shows in their complete form from the week Lennon and Ono cohosted the show are presented. The duo performs a variety of songs and answers a wide range of questions about their beliefs and their life stories.

Milton, Pat (Associated Press). "Vigil for John Lennon." *Metro* (New York) (December 9–11, 2005): 2. Local coverage of the gathering in Central Park to commemorate the 25th anniversary of Lennon's death.

Mitchell, Jack. "A Final Record." *New York Times* (December 8, 2005). Accessed March 4, 2007, at http://www.rense.com/general69/jandyok.htm. An op-ed piece by the New York celebrity photographer. The author shares his memories of a photo session with Lennon and Yoko Ono about a month before Lennon's death.

Moore, Frazier (Associated Press). "Cavett DVD Recalls Talks with Lennon." *Sentinel-Tribune* (Bowling Green, Ohio) (November 17, 2005): 8. Coverage of new DVD featuring 1970s interviews of Lennon and Yoko Ono by late-night talk show host Dick Cavett.

Morris, Jan. "Britain's Finest Hour." *Rolling Stone* 335 (January 22, 1981): 22. How Lennon and The Beatles saved the Empire from its World War II doldrums, though things fell apart again.

Morse, Steve. "Musicians Recall the Lennon They Knew." *Boston Globe* (December 8, 2005). Accessed March 4, 2007, at http://www.boston.com/ae/books/articles/2005/12/08/musicians_recall_the_lennon_they_knew/. A book review of the Yoko Ono–edited collection *Memories of John Lennon*.

Mullin, Jeff. "John Lennon: Dead But Live?" *News & Eagle* (Enid, Oklahoma) (March 15, 2006). Accessed March 15, 2006, at http://www.enidnews.com/opinion/local_story_074005937.html?keyword=topstory. The author takes a humorous slant toward the announcement of a pay-per-view séance to communicate with Lennon. He suggests that if music can be retrieved from Lennon, then attempts should also be made to contact everyone from Bach to Jimi Hendrix.

Nabhan, Shibly. "You Know It Ain't Easy: Remembering the Wedding Odyssey of John and Yoko." *Japan Times* (April 13, 2006). Accessed March 4, 2007, at http://search.japantimes.co.jp/cgi-bin/fm20060413a1.html. The author relates the story of Lennon and Yoko Ono's travails when they tried to get married. The text of "The Ballad of John and Yoko" frames the piece.

Naha, Ed, ed. *John Lennon and the Beatles Forever.* New York: Tower, 1981. A newsstand paperback published at the time of Lennon's murder.

Nash, Alun. "John Lennon and the Influence of Lewis Carroll." *Jabberwocky: The Journal of the Lewis Carroll Society* 7 (1978): 36–39.

Neil, Scott. "Auction to Feature Sailing Log Signed by John Lennon." *Royal Gazette* (Bermuda) (March 28, 2006). Accessed March 28, 2006, at http://www.theroyalgazette.com/apps/pbcs.dll/article?AID=/20060328/NEWS/103280165. The upcoming auction of a sailing log of a trip that Lennon made from Rhode Island to Bermuda is the impetus for the author's recounting of the journey.

Neil, Scott. "'I Guess It's Time To Say Goodbye to Paradise.'" *Royal Gazette* (Bermuda) (December 8, 2005). Accessed February 4, 2006, at http://www.theroyalgazette.com/apps/pbcs.dll/article?AID=/20051208/LIFESTYLE/112080145. The author writes a long piece about Lennon's last summer holiday. The article includes an interview with Bermudian Andy Newmark, who played drums on Lennon's final album *Double Fantasy.*

Neil, Scott. "The Last Summer." *Royal Gazette* (Bermuda) (December 6, 2005). Accessed February 4, 2006, at http://www.theroyalgazette.com/apps/pbcs.dll/article?AID=/20051206/LIFESTYLE/112060158. The author relates the memories of the real estate agent who helped Lennon find a summer cottage in Bermuda.

Neil, Scott. "The Night I Met John Lennon." *Royal Gazette* (Bermuda) (December 7, 2005). Accessed February 4, 2006, at http://www.theroyalgazette.com/apps/pbcs.dll/article?AID=/20051207/LIFESTYLE/112070095. The author shares the experiences of fellow Bermudian journalists who spent an evening with Lennon at a disco during his July 1980 holiday on the island.

Ney, Jutta. "Rock and Roll Revival." *Jazz and Pop* (January 1970): 61.

Ney, Jutta. "'War Is Over' If You Want It: Happy Christmas from John and Yoko." *Jazz and Pop* (March 1970): 31.

"1980: John Lennon Shot Dead." *News.BBC.Co.UK* (December 8, 2005). Accessed February 4, 2006, at /news8.thdo.bbc.co.uk/onthisday/hi/dates/stories/

December/8/newsid_2536000/2536321.stm. A reprint of the BBC bulletin about the death of Lennon.

"1940–1980: Recollections." *Rolling Stone* 335 (January 22, 1981): 18 ff. Friends and acquaintances ranging from Peter Fonda and Murray Kaufman to John Sinclair and Carly Simon and a host of others offer their tributes to Lennon.

Noebel, David A. *The Legacy of John Lennon: Charming or Harming a Generation?* Chicago: Nelson, 1982. Antirock religious writer presents his views of Lennon's impact on youth.

Norman, Philip. "'I Was Never Lovable, I Was Just Lennon.'" *Sunday Times* (December 14, 1980): 33. The Beatles' biographer's thoughts on Lennon on the occasion of his death.

Norman, Philip. *Shout!: The Beatles In Their Generation.* New York: Fireside, 2003. Revised and updated edition of Beatles career biography has significant section on post-break-up years.

O'Donnell, Jim. *The Day John Met Paul.* New York: Hall of Fame, 1994.

"100 Classic Album Covers: "Live Peace in Toronto 1969." *Rolling Stone* 617 (November 14, 1991): 113. The Plastic Ono Band's *Live Peace* album cover is included in *Rolling Stone* magazine's list of classic album covers.

"Ono Not Interested in Bringing out Fresh Lennon Material: Ex-Associate." *WebIndia123.com* (January 13, 2006). Accessed March 4, 2007, at http://in.news.yahoo.com/060113/139/61zjg.html. The article is about songs Lennon co-wrote with Bruce Bierman, who is trying to get them released but is receiving resistance from Yoko Ono.

Ono, Yoko. *Grapefruit: A Book of Instructions and Drawings.* New York: Simon & Schuster, 2000. Lennon wrote the introduction to an earlier edition of this book (included here), and several parts of it influenced aspects of some of his songs, including "Imagine."

Ono, Yoko. *John Lennon: Summer of 1980.* New York: Putnam, 1983. A collection of black-and-white photographs selected by Yoko Ono of the Lennons in New York City in 1980 along with lyrical excerpts from the *Double Fantasy* album. The Lennons are seen in the recording studio, outside the Dakota, in Central Park, in bed, and at a café. The eight photographers—Allan Tannenbaum, Paul Goresh, Roger Farrington, Bob Gruen, David Spindel, Michel Senecal, Jack Mitchell, and Lilo Raymond—share their experiences of photographing the couple.

Ono, Yoko, ed. *Memories of John Lennon.* New York: Harper Entertainment, 2005. Mostly anecdotal reminiscences of Lennon by fellow musicians, music industry executives, disc jockeys, actors, journalists, photographers, friends, relatives, and other acquaintances. The pieces vary in length from a six-word sentence (Norman Mailer) to 20 pages (Elliot Mintz).

Ono, Yoko. "Strawberry Fields Forever." *New York Times* (August 28, 1981): 23.

"Original Lennon Draft Lyric Up for Sale." *Ireland Online* (January 17, 2006). Accessed March 4, 2007, at http://www.breakingnews.ie/ireland/?jp=CWEYAUKFGBCW. An article about the auction of the handwritten lyrics of "A Day in the Life."

O'Toole, Lawrence. "The Lennon Legacy." *Maclean's* (December 22, 1980): 36–39. An appreciation of Lennon published in the Canadian news magazine at the time of his slaying.

Ott, Terry. "Here, There and Everywhere." *Globe and Mail* (December 3, 2005). Accessed March 4, 2007, at http://www.theglobeandmail.com/servlet/story/RTGAM.20051202.bkbeat1203/BNStory/SpecialEvents/. The author submits a mostly positive review of the Spitz biography.

Palmer, Robert. "John Lennon: Guiding Force in Music and Culture of 60's." *New York Times* (December 10, 1980): B7. An overview of Lennon's life and music career written by one of the newspaper's popular music critics.

Palmer, Robert. "Lennon Known as Both Author and Composer." *New York Times* (December 9, 1980): 9. The *Times'* rock critic's appreciation of Lennon written at the time of his murder.

Palmer, Robert. "The Real Way To Remember Lennon." *New York Times* (December 9, 1981): 23. An op-ed piece by the newspaper's rock critic written on the occasion of the first anniversary of Lennon's passing.

Pang, May and Henry Edwards. *Loving John: The Untold Story.* New York: Warner, 1983. Working with Lennon and Ono from 1971 and Lennon's sometime lover from 1973 to 1978, the author tells of her life with Lennon and contradicts some of the standard accounts of Lennon's "lost weekend."

Partridge, Elizabeth. *John Lennon: All I Want Is the Truth.* New York: Viking/Penguin, 2005. A coffee table book with many black-and-white photographs covering the full range of Lennon's career. Although targeted to young adults, the work will appeal to all interested in Lennon.

Patterson, Hannah. "Choruses of Disapproval." *Guardian* (Manchester, England) (October 24, 2006). Accessed October 24, 2006, at http://film.guardian.co.uk/london2006/story/0,,1930439,00.html. The author analyzes the climate that has spawned several films with antiwar messages, including *The U.S. vs. John Lennon.*

Patton, Phil. "Strawberry Fields Forever." *New Times* (October 4, 1974): 73.

Perrin, Timothy. "A Parisian Ode to Lennon." *Globe and Mail* (December 7, 2005). Accessed March 4, 2007, at http://www.theglobeandmail.com/servlet/story/RTGAM.20051206.wlennon1207/EmailBNStory/specialTravel/. A review of an exhibit of Lennon artifacts at the Cité de la Musique in Paris.

Podrazik, Walter J. *Strange Days: The Music of John, Paul, George and Ringo Twenty Years On.* Ann Arbor, MI: Pierian, 1986.

Pollick, Amy. "Lennon's Ex-Wife Shares Relationship Memories." *Decatur Daily* (Alabama) (February 6, 2006). Accessed March 4, 2007, at http://www.decaturdaily.com/decaturdaily/books/060205/book1.shtml. A review of Cynthia Lennon's *John.*

Polskin, Howard. "John Lennon's Murder: Did TV Go Too Far?" *TV Guide* 29 (November 21, 1981): 2–8. An analysis of the media coverage of Lennon's murder published as the first anniversary approached.

"The Pop 100: John Lennon, 'Imagine.'" *Rolling Stone* 855 (December 7, 2000): 73. Lennon's "Imagine" is ranked number 15 among *Rolling Stone* magazine's best pop songs.

Preszler, June. *John Lennon.* Mankato, MN: Capstone, 2005. A biography of Lennon intended for children.

Pujol, Rolando. "The News Bulletin Was 'Unspeakable.'" *amNew York* (December 8, 2005): 8. The author contextualizes the announcement of Lennon's death in the media culture of 1980.

Quantick, David. *Revolution: The Making of the Beatles' White Album*. Chicago: A Capella, 2002. A well-written (with a sense of humor) account of the creation of The Beatles' only double album. The core of the book is a detailed look at the creation of each song. The author gives high praise to Lennon's "Revolution 9."

Quindlen, Anna. "Imagine All the People Mourning in the Rain." *New York Times* (December 9, 1981): 2. An article about the gathering to commemorate the first anniversary of Lennon's death.

Rabinowitz, Dorothy. "John Lennon's Mourners." *Commentary* (February 1981): 58–61. The author suggests that the outpouring of grief at the time of Lennon's assassination was more for the mourners than for Lennon.

Rakobowchuk, Peter. "Youth Stage Bed-In at UN Climate Conference in Memory of John Lennon." *Canadian Press* (December 9, 2005). Accessed February 4, 2006, at http://www.canada.com/nationalpost/story.html?id=0c9a7b 92-068b-40c7-b060-3f37103f0bf4&k=89425. Young environmentalists in Montreal drew attention to their campaign to reduce greenhouse gases by using a bed-in as Lennon and Yoko Ono had done for their peace campaign in Montreal in 1969.

Rappaport, Doreen and Bryan Collier. *John's Secret Dreams: The Life of John Lennon*. New York: Hyperion Books for Children, 2004. A picture book biography of Lennon intended for children.

Reed, Billy. "Beatles Injected Fun into the Serious '60s." *Louisville Courier-Journal* (December 10, 1980): E7. An appreciation of Lennon written at the time of his slaying.

Reed, Rex. "Living Next to Lennon." *Daily News* (New York) (December 14, 1980): Leisure-5. The celebrity chronicler writes of his personal experiences as neighbor of the Lennons in a special tribute section.

Reiter, Naomi. "The Artwork of John Lennon for Sale." *Naples Sun-Times* (Florida) (February 15, 2006). Accessed February 15, 2006, at http://www.zwire. com/site/news.cfm?newsid=16129622&BRD=2605&PAG=461&dept_ id=523946&rfi=6. A short article about an exposition and sale of Lennon's prints and drawings in Naples, Florida.

Reiz, Rose Mary. "Cynthia Lennon Shares John's Story from Her Side." *Flint Journal* (Michigan) (April 2, 2006). Accessed April 2, 2006, at http://www.mlive.com/ news/fljournal/features/index.ssf?/base/features-0/1143973441204750. xml&coll=5. The author submits a positive review of Lennon's ex-wife's memoir.

Rense, Rip. "A Director's Search for John Lennon." *Los Angeles Times* (October 6, 1988): IV–3. A focus on director Andrew Solt at the time of the premiere of the *Imagine* documentary.

Ressner, Jeffrey. "Lennon Film in the Works." *Rolling Stone* 527 (June 2, 1988): 23. A brief article about the upcoming premiere of the *Imagine* film.

Ressner, Jeffrey. "The Making of *Imagine*." *Rolling Stone* (October 6, 1988): 37. An article about the production of the *Imagine* documentary.

Reynolds, Stanley. "The Cruel and Uncompromising Working Class Hero." *Guardian* (Manchester, England) (December 10, 1980). Accessed March 4, 2007, at http://www.guardian.co.uk/thebeatles/story/0,,612490,00.html. At the time of Lennon's passing, an acquaintance reflects on Lennon's personality.

Rich, Frank. "Growing Up with the Beatles." *New York Times* (December 14, 1980): 30. A personal reflection in reaction to the shooting of Lennon.

Robb, Christina. "We Need Him ... We Miss Him." *Boston Globe* (December 10, 1980): 19. An appreciation of Lennon written at the time of his murder.

Robberson, Todd. "John Lennon's First Wife Out To Set the Record Straight." Knight Ridder/Tribune News Service (November 30, 2005). Accessed March 4, 2007, at http://www.azcentral.com/ent/celeb/articles/1201lennonex.html. An interview with Lennon's ex-wife Cynthia on the occasion of the publication of her biography *John*.

Roberts, Richard. "Yesterday's Mourning Before Sunrise." *Philadelphia Evening Bulletin* (December 10, 1980): 1. Local reaction to the slaying of Lennon.

Robertson, John. *The Art and Music of John Lennon*. Secaucus, NJ: Carol, 1991. A detailed account of Lennon's creative activities, including the author's well-considered opinions. Indispensable, though not complete

Robertson, John. *Lennon: 1940–1980*. London: Omnibus Press, 1995. A chronological day-by-day account of Lennon's life, with photo illustrations. An excellent companion to the author's previous book, and more approachable.

Rockwell, John. "The Impassioned Chief of a Generation's Idols: An Appreciation." *New York Times* (December 10, 1980): B7. The author writes of how Lennon kept the focus of what he believed true and cut through the falseness.

Rockwell, John. "Leader of a Rock Group that Defined a Generation." *New York Times* (December 9, 1980): 7. Lennon's obituary by the *Times'* music critic.

Rodgers, Larry. "Silence Still Resonates for Writer." *Arizona Republic* (December 4, 2005). Accessed March 5, 2007, at http://www.azcentral.com/arizonarepublic/ae/articles/1204lennon1204memory.html. The writer remembers a trip from Ohio to New York to be in Central Park for the 10 minutes of silence six days after Lennon's murder.

Rogan, Johnny. *The Complete Guide to the Music of John Lennon*. London: Omnibus Press, 1997. A succinct and valuable commentary on Lennon's solo recorded output.

Rollin, Betty. "Top Pop Merger: Lennon/Ono, Inc." *Look* 33 (March 18, 1969): 36–42.

"The *Rolling Stone* 200: The Essential Rock Collection: John Lennon." *Rolling Stone* 760 (May 15, 1997): 76. Lennon's *Plastic Ono Band* and *Imagine* are included in *Rolling Stone* magazine's list of essential albums.

The Rolling Stones Rock and Roll Circus. Produced by Robin Klein and Iris Keitel. Directed by Michael Lindsay-Hogg. 65 min. plus extras. Abkco Films. 2004. DVD. Lennon appears with an all-star band called The Dirty Mac to perform his recent Beatles number "Yer Blues" and a jam with Ono and violinist Ivy Gitlis. The DVD includes a bonus quad-screen edit of "Yer Blues." The film was made in December 1968 but was unseen by the public until 1996.

Roos, Michael E. "The Walrus and the Deacon: John Lennon's Debt to Lewis Carroll." *Journal of Popular Culture* 18 (Summer 1984): 19–29. The author analyzes Lennon's compositions of 1966 and 1967 in relation to *Alice's Adventures in Wonderland* and *Through the Looking Glass*.

Rose, Lisa. "Lennon Deserves Better than Superficial Documentary: Imagine a Naïve, Simplistic Documentary about the Most Complex, Cynical Member of the Beatles." *nola.com* (October 13, 2006). Accessed October 13, 2006, at http://www.

nola.com/movies/t-p/index.ssf?/base/entertainment-0/1160717105292200. xml&coll=. An unfavorable review of *The U.S. vs. John Lennon* documentary.

Rosen, Jane and Paul Keel. "A Vigil but No Funeral for Lennon." *Guardian* (Manchester, England) (December 10, 1980). Accessed March 5, 2007, at http:// www.guardian.co.uk/print/0,,3935281-110875,00.html. Coverage of the passing of Lennon.

Rosen, Robert. *Nowhere Man: The Final Days of John Lennon.* New York: Soft Skull, 2000.

Rouse, Robert. "Remembering John Lennon—I Read the News Today Oh Boy." *American Chronicle*(December 8, 2005). Accessed March 5, 2007, at http:// www.americanchronicle.com/articles/viewArticle.asp?articleID=4060. A personal remembrance of the impact of Lennon on the author's life.

Rowland, Mark. "John and Yoko: The Long and Winding Road." *Playgirl* (March 1981): 21.

Rugg, Diane. "For Lennon's Fans, Too, the Dream Is Over." *News Tribune* (Woodbridge, New Jersey) (December 10, 1980): 23. The reactions of New Jersey suburban mall shoppers to the slaying of Lennon. The author notes that all Lennon and Beatles recordings were sold out at the mall.

Ruhlmann, William. "John Lennon." In *All Music Guide,* eds. Michael Erlewine, Vladimir Bogdanov, Chris Woodstra, and Stephen Thomas Erlewine. San Francisco: Miller Freeman, 1997: 219–220. A guide to Lennon's recorded output.

Saimaru, Nishi F. *John Lennon: A Family Album.* Tokyo: Fly Communications, 1982.

"Sales Boost for Lennon Prints." *The Times* (London) (January 20, 1970): 3B.

Sander, Ellen. "John and Yoko Ono Lennon: Give Peace a Chance." *Saturday Review* (June 28, 1969): 46–47. In a somewhat unfocused article, the author suggests that Lennon can stop the violence of the era if he is granted a visa.

Sante, Luc. "Beatlephobia." *New York Review of Books* (December 22, 1988): 30–35. A review of the Goldman biography.

Sauceda, James. *The Literary Lennon: A Comedy of Letters: The First Study of All the Major and Minor Writings of John Lennon.* Ann Arbor, MI: Pierian, 1983. A literature professor analyzes *In His Own Write* and *A Spaniard in the Works* in great detail.

Scaggs, Austin. "Lennon Remembered: Two Major John Lennon Exhibitions Open." *Rolling Stone* 855 (December 7, 2000): 25–26. The author notes the opening of the John Lennon Museum in Japan and a major Lennon exhibit at the Rock and Roll Hall of Fame.

Scanlon, Karen. "Slaying Stuns Concert-goers." *Philadelphia News* (December 9, 1980): 4. The reaction to the death of Lennon by concertgoers exiting a Bruce Springsteen concert on the night of the shooting.

Schuster, Peter. *Four Ever.* Stuttgart, Germany: Belser, 1986.

Schwartz, Maryln. "A Parent Takes a Second Look: Beatles Weren't So Bad After All." *Dallas Morning News* (December 11, 1980): 1C. An appreciation written by a parent of Beatle fans written at the time of Lennon's slaying.

Seaman, Frederic. *The Last Days of John Lennon.* New York: Citadel Press, 1992. Fired by Ono for pilfering Lennon materials after his death, this one-time Lennon assistant tells the story from his perspective, indicating that the couple's relationship was faltering and that Ono was cold and calculating after Lennon's murder.

Search for Liberation: Featuring a Conversation between John Lennon and Swami Bhaktivedanta. Los Angeles: Bhaktivedanta Book Trust, 1981. Slim volume purports to be transcript of Lennon and Harrison in conversation with noted Swami and guru about various sacred teachings, and—although it reads plausibly enough with Harrison much more earnest and Lennon skeptical—it is not made clear what the source for the transcript is.

Semley, John. "John Lennon Was a Pussy." *McGill Tribune* (October 24, 2006). Accessed October 24, 2006, at http://www.mcgilltribune.com/media/ storage/paper234/news/2006/10/24/AE/Pop-Rhetoric.John.Lennon. Was.A.Pussy-2386491.shtml?norewrite200610251323&sourcedomain=www. mcgilltribune.com. On the occasion of the release of *The U.S. vs. John Lennon* documentary, the author rails against the Lennon legend.

Shames, Lawrence. "John Lennon, Where Are You?" *Esquire* (November 1980): 31–38 ff. In a long cover story, the author describes his journey to discover what Lennon has been up to during his long period of public silence. He visits one of Lennon's dairy farms, the estates in Long Island, New York, and Palm Beach, Florida, and interviews former Lennon collaborator David Peel. This article reputedly influenced Lennon's killer.

"Sharing the Grief." *Rolling Stone* 335 (January 22, 1981): 20 ff. A description of what Lennon's former band mates, his wife and others close to him, and common fans did in the days following his death.

Sharp, Ken. "The Making of John Lennon and Yoko Ono's *Double Fantasy:* An Interview with Producer Jack Douglas." *Goldmine* (March 23, 2001): 14–19. An intriguing interview that includes Douglas's shocking confession that he took it upon himself to deprive the world of Lennon's last recorded comments.

Shatskin, Mike, Lyn Belanger, and Jo Kearns. *A Tribute to John Lennon.* New York: Proteus, 1981. A newsstand biography printed on the occasion of Lennon's passing.

Sheff, David. "In Praise of John Lennon: The Liverpool Lad as Musician, Husband, Father and Man." *People Weekly* (December 22, 1980): 26–36. In a photo-filled tribute cover story, the author, who conducted the *Playboy* interview with the Lennons, relates his experiences during the interview process.

Sheff, David. "Yoko and Sean: Starting Over." *People Weekly* (December 13, 1982): 42–45.

Sheff, David and Victoria Sheff. "The Betrayal of John Lennon." *Playboy* (March 1984): 84–87 ff. Detailed article covers the shocking behind-the-scenes stories of former Lennon and Ono confidants and associates regarding Lennon's legacy and estate in the first three years after his death. The tawdry details run the gamut from stolen trinkets through missing diaries and recordings to death threats.

"Shell Found at Lennon House." *The Times* (London) (May 23, 1970): 3F.

Shevy, Sandra. *The Other Side of Lennon.* London: Sidgwick & Jackson, 1990.

Shields, Nelson T. "New Hope for Gun Controls: Lennon Murder May Bring Young People into the Battle." *Los Angeles Times* (December 21, 1980): IV-5.

Sholin, Dave. "John and Yoko on Marriage, Children and Their Generation." *Ms.* (March 1981): 58 ff. Excerpts from the interview that the author carried out for the RKO Radio Network on December 8, 1980. The focus is on child-rearing, marriage, working as a couple, and feminism.

Shotton, Pete and Nicholas Schaffner. *John Lennon: In My Life*. New York: Stein and Day, 1983. Shotton, a former member of The Quarry Men and Lennon's close friend from the time of their youth, tells his insider story.

Singh, Anita. "Angry John Lennon Letter Set for £15,000 Auction Sale." *Daily Post* (Liverpool) (May 18, 2006). Accessed May 18, 2006, at http://icliverpool.icnetwork.co.uk/0800beatles/0050news/tm_objectid=17096110&method=full&siteid=50061&headline=angry-john-lennon-letter-set-for--pound-15-000-auction-sale-name_page.html. A letter Lennon sent in 1971 to an American journalist who accused the early Beatles of exploiting black American music is auctioned.

Singleton, Don. "A Life that Revolutionized the World." *Daily News* (New York) (December 10, 1980): 61. First of a series of articles presenting an in-depth look at Lennon's life and career.

Smith, David. "Lennon Jukebox Reveals Beatles' Musical Debts." *Guardian* (Manchester, England) (March 7, 2004). Accessed March 5, 2007, at http://arts.guardian.co.uk/news/story/0,11711,1164013,00.html. An article about the 40-plus artists represented on Lennon's jukebox and their influences on The Beatles' recordings.

Smith, Harold. "Lennon's 'Last Temptation.'" *Christianity Today* (November 4, 1988): 14–15. Using the publication of Goldman's biography as a launching pad, the author suggests that the sixties generation may be ready for "true" truth.

Snell, Conrad. *John Lennon 4 Ever: The Biography*. New York: Crown Summit Books, 1981. A newsstand paperback biography published at the time of Lennon's killing.

Snyder-Scumpy, Patrick. "People and Things that Went Before." *Crawdaddy* (June 1973): 48.

Soeder, John. "Fans Still Imagine a World with John Lennon." *Plain-Dealer* (Cleveland, Ohio) (December 8, 2005). Accessed March 5, 2007, at http://abbeyroadontheriver.com/news/23.html. An anniversary wrap-up that includes quotes from the author's conversations with Cynthia Lennon, James Henke (of the Rock and Roll Hall of Fame), and Bob Spitz (Beatles' biographer).

Solt, Andrew and Sam Egan. *Imagine: John Lennon*. New York: Macmillan, 1988. A coffee table volume prepared to coincide with the release of the biographical documentary film and record album collection of the same name.

Sooke, Alastair. "Singing to the Gallery." *Telegraph.co.uk* (September 2, 2006). Accessed September 2, 2006, at http://www.telegraph.co.uk/arts/main.jhtml?xml=/arts/2006/09/02/bacandice02.xml. The author witnesses video installation artist Candice Breitz creating her latest work, which will be culled from more than two dozen people singing their way through Lennon's *Plastic Ono Band* album.

"Sorrow, Tributes around the World." *Philadelphia Inquirer* (December 10, 1980): A15. International reaction to the passing of Lennon.

Spencer, Scott. "John Lennon." *Rolling Stone* 335 (January 22, 1981): 13. In the introduction to a special tribute issue to Lennon, the stunned author struggles to write of the meaning of the death of the musician.

Spitz, Bob. *The Beatles: The Biography.* New York: Little, Brown, 2005. Massive tome includes well-researched unfolding of Lennon's early years.

Sragow, Michael. "John Lennon Documentarians Aim To Give Us Some Truth." *Baltimore Sun* (October 1, 2006). Accessed October 1, 2006, at http://www. baltimoresun.com/features/custom/aetoday/bal-ae.lennon01oct01,0,1402 999.story?coll=bal-aetoday-headlines. A favorable review of *The U.S. vs. John Lennon* documentary that includes interviews with its makers David Leaf and John Scheinfeld.

Stannard, Neil and John Tobler. *Working Class Heroes.* New York: Avon, 1985.

Starr, Ringo. *Postcards from the Boys.* San Francisco: Chronicle Books, 2004. A collection of postcards sent to Starr individually by Lennon and the other Beatles, with Starr's memoir commentary based on the posts.

"Stars Are Shocked after Murder of Lennon." *Philadelphia Evening Bulletin* (December 10, 1980): A8. A survey of remarks by celebrities regarding Lennon's murder.

Stecklow, Steve. "Springsteen, Audience Remember Lennon." *Philadelphia Evening Bulletin* (December 10, 1980): A8. A review of the Bruce Springsteen concert held at Philadelphia's Spectrum the night after Lennon's death.

Stephens, Christopher J. "All Those Years Ago." *National Ledger* (November 23, 2005). Accessed March 5, 2007, at http://www.nationalledger.com/cgi-bin/ artman/exec/view.cgi?archive=1&num=1794. A brief article that posits Lennon's death as the dividing line between the idealism of the 1960s, the cynicism of the 1970s, and the greed of the 1980s.

Stevens, John. *The Songs of John Lennon: The Beatle Years.* Boston: Berklee Press, 2002. The music professor author provides musicological analysis of 25 Beatle songs composed by Lennon from "You Can't Do That" to "Come Together."

Stockdale, Tom. *John Lennon.* Broomall, PA: Chelsea House, 1997.

Stokes, Geoffrey. "Some Years in the Life." *Rolling Stone* (December 25, 1980): 107.

Stone, Steve, ed. *John Lennon: All You Need Is Love.* New York: Marjam, 1980. A newsstand biography published on the occasion of Lennon's murder.

Strauss, Robert. "Lennon Was Always the Leader." *Philadelphia News* (December 9, 1980): 4. A profile of Lennon written at the time of his death.

Strauss, Robert. "Lennon's Dream Girl." *Philadelphia News* (December 9, 1980): 20.

Sullivan, Henry W. *The Beatles with Lacan: Rock 'n' Roll as Requiem for the Modern Age.* New York: Peter Lang, 1995. The Oxford- and Harvard-educated scholar psychoanalyzes the significance of The Beatles. One chapter is devoted to Lennon, including his solo years.

Sullivan, Mark. "'More Popular than Jesus': The Beatles and the Religious Far Right." *Popular Music* 6 (Summer 1987): 313–326.

Swan, Christopher. "Fellow Voyagers." *Christian Science Monitor* (December 11, 1980): 7. A fond appreciation of Lennon at the time of his slaying.

Sweet Toronto. Produced by Alan Douglas. Directed by D. A. Pennebacker. 56 min. Pioneer Artists. 2001. DVD. The Plastic Ono Band's live debut at the Toronto Rock and Roll Revival Festival is highlighted, with brief footage of some classic rock acts as a warm-up. The collection also includes a few minutes of Ono attending an art exhibit of some of Lennon's sketches.

Swenson, John. *The John Lennon Story.* New York: Leisure, 1981.

Takiff, Jonathan. "Lennon Rocked an Era." *Philadelphia News* (December 9, 1980): 5. An obituary and appreciation of Lennon.

Taylor, Derek. *As Time Goes By: Living in the Sixties with John Lennon, Paul McCartney*. Ann Arbor, MI: Pierian, 1983. Former Beatles press agent provides insights into the fall of Apple and the end of The Beatles.

Teeman, Tom. "Give Me a Chance, Says Yoko." *The Australian* (July 10, 2006). Accessed July 10, 2006, at http://www.theaustralian.news.com.au/story//0,20867,19733568-16947,00.html. The author speaks with Lennon's second wife in a rare, substantial interview.

Terry, Carol. *Here, There and Everywhere: The Beatles First International Bibliography*. Ann Arbor, MI: Pierian, 1990. A comprehensive bibliography of Beatles' reference sources.

Tezer, Adnan. "DVD Review: Imagine—Deluxe Edition." *Monsters and Critics* (December 19, 2005). Accessed March 5, 2007, at http://dvd.monstersand-critics.com/reviews/article_10634.php/DVD_Review_Imagine_-_Deluxe_Edition. A mostly positive review of the content of the re-release of the film *Imagine*. The reviewer is disappointed with the visual and audio quality.

Thibodeau, Timothy M. "Won't You Please Help Me: The Life and Death of the Beatles." *National Review* (April 6, 2006). Accessed April 6, 2006, at http://www.nationalreview.com/comment/thibodeau200604060625.asp. In a long, well-thought out piece, the author uses the 2005 Spitz biography as a launchpad to discuss the demise of the group, with a special emphasis on Lennon.

"The Thinking Man's Beatle." *Philadelphia Evening Bulletin* (December 9, 1980): A3. An appreciation of Lennon written on the occasion of his murder.

Thomson, Elizabeth and David Gutman, eds. *The Lennon Companion: Twenty-Five Years of Comment*. Cambridge, MA: Da Capo, 2004. An excellent collection of articles evaluating Lennon's work from the early Beatle days to after his death.

Tianen, Dave. "All You Need Is Music." *Milwaukee Journal Sentinel* (November 30, 2005). Accessed March 5, 2007, at http://www.jsonline.com/story/index.aspx?id=374397. A look at the major recording milestones of The Beatles and Lennon as a solo artist.

Tianen, Dave. "Multimedia: A Look at Lennon." *Milwaukee Journal Sentinel* (November 30, 2005). Accessed March 5, 2007, at http://www.jsonline.com/story/index.aspx?id=374336. An annotated list of books and other items that were released to correspond with the anniversary of Lennon's death.

Tianen, Dave. "We Are Still Trying To Decide If Lennon Was Saint, Sinner or Someone in Between." *Milwaukee Journal Sentinel* (November 30, 2005). Accessed March 5, 2007, at http://www.jsonline.com/story/index.aspx?id=374332&format=print. The image of Lennon 25 years after his death based on interviews with author Bob Spitz and *Life* magazine editorial director Bob Sullivan.

"The Top 100: The Best Albums of the Last Twenty Years: *Imagine*." *Rolling Stone* 507 (August 27, 1987): 125. The *Imagine* album is ranked number 61 among *Rolling Stone* magazine's best 100 albums of the years 1967–1987.

"The Top 100: The Best Albums of the Last Twenty Years: *Plastic Ono Band*." *Rolling Stone* 507 (August 27, 1987): 52. The *John Lennon/Plastic Ono Band* album is ranked number four among *Rolling Stone* magazine's best 100 albums of the years 1967–1987.

Torre, Nestor U. "Documentary Tackles Beatles' Contentious Breakup." *Inquirer* (Philippines) (April 8, 2006). Accessed March 5, 2007, at http://www.

paulmccartney.name/Documentary_tackles_Beatles_contentious_breakup/844. htm. The author discusses various theories that led to the breakup of Lennon's popular band and a new documentary that covers the subject.

Towarnicky, Carol. "Lennon … at 40." *Philadelphia Daily News* (October 9, 1980): 29. A profile of Lennon as he reaches middle age.

Trakin, Roy. "Lennon's Musical Journey." *Daily News* (New York) (December 14, 1980): Leisure-7. A one-page synopsis of Lennon's album-by-album contributions to The Beatles and comments about his solo albums in a special tribute section.

"Trashing the Lennon Legend." *Florida Times-Union* (Jacksonville) (August 7, 1983): 4. A review of John Green's book *Dakota Days*.

Travis, Alan. "The Night Yogi and Boo-Boo Helped Semolina Pilchard Snare a Beatle." *Guardian* (Manchester, England) (August 1, 2005). Accessed March 5, 2007, at http://www.guardian.co.uk/uk_news/story/0,,1539997,00.html. An article about the Lennon and Ono drug bust in 1968 by Detective Sergeant Norman "Nobby" Pilcher and his drug-smelling dogs.

Traynor, Luke. "They Were Going To Get Back Together." *Liverpool Echo* (December 8, 2005). Accessed March 5, 2007, at http://www.jobs-merseyside.co.uk/news/tm_objectid=16461158&method=full&siteid=50061&headline=they-were-going-to-get-back-together-name_page.html. The author posits a possible Beatles reunion based on a clause in a contract Paul McCartney signed with CBS in 1979, and legal action by Lennon in 1980.

Tremlett, George. *The John Lennon Story.* London: Futura, 1976.

"Tribute to John Lennon on the Anniversary of His Death." *New York Times* (December 9, 1982): 21. A local report about a New York City tribute to Lennon two years after his death.

"Trouble Seemed So Far Away." *The Times* (London) (December 8, 1981): 5D. A report looking back one year after the shooting of Lennon.

Turner, Gustavo F. "Fans Still Book the Beatles." *Dallas Morning News* (December 8, 2005). Accessed March 5, 2007, at http://www.wfaa.com/sharedcontent/dws/ent/stories/DN-beatlesbook_1208gl.State.Edition1.169adb7a.html. A harsh review of Spitz's Beatles biography of 2005.

"2 John Lennon Memorials Draw 4,000 in Liverpool." *New York Times* (March 30, 1981): 20. The coverage of memorial services for Lennon in his hometown several months after his death.

Udovitch, Mim. "On Being a Prick: Albert Goldman's Last Emission." *Village Voice* (September 27, 1988): 53–54. A negative review of the Goldman biography.

"U.S. Ban on Beatles over Religion." *The Times* (London) (August 5, 1966): 8E. The reaction across the country to Lennon's statement about The Beatles and Jesus Christ.

The U.S. vs. John Lennon. Directed by David Leaf and John Scheinfeld. 1 hr. 45 min. Lionsgate, 2006. A feature-length documentary about Lennon's political activism, immigration troubles, and harassment by the U.S. federal government.

Walters, Ray. "Paperback Talk: Beatlemania." *New York Times Book Review* (December 28, 1980): 19.

"War Is Over! If You Want It." *New York Times* (December 21, 1969): 16.

Warman, Christopher. "Lennon and Picasso Works Compared." *The Times* (London) (March 13, 1969): 10A.

Wenner, Jann. "Endpaper." *Rolling Stone* 335 (January 22, 1981): 18 ff. The *Rolling Stone* publisher has the final word in a special tribute issue to Lennon. He speaks of Lennon's friendship and his support of the magazine in its nascent years.

Wenner, Jann. "John Lennon." *Rolling Stone* (January 21, 1971): 36–43.

Wenner, Jann. "John Lennon in *How I Won the War.*" *Rolling Stone* 1 (November 9, 1967): 16. A review of *How I Won the War* with a focus on Lennon.

Wenner, Jann. *Lennon Remembers: New Edition.* New York: Verso, 2000. Extensive interview conducted by the *Rolling Stone* publisher in December 1970, originally published in book form in 1971. Retranscribed and republished in 2000 with a new introduction by Wenner and a "Forward" by Ono. In the reading of the interview Lennon comes across as vitriolic. But upon hearing it, his humor, relaxed stance, and matter-of-fact delivery lessen the harshness considerably.

Wenner, Jan. "Man of the Year.'" *Rolling Stone* 51 (February 7, 1970): 24–25. The *Rolling Stone* publisher offers his reasons for why Lennon is the "man of the year" of 1969.

"What He Meant Was..." *New York Times* (August 16, 1966): 38. An article about Lennon's controversial remarks about the popularity of The Beatles versus Jesus.

Whitburn, Joel. *Top Pop Albums, 1955–1996.* Menomonee Falls, WI: Record Research, 1996. The bible of *Billboard* best-seller information for record albums.

Whitburn, Joel. *Top Pop Singles, 1955–1996.* Menomonee Falls, WI: Record Research, 1997. The ambitious, exhaustively researched compendium of *Billboard* best-seller information for 45-RPM singles.

Wicker, Tom. "You, Me and Handguns." *New York Times* (December 12, 1980): 35. An op-ed piece about gun control sparked by Lennon's death.

Wiegand, Rolf. "Reflections on John Lennon." *Cincinnati Enquirer* (December 14, 1980): B4. An appreciation written upon the passing of Lennon.

Wiener, Jon. *Come Together: John Lennon in His Time.* Chicago: University of Illinois Press, 1990.

Wiener, Jon. "Crushing a Dead Beatle." *Los Angeles Times* (September 4, 1988): II-9. The expert on Lennon's immigration issues gives his opinion of the then recently published Goldman biography.

Wiener, Jon. *Gimme Some Truth: The John Lennon FBI Files.* Los Angeles: University of California Press, 2001. The entire story of Lennon's harassment by the U.S. federal government through the Nixon administration and beyond, detailing his immigration struggles.

Wiener, Jon. *Professors, Politics and Pop.* New York: Verso, 1991. Includes the chapter "John Lennon Versus the FBI," which describes the Nixon administration's campaign to deport John Lennon in the early 1970s and the author's research into the FBI files regarding the same. The essay was originally published in *The New Republic* (May 2, 1983).

Wiener, Jon. "The U.S. vs. John Lennon." *Truthdig* (September 17, 2006). Accessed March 5, 2007, at http://www.zmag.org/content/showarticle.cfm?SectionID=30&ItemID=10982. The author, who acted as the historical consultant for the documentary *The U.S. vs. John Lennon,* provides some of the background for the events depicted in the film and provides a wider background on the actions the U.S. government has taken to prevent many artists from entering or settling in the country.

Wiener, Jon. "The U.S. vs. John Lennon." *CBSNews.com* (September 16, 2006). Accessed September 16, 2006, at http://www.cbsnews.com/stories/2006/09/ 15/opinion/main2014623.shtml.The author compares the Lennons' activities as depicted in the documentary *The U.S. vs. John Lennon* with the Vote for Change concerts that were held for the 2004 presidential election. The article is reprinted from *The Nation*.

Wigney, Allan. "Hey Hey Johnny: Elton Coaxed Icon Back." *Ottawa Sun* (Canada) (July 17, 2006). Accessed July 17, 2006, at http://www.ottawasun.com/ Showbiz/Music/2006/07/16/1686942-sun.html. The author summarizes the events that led to Elton John working with Lennon on "Whatever Gets You through the Night."

Wigston, Nancy. "John Lennon and the Flaming Red Rabbi." *Canadian Jewish News*. Accessed February 4, 2006, at http://www.cjnews.com/viewarticle. asp?id=8403. The author relates the story of how 70-year-old Rabbi Abraham Feinberg influenced and contributed to Lennon's "Give Peace a Chance." The details of the hotel room where the song was recorded are also unfolded.

Wilder, Eliot. "John Lennon: Sometime in New York City." *Portland Phoenix* (December 23–29, 2005). Accessed March 5, 2007, at http://www.portlandphoenix. com/music/otr/documents/05163197.asp. A negative review of the re-release on compact disc.

Williams, Paul. *The Map, Rediscovering Rock and Roll (A Journey)*. South Bend, IN: And Books, 1988. In this wide-ranging memoir, the pioneering rock music critic recounts his time with Lennon and Yoko Ono (and Timothy and Rosemary Leary) in Montreal at the time of the recording of "Give Peace a Chance."

Williams, Richard. "Solo Beatles." *The Times* (London) (January 23, 1971): 17E.

Wilmington, Michael. "'Imagine' John Lennon on a Pedestal." *Los Angeles Times* (October 6, 1988): VI–1 ff.

Winn, James Anderson. "The Beatles as Artists: A Meditation for December Ninth." *Michigan Quarterly Review* 28 (Winter 1984): 1–20.

Winn, Steven. "John Lennon's Strange Sort of Immortality, Now 25 Years Long." *San Francisco Chronicle* (December 8, 2005). Accessed February 6, 2006, at http:// www.sfgate.com/cgi-bin/article.cgi?f=/c/a/2005/12/08/DDG9QG409R1. DTL). On aging and nostalgia, and Lennon's place in our culture.

"WMCA Bans New Single, 'Ballad' by Beatle Lennon." *New York Times* (May 24, 1969): 70. An article about the New York radio station not playing "Ballad of John and Yoko" because of the controversial lyric in the refrain.

Woffinden, Bob. *The Beatles Apart*. New York: Proteus, 1971.

Wolfe, Arnold Sidney. *Irony, Ambiguity and Meaning in CBS Television News Coverage of the Death of John Lennon*." Doctoral dissertation: Northwestern University, 1988. Abstract available in *Dissertation Abstracts International* (November 1988): 989A.

Wolfe, Tom. "A Highbrow under All That Hair." *Book Week* (May 3, 1964): 4. The best-selling author's perspective on Lennon's volume *In His Own Write*.

Wood, Michael. "John Lennon's Schooldays." *New Society* (June 27, 1968): 948.

Wooley, Bryan. "John Lennon and the Death of the '60s." *Dallas Times Herald* (December 10, 1980): 9.

Wootton, Richard. *John Lennon*. New York: Random House Books for Children, 1985. A biography of Lennon for children.

"Worldwide Mourning Continues for Lennon." *Philadelphia Evening Bulletin* (December 10, 1980): A7. An article about international reaction to the slaying of Lennon.

"Writer Presents Different Picture of Dakota Days." *Florida Times-Union* (Jacksonville) (July 1, 1983): D16. A review of John Green's memoir *Dakota Days*.

"Yoko Ono Asks Mourners To Give to Foundation Lennon Favored." *New York Times* (December 10, 1980): 7. Local newspaper coverage related to Lennon's murder.

"Yoko Ono Joins Vigil for John Lennon." *CNN.com* (December 9, 2005). Accessed February 4, 2006, at http://www.cnn.com/2005/SHOWBIZ/Music/12/09/lennon.tributes/. A report of Yoko Ono's brief appearance at the "Imagine" mosaic in the Strawberry Fields section of Central Park on the 25th anniversary of his death. The report includes quotes from fans at Strawberry Fields and in Liverpool for the anniversary.

"Yoko Ono Loses Baby." *New York Times* (October 17, 1969): 41. An article about one of Yoko Ono's miscarriages.

Yorke, Ritchie. "John, Yoko & Year One." *Rolling Stone* 51 (February 7, 1970): 18–21. The author submits a detailed account of the Lennons' week-long trip to Canada in December 1969, which included meetings with comedian Dick Gregory, Prime Minister Pierre Trudeau, and media analyst Marshall McLuhan. A transcript of a portion of the McLuhan meeting is included.

Yorke, Ritchie. "Lennon on Toronto: 'Bloody Marvelous.'" *Rolling Stone* 44 (October 18, 1969): 6. Lennon's enthusiastic reflections two days after the Toronto Rock and Roll Revival performance in 1969.

Yorke, Ritchie. "A Private Talk with John." *Rolling Stone* 51 (February 7, 1970): 22–23. An interview with Lennon that includes a discussion about the future of The Beatles and the artist's reflections on his December 1969 trip to Canada.

Young, Paul. *The Lennon Factor*. New York: Stein and Day, 1972.

Zeidler, Sue. "Lennon Friend Attacks TV Séance To Reach Ex-Beatle." *Reuters* online news wire service (March 21, 2006). Accessed March 21, 2006, at http://today.reuters.com/News/newsArticle.aspx?type=entertainmentNews&storyID=2006-03-21T231754Z_01_N21338578_RTRUKOC_0_US-MEDIA-LENNON.xml. Elliot Mintz, Yoko Ono's spokesperson, criticizes the upcoming séance as well as the film in production that focuses on Lennon's assassin.

Zeidler, Sue. "Court Battle over Lennon FBI Files Rages On." *Reuters* online news wire service (December 7, 2005). Accessed on March 5, 2007, at http://www.michaelmoore.com/words/latestnews/index.php?id=5106. A summary of the struggle to obtain access to Lennon's file through the Freedom of Information Act. Ten pages were yet to be released at the time the article was published.

Zelnick, C. R. "Lennon Fight To Stay in U.S. Raises Legal Points." *Christian Science Monitor* (September 8, 1975): 7.

Zito, Tom. "The Peaceful Man behind the Glasses." *Washington Post* (December 9, 1980): B1. An appreciation of Lennon written at the time of his death.

Index

About the Authors

BEN URISH has taught courses in Popular Music at Temple University, and has made popular music a large component in classes on mass media and American cultural history at Michigan State University.

KEN BIELEN has taught courses in Popular Music at Bowling Green State University and has researched and written extensively on the subject. He is the author of *The Lyrics of Civility* (1999).